Fodor's 94
Boston

W9-ARR-782

Fodor's Travel Publications, Inc.
New York • Toronto • London • Sydney • Auckland

ISBN 0–679–02503–0

Fodor's Boston

Editors: Jillian L. Magalaner, Marcy S. Pritchard
Editorial Contributors: Helena Bentz, Mary H. Frakes, Kimberly Grant, Jane Holtz Kay, Julia Lisella, Valerie Martone, Anne Merewood, Kay Howe Scheller, William Scheller, Mary Ellen Schultz, Katherine Minton Tatum, Christina Tree
Creative Director: Fabrizio La Rocca
Cartographer: David Lindroth
Illustrator: Karl Tanner
Cover Photograph: David Brownell/Image Bank

Design: Vignelli Associates

Special Sales

MANUFACTURED IN THE UNITED STATES OF AMERICA
10 9 8 7 6 5 4 3 2 1

Contents

Maps

Foreword

Perhaps no one today would speak of the Boston State House as "the hub of the solar system," as Oliver Wendell Holmes once did, yet Boston itself is very much at the heart of American history. Reminders of the American past are everywhere here, and visitors will come upon them frequently as they explore Boston, Cambridge, and the towns west and north of Boston to which this book takes the reader.

While every care has been taken to ensure the accuracy of the information in this guide, the passage of time will always bring change, and consequently the publisher cannot accept responsibility for errors that may occur.

All prices and opening times quoted here are based on information supplied to us at press time. Hours and admission fees may change, however, and the prudent traveler will avoid inconvenience by calling ahead.

Fodor's wants to hear about your travel experiences, both pleasant and unpleasant. When a hotel or restaurant fails to live up to its billing, let us know and we will investigate the complaint and revise our entries where the facts warrant it.

Send your letters to the editors of Fodor's Travel Publications, 201 E. 50th Street, New York, NY 10022.

Highlights'94 and Fodor's Choice

Highlights '94

The ongoing **Central Artery/Third Harbor Tunnel project,** a massive public-works project to depress and enlarge the main north–south highway cutting through Boston, may encourage more Boston tourists to leave their cars at home or in hotel parking garages in 1994 and beyond (the project is scheduled for completion in 2001). The 7-mile-long $5-billion project involves replacing the artery with an underground highway. A seaport access road will be built from the end of the Massachusetts Turnpike to the South Boston waterfront, and a tunnel will be constructed under the harbor from South Boston to Logan International Airport, connecting with Route 1A. In 1994, most construction projects will be off the tourist paths, in the industrial section of South Boston and at the airport. The bulk of the work along I–93, as it passes through downtown Boston, involves moving utility cables during non-rush hours. Interruptions will be minimized and temporary detours (weekend-long or week-long) are scheduled; steel plates will cover the construction during off-hours. By keeping the existing elevated highway in service during construction, traffic problems should be mitigated, but the "Big Dig" is as good an excuse as any for taking public transportation around the city.

Boston now has its very first **centralized bus station,** linking buses to the commuter rail, Amtrak, the Red Line, and Logan Link at South Station. The $80-million project includes a two-level bus station, with 29 berths built over the train tracks, from which all intercity buses depart. Eventually, Peter Pan and Plymouth & Brockton (located across the street) will join Greyhound in the new facility when they are displaced as a result of the Central Artery project.

In May 1993 the **Harborside Hyatt Hotel** (tel. 617/568–1234) opened at Logan International Airport. The 14-story hotel includes two levels of public space, twelve floors allowing for 270 guest rooms, a restaurant, lobby bar, and health club. A two-story atrium, as well as many of the guest rooms and other public spaces, overlooks Boston's skyline and waterfront. The hotel is adjacent to the Airport Water Shuttle, which docks at Rowes Wharf a few blocks from the financial district and downtown, and it will be accessible via the upcoming Third Harbor Tunnel.

In time for its centennial celebration in 1995, the main building of the **Boston Public Library**—the first lending library in the country—is undergoing phase one of its $50-million renovation project: A new staircase has been added to the basement level where new space for maps and government documents will be created. Perhaps Boston's best-kept secret, the courtyard, will be completely open again in

1994; Harvard's Fogg Art Museum has cleaned a number of the BPL's now-brilliant murals. You may wish to take the hour-long art and architecture tours led by well-versed historians at the BPL.

The **John F. Kennedy Library** reopened in November 1993 after completely renovating its exhibits, now geared to address a new generation of visitors who did not grow up in the time of JFK.

At the Charlestown Navy Yard, the **USS *Constitution*** resurfaced in October 1993 after a year in drydock, during which major inspections and repair assessments were made. She is now ready to resume her duties in the city's annual 4th of July celebration. After the ship celebrates her 200th anniversary in 1997, she will undergo a major overhaul.

The five-year **Prudential Center** project—the rebuilding of 225,000 square feet of retail space in arcades linking St. Botolph St. to the Back Bay Train Station and Copley Place to the Hynes Convention Center—was completed, and more than 70 shops and services tenanted, in the fall of 1993.

In the autumn of 1993, the **Boston Children's Museum** began construction of a new wing, which includes a 50-foot-tall "wave" of copper extending out into a barge, linking the museum to the Computer Museum next door and creating a shared front lobby. This addition, set to open in late 1994, will contain a waterfront education center. Inside the Children's Museum, the "Teen Tokyo" interactive exhibit (which runs through 1995) includes an authentic Japanese subway car that simulates a crowded Tokyo ride, a 6-foot replica of a sumo wrestler, a karaoke box, Japanese rock videos, and a re-creation of a 16-year-old Japanese boy's bedroom.

A plus for families is **"Kids Love Boston,"** a new publication from the Convention and Visitors Bureau. It highlights tours and attractions geared to families and contains information on hotel packages for families offered by 26 hotels. It identifies which hotels have an ice-cream parlor for kids, which will lend a Polaroid camera or bicycles for the day, and which have camplike activities organized for children.

In 1994, Boston will host part of soccer's **World Cup** competition. Foxboro Stadium, 30 miles southwest of Boston, hosts first-round games on June 21, 23, 25, and 30, qualifying games on July 5th, and quarterfinal games on July 9th. Special transportation is available to the stadium and other activities are scheduled to coincide with the games. North End Italians are avid soccer fans, so if you can't make it to Foxboro, head to one of the cafés on Hanover Street for lively TV viewing.

Fodor's Choice

No two people will agree on what makes a perfect vacation, but it's fun and helpful to know what others think. We hope you'll have a chance to experience some of Fodor's Choices yourself while visiting Boston. For detailed information about each entry, refer to the appropriate chapters within this guidebook.

Favorite Sights

Commonwealth Avenue when the magnolia trees are in bloom

Louisburg Square under a blanket of newly fallen snow

The Public Garden at twilight on a clear winter's night

Boston from the top of the Prudential or the Hancock Towers

The first spring day the sculls and the sailboats are sighted on the Charles River

Jazz

The Regattabar at the Charles Hotel

The *Boston Globe* jazz festival in the spring

Works of Art

The Spirit of '76 in Marblehead

Daniel Chester French's *Minuteman* statue in Concord

Asaroton, by Mags Harries, in the Haymarket

Titian's *Rape of Europa* in the Gardner Museum

All the Impressionist paintings in the Museum of Fine Arts

Bars

The Hampshire House

The Ritz-Carlton

Jacob Wirth's

The revolving rooftop lounge of the Hyatt Regency at night

Day Trips

Plum Island in Newburyport

Boston Harbor Islands

Rockport on the North Shore

Favorite Walks

Along the Esplanade

The Freedom Trail in the North End

From the Ritz-Carlton Hotel, down Newbury Street to Gloucester Street, right on Gloucester to Commonwealth Avenue, and right on Commonwealth to the Public Garden

Memorial Drive in Cambridge from MIT to Harvard

Anywhere in the Arnold Arboretum

Hotels

The Boston Harbor Hotel at Rowes Wharf *(Very Expensive)*

The Ritz-Carlton *(Very Expensive)*

The Copley Square Hotel *(Moderate)*

The Lenox Hotel *(Very Expensive)*

Restaurants

Julien *(Very Expensive)*

Ristorante Toscano *(Expensive–Very Expensive)*

Biba *(Moderate–Expensive)*

Bertucci's *(Inexpensive)*

Legal Seafoods *(Moderate)*

Eastern Massachusetts

NEW HAMPSHIRE

Lawrence

113

Lowell

3

Merrimack R.

125

93

38

110

28

27

225

Reading

2

495

128   95   Woburn

Concord

Lexington   Malden

4   Medford

117

Lincoln   2

Somerville

126   Cambridge

27   Waltham

Weston   20   Charles R.

90

Brookline

9

1

1A   203

9   Wellesley

90   Framingham   Natick

Charles R.

135   126   95

16

128

Norwood   95

109   27

1A

146   Sharon

126

0   10 miles

0   15 km

128

1

RHODE ISLAND   Woonsocket

106

495

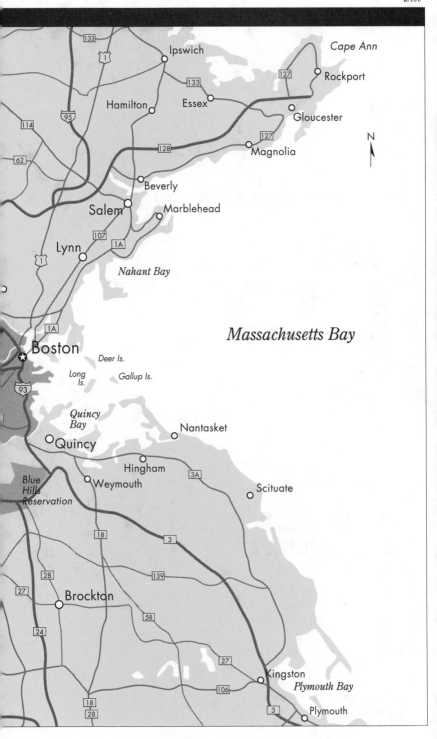

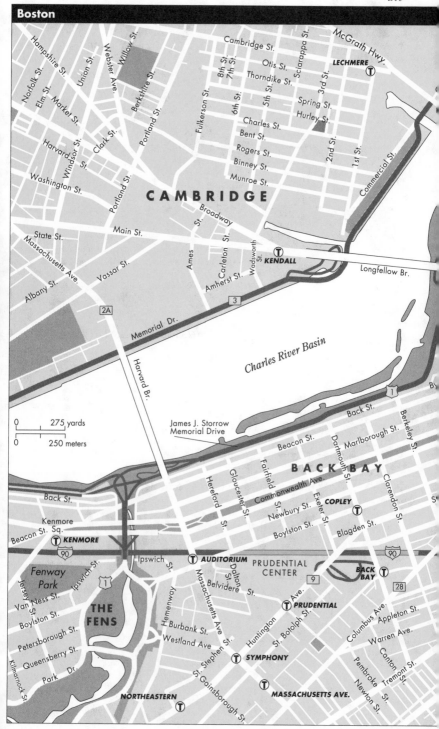

Hampshire St.
Union St.
Webster Ave.
Willow St.
Berkshire St.
Cambridge St.
Otis St.
Sciarappa St.
McGrath Hwy.
LECHMERE (T)
Norfolk St.
Elm St.
Market St.
Clark St.
Portland St.
8th St.
7th St.
Thorndike St.
6th St.
5th St.
Spring St.
Hurley St.
3rd St.
Fulkerson St.
Harvard St.
Windsor St.
Charles St.
Bent St.
Rogers St.
Binney St.
Munroe St.
2nd St.
1st St.
Commercial St.
Washington St.

CAMBRIDGE

State St.
Massachusetts Ave.
Main St.
Broadway
St.
Ames
Carleton St.
Wadsworth St.
KENDALL (T)
Longfellow Br.
Albany St.
Vassar St.
Amherst St.
Am003
[3]
[2A]
Memorial Dr.
Harvard Br.
Charles River Basin
[1]
By
0 275 yards
0 250 meters
Back St.
James J. Storrow
Memorial Drive
Beacon St.
Marlborough St.
Berkeley St.
Back St.
Fairfield St.
Dartmouth St.
BACK BAY
Kenmore
Sq.
Gloucester St.
Commonwealth Ave.
Exeter St.
COPLEY (T)
Clarendon St.
Beacon St.
KENMORE (T)
Hereford St.
Newbury St.
Boylston St.
Blagden St.
[90]
Ipswich St.
(T) *AUDITORIUM*
Dalton St.
PRUDENTIAL CENTER
[9]
BACK BAY (T)
[90]
Fenway Park
[1]
Belvidere St.
[28]
Jersey St.
Van Ness St.
Boylston St.
THE FENS
Hemenway
Massachusetts Ave.
Burbank St.
Huntington Ave.
(T) *PRUDENTIAL*
St. Botolph St.
Columbus Ave.
Appleton St.
Petersborough St.
Westland Ave.
Warren Ave.
Queensberry St.
St. Stephen St.
Conton St.
Pembroke St.
Tremont St.
Park Dr.
NORTHEASTERN (T)
St. Gainsborough St.
(T) *SYMPHONY*
(T) **MASSACHUSETTS AVE.**
Newton St.
Kilmarnock St.

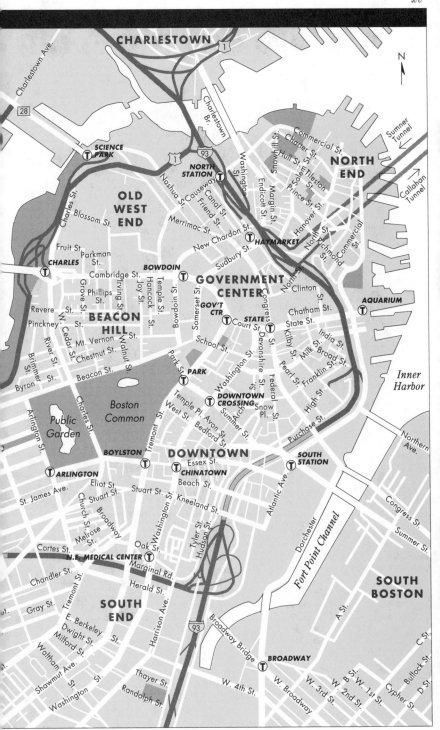

World Time Zones

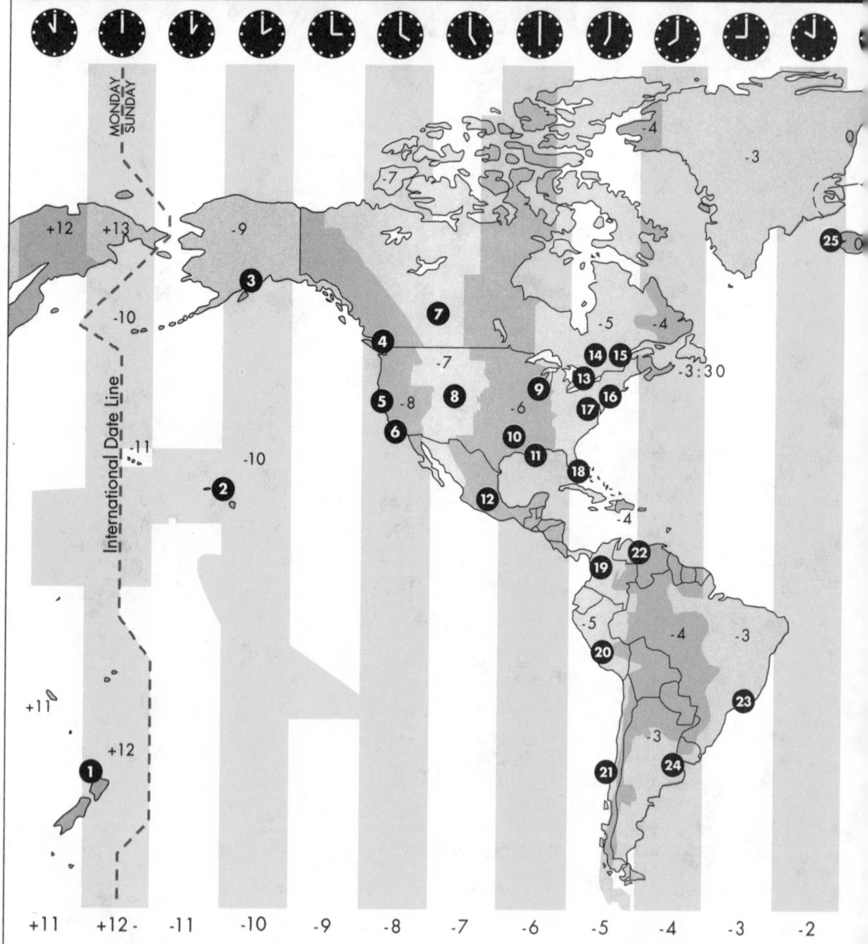

+12 +13

-9

-10

International Date Line

MONDAY
SUNDAY

-11

-10

+11

+12

-4

-3

25

7

-5

-4

14 15

13

-3:30

3

4

-7

5 -8

8

9

16

6

17

10

11

18

2

12

-4

19 22

-5

-4

-3

20

-3

23

21 24

+11   +12 -   -11   -10   -9   -8   -7   -6   -5   -4   -3   -2

Numbers below vertical bands relate each zone to Greenwich Mean Time (0 hrs.).
Local times frequently differ from these general indications,
as indicated by light-face numbers on map.

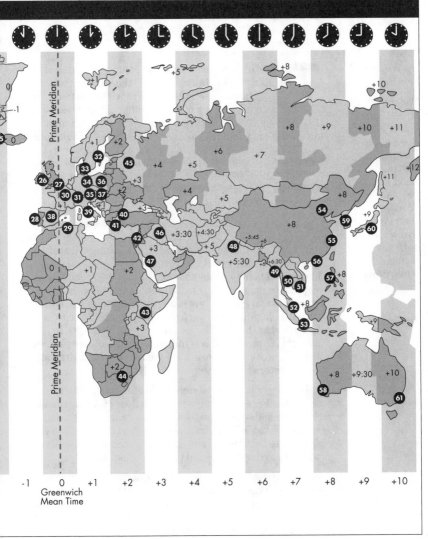

Introduction

By William G. Scheller

The author of More Country Walks Near Boston *and* New Hampshire: Portrait of the Land and Its People, *William Scheller contributes frequently to national and regional publications.*

Two destinations named Boston occupy the clutch of irregularly shaped peninsulas at the westernmost recess of Massachusetts Bay. The tourist's Boston is the old city, soul and anchor of that peculiar thing called New England civilization and the cradle of American independence. Its most famous buildings are not merely civic landmarks but national icons; its great citizens are not the political and financial leaders of today but the Adamses, Reveres, and Hancocks who live at the crossroads of history and myth. This city is 360 years old, far older than the republic it helped to create in the days of its vigorous youth.

The other Boston, built no less by design than the original, is barely three decades old and every bit as young and vigorous as Paul Revere's town. This is the business traveler's destination, the new Boston created by high finance and higher technology as an answer to those who thought the city had become scarcely more than a museum. It is a place of granite and glass towers rising along what once had been rutted village lanes, dwarfing the commercial structures that stood as the city's largest just a generation ago. In this new city, Samuel Adams is the name of a premium beer, and John Hancock is an insurance company with a dramatic headquarters tower designed by I. M. Pei.

It is entirely possible to come to Boston intent on visiting either the Freedom Trail or the 48th floor of Amalgamated Software and to get exactly what you want out of the experience. With a little extra time and effort, though, you can appreciate both the old and the new Boston and understand why they are really one and the same American city.

Boston is where the Mystic and the Charles flow together to form the Atlantic Ocean. That's the old attitude, and it has been reinforced by local anecdotes, such as the one about the Boston lady who said she had driven to the West Coast "by way of Dedham," and the one about the two Bostonians who blamed a spate of hot San Francisco weather on the fact that the sea was 3,000 miles distant. "The Bostonian who leaves Boston ought to be condemned to perpetual exile," a character says in William Dean Howells's *The Rise of Silas Lapham;* years later, Leverett Saltonstall, the Brahmin senator, said that "the real New England Yankee is a person who takes the midnight train home from New York."

The sayings and stories reinforce the popular notion that Boston is an exceedingly self-important town. Yet Bostonians are not the only people who take the place so seriously. Boston, in reality and in myth, surely looms larger than any other settlement of 600,000 souls in the United States, with the possible exception of San Francisco. The reason for this is hard to come by, but it has to be more than merely the result of masterful self-promotion on the part of a city where "the Lowells speak only to the Cabots, and the Cabots speak only to God" and the common folk used to vote "often and early for James Michael Curley."

Boston has an odd combination of reputations to live up to. For years, the standard line was that it was staid, respectable, and quick to raise its eyebrows at anything or anyone smacking of impropriety. It was a town in which the Watch and Ward Society recommended the books and plays that ought to be banned, where the major social outlets were evenings at the Symphony and afternoons at the Club, and where the loudest noise was the sound of dust and interest collecting on old Yankee money. More recently, word has gone around that Boston's enormous population of undergraduate and graduate students, artists, academics, and smart young professionals who graduated and stayed on have made the town a haven for foreign movies, late-night bookstores, racquetball, sushi restaurants, unconventional politics, and progressive rock bands.

Neither view is closer to the truth than the other, and neither will do on its own. Nor can the tempting but ultimately glib idea of homogenization prevail; for all its age and small physical size, Boston is one of the least socially homogeneous cities on earth. Sure, men with three last names sit in leather wing chairs at the Somerset Club, but in most of the city the prevailing idea of a club is the Holy Name Society or the Sons of Italy. Yes, you will see lampposts and litter barrels plastered with ads for performances by radical dance collectives, but Boston's big political concerns revolve around which shade of Democrat is running for high city office (a Republican would as soon swim to Provincetown) and how he will dispense help to the homeless, asphalt to the potholes, and goodwill to the high-tech barons. Women stockbrokers with Harvard M.B.A.s eat *gelato* and play racquetball; at the same time, guys in South Boston eat potato chips and play the numbers. Despite its small size, Boston compartmentalizes itself so neatly that you can come here and find as staid or as hip a city as you desire, and effectively ignore the city you chose not to find—even if you stay around for years.

In considering the roots of the Boston image and the Boston reality, we have to recognize two overwhelming influences on the Boston we know today. The first is Anglo-Saxon, a.k.a. Yankee or Brahmin. The second is unquestionably Irish, despite the diversity of the races and nationalities that have disembarked on the wharves of Boston during the past 150 years. Though there may never have been much love lost between the two factions, Boston is their mutual creation.

Most of the Yankees' ancestors left England in the 17th or the 18th century on a wing and a prayer, with little more than the clothes on their backs and a willingness to apprentice or even indenture themselves to compatriots who had already become established. There was nothing aristocratic about them then, and there is nothing aristocratic about them today—assuming we encounter them as the unspectacular yeomen and urban-suburban *bourgeoisie* who constitute the base coat of New England's overlay of populations. In the 1700s and early 1800s, however, some of them began to acquire fortunes to go with their ancient lineage, and thus the Brahmin was born. The term was first used by Dr. Oliver Wendell Holmes in *The Autocrat of the Breakfast-Table:* "He comes of the Brahmin caste of New England. This is the harmless, inoffensive, untitled aristocracy." Holmes himself was a sterling example of a Brahmin, as was his son and namesake the Supreme Court justice. Although not spectacularly wealthy, the Holmeses were vastly learned and endowed with a sense of civic responsibility. When combined with pedigree, these qualities counted as much as money in establishing the Brahmin mystique.

Money counted less and less as the years separated the Brahmins from their merchant-prince and industrialist ancestors who provided them with their China-trade porcelain, Back Bay town houses, and summer homes in Nahant. It became something you had but didn't talk about, something you devoted no great amount of time to multiplying. One theory as to why Boston lost out to New York in the struggle for financial supremacy in post–Civil War America credits the practice of tying up family legacies in trusteeships so that potential venture capital was inaccessible to one's heirs. But the best explanation is probably the simplest: making money with gusto began to seem gauche, a frenetic activity best left to ostentatious New Yorkers. It was thought far better to husband your resources and live a seemly life.

At worst, this attitude created a race of "cold-roast Bostonians," thin-lipped and tight with a dollar, as conservative in the realm of social and aesthetic ideas as they were with their portfolios. At best, it produced an atmosphere in which people spent their energies on public beneficence and the cultivation of the life of the mind rather than on commerce. Organizations such as the Appalachian Mountain Club, the American Ornithological Union, and the Massachusetts Trustees of Public Reservations were talked into vigorous existence over sherry and biscuits in the homes of comfortable men. Colonel Henry Lee Higginson founded the Boston Symphony and financed it for years out of his own pocket. Scholars such as Francis Parkman and Samuel Eliot Morison, secure in social standing and without pressing material needs, worked as hard writing history as their ancestors had making money. And men like Thomas Appleton cultivated salons in which good conversation for its own sake was the prized commodity.

Most important, the old Yankee money poured into education; the investment in scores of colleges and universities, more than anything else, has helped establish the region's present character.

Putting money into college endowments was the logical extension of the acute concern with education that the Puritans brought to Boston in 1630 and that manifested itself during that first decade in John Harvard's donation of his library to form the cornerstone of Harvard College. Finally, it was the means by which the idea of cold-roast Boston as a stodgy, intolerant, and unchanging place was laid to rest. The strains of dynamism and liberality evident in the intellectual and economic climate of Boston today are owed to the tremendous influx of fertile minds that the great investment in education made possible. People come here for schooling and never go home. Scientific and humane inquiry have reached critical mass in Boston, and the reactions go on and on. In time they may reach even to Boston's public schools, whose largely poor and minority children are too easily forgotten when municipal budgets and priorities must be set.

A s Boston is a city of colleges, it is also a city of neighborhoods. Neighborhoods are traditionally the bastions of continuity in a big city, places where a certain outlook and sense of parochial identity are preserved. Ironically, Boston's ethnic groups, the Irish in particular, have managed to maintain the conservative, tradition-minded neighborhood spirit cultivated by the Yankees when all Boston was the neighborhood. If any custom replaced beans and brown bread on Saturday night in the Back Bay, it was fish during Lent in Charlestown and Southie. The Irish, in this century, have been the keel of Boston.

The Irish began to arrive in the late 1840s, when the potato famine devastated their home island. Boston had never seen such an invasion of immigrants and was anything but ready. The famous "No Irish Need Apply" signs went up, although the rapid growth of the city made it necessary for the natives to give the Irish jobs. There were only so many farm girls willing to come to the city and enter domestic service, and few businesses during the boom time of the Civil War era could afford the Waltham Watch Company's "Yankees only" employment strictures.

The Irish found their way into jobs and into the social structure, and they found two avenues particularly appealing: the civil service, particularly in the police and fire departments, and local politics. The venture into politics was in large part a defensive maneuver, a means of consolidating power in municipal institutions when it was denied them in the social and economic spheres. The first Irish mayor was elected in 1886, and by 1906 John F. Fitzgerald, the legendary "Honey Fitz," held the office. He was fiercely Irish, the most flamboyant and assertive Boston politician, until Mayor Curley himself appeared and defined big-city machine politics in a way only Chicago's Richard Daley—and, some say, retired Boston mayor Kevin White—have surpassed.

The wresting of political power from the Yankees allowed the Irish and their more recently arrived ethnic allies to take care of their own, and loyalty and votes were the mortar in the agreement. Similarly, civil service and other relatively secure blue-collar positions were a path to the kind of security that translated itself into stable, parish-oriented neighborhoods made up of row upon row of triple-decker apartment buildings, the wooden monoliths known in Boston as "Irish battleships." While you are in the area, read one of Mike Barnicle's *Boston Globe* columns, which often recall the spirit of these neighborhoods. (Barnicle has long since decamped for the suburbs.)

The Irish and other ethnics, then, are the inheritors and guardians of the old Boston insularity and stability. It was neighborhood (not just Irish) discomfiture at the violation of this state of affairs that produced the terrible antagonisms associated with court-ordered school busing in the early 1970s. The new minorities—blacks, Hispanics, Asians—often find themselves in a situation similar to that faced by the new arrivals in the last century.

Nowadays working-class white enclaves and poor minority neighborhoods alike worry about the effects of gentrification, loosely defined as the migration of upper-middle-class, white-collar workers and professionals (yesterday's would-be suburbanites) into the core of the city, where there are town houses to be restored and apartments to be converted into condominiums. Boston was made to order for this implosion of the affluent because it has so much solid housing stock within walking distance of downtown. The prime gentrification areas are the South End, the Italian North End, Charlestown, and part of Dorchester. In Cambridge, the Central Square area is changing its tone. The South End, the most racially and ethnically mixed Boston neighborhood, stands to lose some of its diversity as poorer residents are displaced by the new gentry. In Charlestown and the North End, the white working class and older citizens are most likely to suffer from the disruption. Many people can move to blue-collar suburbs such as Malden or Revere, and graduate students priced out of Cambridge can always go to Somerville; the situation is more difficult for the low-income minorities and pension-dependent elderly. The disappearance of inexpensive rental housing has led to an increase in homelessness in Boston.

A lot can be said for gentrification. Places like Union Park in the South End and some of the streets around the Bunker Hill Monument in Charlestown look better than they have in years, and the city can certainly use the tax base. New businesses flourish, often selling kiwi fruit and the *Wall Street Journal* across from *bodegas* (Hispanic groceries) and tired old luncheonettes. Yet there are people who insist that the reclaimed blocks are pretty but sterile and that the old neighborhood identities have gone. One thing is certain: We have not seen the end of this new movement, which is beginning to spill over into traditional working-class neighborhoods such as South Boston. The threat to supplies of affordable housing stock is real enough; of the thousands of condominium units created in Boston in recent years, only a handful have been in new buildings. The majority have represented an upscaling of older rental units.

The appearance of the new gentry is evidence of the success of Boston's 30-year attempt to redefine its place in New England and the world. By the 1950s, Boston was living on its past. The industrial base had eroded, the population had begun to decrease (it is still about 100,000 below its peak), and the high-tech era had yet to begin. To the successive mayors Hynes, Collins, and White, and to the fiscal nabobs who made up the private advisory group known as "the Vault," it seemed to make sense to play up the service aspects of the local economy and at the same time to launch vast tear-down-and-start-over projects like the Prudential Center, Government Center, and Charles River Park. By the 1970s the emphasis had shifted from new construction to recycling old buildings, except downtown, where office towers rose at a frantic pace during the boom years of the 1980s. Other new projects included Copley Place, in the Back Bay, and several adjoining Park Square in Boston and Harvard and Kendall squares in Cambridge. Whether the physical plant was to be new or recycled, the objective—especially during the 16-year tenure of Mayor Kevin White—was the same: Boston was going to be a "world city," divested of its provinciality and standing shoulder to shoulder with New York and San Francisco, Frankfurt and Paris. Hotels and restaurants began to multiply. Logan Airport expanded. Banking flourished; once the Athens of America, Boston now wanted to become the Zürich. To paraphrase Carl Sandburg, Boston would be a player with computers and the nation's data handler. And the universities would continue to provide both an intellectual patina and a steady stream of technical accomplishments.

To a significant degree the plan has worked, and the legions of condo buyers and town-house restorers are part of a new order only recently slowed by the recession of the early 90s. What remains are the questions of how the old neighborhoods will fit in, whether the public school system can be salvaged, and whether there will be a middle class of any size in Boston as the century draws to a close.

Given a population with such divergent antecedents, and one caught up in such a vast civic overhaul, it is difficult to point to a "typical" Bostonian. We see a number of types—Cambridge academics, North Shore Brahmin ladies in town for the Friday afternoon symphony, business-suited young women with rucksacks and running shoes—but generalizations fail us. Even the famous old Boston accent is hard to pin down, beyond a few broad As and dropped Rs; there are so many emigrants from other parts of the country that the native speech has become hopelessly diluted. (One thing is certain: *No one* talks like the Kennedys, who developed an Irish Brahmin accent all their own.)

Your essential Bostonian does love sports and politics, probably because both are vehicles for argument. And argument is an ancient Celtic pastime, one the Yankees cultivated when Calvinists and freethinkers went toe-to-toe. The disputations could well be carried past recent Red Sox trades and the City Council to questions of whether Boston is on its way up or down, whether it is forward-thinking or preoccupied with the past, whether the "world city" label fits or not, whether Boston is fashionable or dowdy, progressive or conservative, wise to the world or just kidding itself. Go into a bar (or into the Union Boat Club, if you're a member) and pick your topic. You may well decide that it is sheer contentiousness, often mixed with respectable intelligence and more than a little rectitude, that put Boston on the map.

Boston, at least north and east of Massachusetts Avenue, is a compact city whose neighborhoods can be divided along precise lines. The city proper, at the tip of the Shawmut Peninsula, consists of Beacon Hill, the North End (largely Italian), the downtown retail and financial district, and Chinatown. Opposite the mouth of the Charles is Charlestown, and across the inner harbor to the north and east is East Boston and the airport. South Boston, much of it landfill, juts due east toward the outer harbor and its cluster of islands; it is not to be confused with the South End, which hugs the Huntington Avenue flank of the Back Bay and is bordered by Chinatown and Roxbury.

The Back Bay, with its orderly grid of streets, extends along the Charles opposite Cambridge, ending at Kenmore Square.

South of Kenmore Square are the Back Bay Fens; here are clustered two important art museums and a much-loved baseball park. Farther south is Roxbury, a largely black neighborhood that merges along its eastern border with biracial but poorly integrated Dorchester, and Jamaica Plain, one of the first of the "streetcar suburbs" brought into existence by turn-of-the-century trolley lines. West of Kenmore Square is the separate municipality of Brookline, which almost completely cuts off Allston and Brighton, two residential and industrial Boston neighborhoods, from the rest of the city. Brookline, long home to many of the Boston area's Jewish families, now shares with Allston and Brighton an increasing number of Asian residents.

Farther south still are West Roxbury, Roslindale, Hyde Park, and Mattapan, virtual suburbs within the city. People here are more likely to identify themselves as coming from these neighborhoods than as hailing from Boston itself. After all, parts of them are farther from Beacon Hill than Cambridge, Medford, or Winthrop.

Boston's neighborhoods and the surrounding suburbs have one thing in common aside from the Red Sox and zip codes beginning with 02. This is the Massachusetts Bay Transit Authority, or "T." The T's services are divided among conventional buses, buses that run like trolleys off overhead wires, real subway and elevated trains, and the Green Line, a trolley system that runs partly underground and partly at street level. The Green Line connects Lechmere Station, just across the Charles River from the Museum of Science, with Government Center, Park Street, and Copley Square; after Copley, it branches into lines serving Jamaica Plain, Boston College, Cleveland Circle, Brookline, and Newton. The Red Line, using conventional subway equipment, runs between Alewife Brook Parkway (in suburban Cambridge) and downtown by way of Harvard Square; from downtown, branches run to Mattapan by way of Dorchester, and to Braintree by way of Quincy. The Orange Line connects Malden (north of Boston) with downtown by way of Charlestown and continues along an all-new underground route through Roxbury to Forest Hills, Jamaica Plain. The Blue Line runs north from downtown to Logan Airport, East Boston, and Revere.

Few people speak well of any of these lines, although taking public transport is always better than driving. Better still, bring comfortable shoes or a bicycle.

1 Essential Information

Before You Go

Visitor Information

For general information and brochures, contact the **Greater Boston Convention and Visitors Bureau** (Box 490, Prudential Tower, Boston, MA 02199, tel. 617/536–4100).

For maps and brochures on Boston and the rest of Massachusetts, contact the **Massachusetts Office of Travel and Tourism** (100 Cambridge St., 13th floor, Boston, MA 02202, tel. 617/727–3201 or 800/447–MASS).

Tours and Packages

Should you buy your travel arrangements to Boston packaged or do it yourself? There are advantages either way. Buying packaged arrangements saves you money, particularly if you can find a program that includes exactly the features you want. You also get a pretty good idea of what your trip will cost from the outset. You have two options: independent packages and fully escorted tours (though the ones available here include Boston as part of a longer New England itinerary). Each has its advantages.

Escorted tours are most often via motorcoach, with a tour director in charge. They're ideal if you don't mind having limited free time and vacationing with strangers. Your baggage is handled, your time rigorously scheduled to pack in maximum sightseeing, and most meals planned. Escorted tours are therefore the most hassle-free way to see a destination, as well as the least expensive. Independent packages allow plenty of flexibility. They generally include airline travel and hotels, with certain options available, such as sightseeing, car rental, and excursions. Independent packages are more expensive than escorted tours.

Travel agents are your best source of recommendations for both tours and packages. They will have the largest selection, and the cost to you is the same as buying direct. Whatever program you ultimately choose, be sure to find out exactly what is included: taxes, tips, transfers, meals, baggage handling, ground transportation, entertainment, excursions, sports or recreation (and rental equipment if necessary). Ask about the level of hotel used, its location, the size of its rooms, the kind of beds, and its amenities, such as pool, room service, or programs for children, if they're important to you. Find out the operator's cancellation penalties. Nearly everyone charges them, and the only way to avoid them is to buy trip-cancellation insurance (*see* Trip Insurance, *below*). Also ask about the single supplement, a surcharge assessed to solo travelers. Some operators do not make you pay it if you agree to be matched up with a roommate of the same sex, even if one is not found by departure time. Remember that a program that has features you won't use, whether for rental of sporting equipment or discounted museum admissions, may not be the most cost-wise choice for you. Don't buy a Rolls-Royce, even at a reduced price, if all you want is a Chevy!

Fully Escorted Tours Escorted tours are usually sold in three categories: deluxe, first-class, and tourist or budget class. The big differences among the categories are the price and the level of accommodations. Some operators specialize in one category, while others offer a range. To judge just how fast-paced the tour is, review the itinerary carefully. If you are in a different hotel each night, you will be getting up early each day to head out, travel to your next destination, do some sightseeing, have dinner, and go to bed, then you'll start all over again. If you want some free time, make sure it's mentioned in the tour brochure; if you want to be escorted to every meal, confirm that any tour you consider does that. Also, when comparing programs, be sure to find out if the motorcoach is air-conditioned and has a restroom on board. Make your selection based on price and stops on the itinerary.

Top operators include **Maupintour** (Box 807, Lawrence, KS 66044, tel. 800/255–4266 or 913/843–1211) and **Tauck Tours** (11 Wilton Rd., Westport, CT 06881, tel. 800/468–2825 or 203/226–6911) in the deluxe category; **Gadabout Tours** (700 E. Tahquitz Way, Palm Springs, CA 92262, tel. 800/952–5068 or 619/325–5556) and **Globus-Gateway** (95-25 Queens Blvd., Rego Park, NY 11374, tel. 800/221–0090 or 718/268–7000) in the first-class range; and Globus's sister operator, **Cosmos** (at the same address) in the budget category.

Independent Packages
Independent packages are offered by airlines, tour operators who may also do escorted programs, and any number of other companies from large, established firms to small, new entrepreneurs. Boston packages are available from **American Airlines Fly AAWay Vacations** (tel. 800/321–2121), from **United Airlines Vacation Planning Center** (tel. 800/328–6877), which will customize a tour with your choice of hotel plus airfare and rental car, and **SuperCities** (Box 1789, Minneapolis, MN 55440, tel. 800/333–1234).

Their programs come in a wide range of prices based on levels of luxury and options—in addition to hotel and airfare, sightseeing, car rental, transfers, admission to local attractions, and other extras. Note that when pricing different packages, it sometimes pays to purchase the same arrangements separately, particularly when a rock-bottom promotional airfare is being offered.

Tips for British Travelers

Tourist Information
Contact the **United States Travel and Tourism Administration** (Box 1EN, London W1A 1EN, tel. 071/495–4466).

Passports and Visas
British citizens need a valid 10-year passport.

A visa is not necessary unless 1) you are planning to stay more than 90 days; 2) your trip is for purposes other than vacation; 3) you have at some time been refused a visa, or refused admission to the United States, or have been required to leave by the U.S. Immigration and Naturalization Service; or 4) you do not have a return or onward ticket. You will need to fill out the Visa Waiver Form, 1–94W, supplied by the airline.

To apply for a visa or for more information, call the U.S. Embassy's Visa Information Line (tel. 0891/200–290; calls cost 48p per minute or 36p per minute cheap rate). If you qualify for visa-free travel but want a visa anyway, you must apply in writing, enclosing a SAE, to the U.S. Embassy's Visa Branch (5 Upper Grosvenor St., London W1A 2JB), or, for residents of

Northern Ireland, to the U.S. Consulate General (Queen's House, Queen St., Belfast BTI 6EO). Submit a completed Nonimmigrant Visa Application (Form 156), a valid passport, a photograph, and evidence of your intended departure from the United States after a temporary visit. If you require a visa, call 0891/234-224 to schedule an interview.

Customs British visitors aged 21 or over may import the following into the United States: 200 cigarettes or 50 cigars or 2 kilograms of tobacco; one U.S. liter of alcohol; gifts to the value of $100. Restricted items include meat products, seeds, plants, and fruits. Never carry illegal drugs.

Insurance Most tour operators, travel agents, and insurance agents sell specialized policies covering accident, medical expenses, personal liability, trip cancellation, and loss or theft of personal property. Some policies include coverage for delayed departure and legal expenses, winter sports, accidents, or motoring abroad. You can also purchase an annual travel-insurance policy valid for every trip you make during the year in which it's purchased (usually only trips of less than 90 days). Before you leave, make sure you will be covered if you have a preexisting medical condition or are pregnant; your insurers may not pay for routine or continuing treatment, or may require a note from your doctor certifying your fitness to travel.

The Association of British Insurers, a trade association representing 450 insurance companies, advises extra medical coverage for visitors to the United States.

For advice by phone or a free booklet, "Holiday Insurance," that sets out what to expect from a holiday-insurance policy and gives price guidelines, contact the Association of British Insurers (51 Gresham St., London EC2V 7HQ, tel. 071/600–3333; 30 Gordon St., Glasgow G1 3PU, tel. 041/226–3905; Scottish Provincial Bldg., Donegall Sq. W, Belfast BT1 6JE, tel. 0232/249176; call for other locations).

Tour Operators Tour operators offering packages to Boston include **Albany Travel (Manchester) Ltd.** (Royal London House, 196 Deansgate, Manchester M3 3NF, tel. 061/833–0202); **British Airways Holidays** (Atlantic House, Hazelwick Ave., Three Bridges, Crawley, West Sussex RH10 1NP, tel. 0293/611611); **Greyhound World Travel Ltd.** (Sussex House, London Rd., East Grinstead, West Sussex RH19 1LD, tel. 0342/317317); **Key to America** (15 Feltham Rd., Ashford, Middlesex TW15 1DQ, tel. 0784/248777); **Kuoni Travel** (Kuoni House, Dorking, Surrey RH5 4AZ, tel. 0306/742222); **North American Vacations** (Acorn House, 172/174 Albert Rd., Jarrow, Tyne & Wear NE32 5JA, tel. 091/483–6226); **Thomson Citybreaks** (Greater London House, Hampstead Rd., London NW1 75D, tel. 081/200–8733).

Airfares Fares vary enormously. Fares from consolidators are usually the cheapest, followed by promotional fares such as APEX. A few phone calls should reveal the current picture. When comparing fares, don't forget to figure airport taxes and weekend supplements. Once you know which airline is going your way at the right time for the least money, book immediately, since seats at the lowest prices often sell out quickly. Travel agents will generally hold a reservation for up to 5 days, especially if you give a credit card number.

Four airlines fly direct to Boston: British Airways (tel. 081/897–4000) and American Airlines (tel. 0800/010151), departing Heathrow; and Northwest (tel. 0345/747800) and Virgin Atlantic (tel. 0293/747747) from Gatwick. Northwest also serves Prestwick.

Car Rental In the United States you must be 21 to rent a car; rates may be higher for those under 25. Extra costs cover child seats, compulsory for children under 5 (about $3 per day); additional drivers (around $1.50 per day); and the all-but-compulsory Collision Damage Waiver. To pick up your reserved car, you will need the reservation voucher, a passport, a United Kingdom driver's license, and a travel insurance policy covering each driver.

When to Go

Where the weather is concerned, the best times to visit Boston are late spring and the months of September and October. Like other American cities of the northeast, Boston can be uncomfortably hot and humid in high summer and freezing cold in the winter. Yet the city is not without its pleasures in these seasons. In summer, there are Boston Pops concerts on the Esplanade, harbor cruises, and scores of sidewalk cafés. In winter there is Christmas shopping on Newbury Street, First Night festivities on New Year's Eve, the symphony, the theater, and college drama and music seasons. And a lot can be said for winter afternoon light on red brick.

Each September, Boston and Cambridge welcome thousands of returning students, along with the perennially wide-eyed freshmen beginning their four-year (or longer) stays in Boston. University life is a big part of the local atmosphere, and it begins to liven considerably as the days grow shorter.

Autumn is a fine time to visit the suburbs. The combination of bright foliage and white church steeples may have been photographed countless times, but it will never become clichéd. The shore routes are less crowded in spring and fall, nearly all the lodging places and restaurants are open, and the Atlantic is as dramatic as ever.

For a classic shore vacation, summer is the only time to go. Select your preference—sailing, swimming, surfcasting, or just lying in the sun—and make your reservations early in the year.

Climate What follows are the average daily maximum and minimum temperatures for Boston.

Jan.	36F	2C	May	66F	19C	Sept.	71F	22C
	20	-7		49	9		55	13
Feb.	37F	3C	June	75F	24C	Oct.	62F	17C
	21	-6		58	14		46	8
Mar.	43F	6C	July	80F	27C	Nov.	49F	9C
	28	-2		63	17		35	2
Apr.	54F	12C	Aug.	78F	26C	Dec.	40F	4C
	38	3		62	17		25	-4

Information Sources For current weather conditions for cities in the United States and abroad, plus the local time and helpful travel tips, call the **Weather Channel Connection** (tel. 900/WEATHER; 95¢ per minute) from a touch-tone phone.

Festivals and Seasonal Events

Top seasonal events in Boston include Chinese New Year in late January or early February, the Boston Marathon in April, the Cambridge River Festival in July, and Harborfest (Boston's Fourth of July celebration), which is followed by a Boston Pops concert and fireworks. For dates and details, request a Calendar of Events from the **Greater Boston Convention and Visitors Bureau** (Box 490, Prudential Tower, Boston, MA 02199, tel. 617/536–4100).

Early Feb. Chinese New Year is celebrated in Boston's Chinatown, with special events at the Children's Museum, *300 Congress St., Museum Wharf, tel. 617/426–8855.*

Mid-Feb.–mid-Mar. The Boston Festival spotlights the city as a major winter destination. Scheduled events include an ice skating party in the Public Garden and Valentine's Day parties. *Tel. 617/536–4100.*

Mid-Mar. Annual Spring New England Flower Show blooms at the Bayside Expo Center. *Tel. 617/536–9280.*

Mid-Mar. St. Patrick's Day Parade is celebrated by many more than the city's substantial Irish population. Tel. 617/536–4100.

Mid-Apr. (Patriot's Day). Reenactment of Paul Revere's Ride from Hanover Street in Boston's North End to Lexington. *Tel. 617/536–4100.*

Mid-Apr. (Patriot's Day). Boston Marathon stretches from Hopkinton to Back Bay Boston. *Boston Athletic Association, tel. 617/236–1652.*

Mid-Apr.–mid-May. Big Apple Circus comes to Boston in conjunction with the Children's Museum. *Marine Industrial Park, 66 Summer St., tel. 617/423–6996.*

Mid-May. Art Newbury Street includes open houses at galleries and jazz and classical ensembles playing in the street. *Tel. 617/267–7961.*

Mid-May. Greater Boston Kite Festival is a high-flying event at Franklin Park. *Tel. 617/725–4505.*

Mid-May. Lilac Sunday at the Arnold Arboretum, from sunrise to sunset, celebrates 400 varieties of lilac in bloom. *Tel. 617/524–1718.*

June. Lowell Folk Festival attracts more than 100,000 music lovers to Lowell.

Mid-June. Bunker Hill Weekend is an authentic reenactment of the Battle of Bunker Hill in Charlestown, culminating in a parade. *Tel. 617/242–5641.*

Early July. Harborfest, Boston's annual Fourth of July celebration, takes place on Boston Harbor and along the Waterfront. *Tel. 617/227–1528.*

July 4. Boston Pops Concert and Fireworks Display is an annual extravaganza of music at the Hatch Shell and fireworks on the Esplanade along the Charles River. *Tel. 617/266–1492.*

Early July. Chowderfest takes place on the Harbor Terrace of the New England Aquarium on Central Wharf. *Tel. 617/227–1528.*

Mid-July. Cambridge River Festival features numerous outdoor events off Memorial Drive along the Charles River. *Tel. 617/349–4380.*

Late Aug. August Moon Festival breaks out in the streets of Chinatown. *Tel. 617/542–2574.*

Early Sept. Labor Day Festival in Lowell honors organized labor throughout the country.

Early Oct. Columbus Day Parade moves from East Boston to the North End. *Tel. 617/725–3952.*

Mid-Oct. Head of the Charles Regatta draws college crew teams from all over and spectators with blankets and beer. *Tel. 617/421–4356.*

Late Nov.–late Dec. Bells of Boston performs handbell ringing on weekends at Faneuil Hall. *Tel. 617/523–3886.*

Dec. Art Newbury Street/Fashion Newbury Street is sponsored by the galleries and shops along Newbury St. *Tel. 617/267–7961.*

Early Dec. Holiday Lighting of 25,000 bulbs takes place on Boston Common and at the tree in front of the Prudential Center. *Tel. 617/725–4033 and 617/236–3744.*

Mid-Dec. Boston Tea Party Reenactment takes place at the Boston Tea Party ship and museum at the Congress Street Bridge. *Tel. 617/338–1773.*

Mid-Dec. Christmas Revels in Cambridge celebrates the winter solstice with traditional dances, processionals, carols, and folk music. *Tel. 617/621–0505.*

New Year's Eve. First Night Celebration, a full day and night of outdoor and indoor concerts and festivities, culminates in fireworks over the Charles River. *Tel. 617/542–1399.*

What to Pack

Boston is generally regarded as one of the "dressier" American cities, although standards and expectations vary from one part of town to another. In Cambridge it is perfectly acceptable, in all but the best restaurants, to dress like a reasonably neat student regardless of your age; jeans and a sports shirt will get you in almost anywhere. For downtown Boston, Beacon Hill, and the Back Bay, however, more conservative dress is in order, especially in the evening. Many restaurants require that men wear jacket and tie. Women can wear anything from business clothes to casual dresses or slacks. Although elegant cocktail outfits are not required anywhere, there are plenty of restaurants where you can wear them and not feel overdressed. Winters are cold and snowy, so come prepared with heavy coats and sweaters, and take along snow boots or sturdy shoes with a good grip for those icy sidewalks.

Luggage Regulations Free baggage allowances on an airline depend on the airline, the route, and the class of your ticket. In general, on domestic flights and on international flights between the United States and foreign destinations, you are entitled to check two bags—neither exceeding 62 inches, or 158 centimeters (length + width + height), or weighing more than 70 pounds (32 kilograms). A third piece may be brought aboard as a carry-on; its total dimensions are generally limited to less than 45 inches (114 centimeters), so it will fit under the seat in front of you or in the overhead compartment. There are variations, so ask in advance. The Federal Aviation Administration safety regulation that pertains to carry-on baggage on U.S. airlines requires only that carry-ons be properly stowed, and allows the airline to limit allowances and tailor them to different aircraft and operational conditions. Charges for excess, oversize, or overweight pieces vary, so inquire before you pack.

Safeguarding Your Luggage Before leaving home, itemize your bags' contents and their worth; this list will help you estimate the extent of your loss if your bags go astray. To minimize that risk, tag them inside and out with your name, address, and phone number. (If you use your home address, cover it so that potential thieves can't see it.) At check-in, make sure that the tag attached by baggage handlers bears the correct three-letter code for your destination. If your bags do not arrive with you, or if you detect damage, do not leave the airport until you've filed a written report with the airline.

Baggage Insurance In the event of loss, damage, or theft on domestic flights, airlines limit their liability to $1,250 per passenger. Excess-valuation insurance can be bought directly from the airline at check-in but leaves your bags vulnerable on the ground. Insurance for lost, damaged, or stolen luggage is available as part of comprehensive travel insurance policies, including those issued by **Access America, Inc.,** underwritten by BCS Insurance Company (Box 11188, Richmond, VA 23230, tel. 800/284–8300); **Carefree Travel Insurance,** underwritten by The Hartford (Box 310, 120 Mineola Blvd., Mineola, NY 11501, tel. 516/294–0220 or 800/ 323–3149); **Tele-Trip** (Mutual of Omaha Plaza, Box 31762, Omaha, NE 68131, tel. 800/228–9792), a subsidiary of Mutual of Omaha; **The Travelers Companies** (1 Tower Sq., Hartford, CT 06183, tel. 203/277–0111 or 800/243–3174); **Travel Guard International,** underwritten by Transamerica Occidental Life Companies (1145 Clark St., Stevens Point, WI 54481, tel. 715/345–0505 or 800/782–5151); and **Wallach and Company, Inc.** (107 W. Federal St., Box 480, Middleburg, VA 22117, tel. 703/687–3166 or 800/237–6615), underwritten by Lloyds, London.

Getting Money from Home

Cash Machines Automated-teller machines (ATMs) are proliferating; many are tied to international networks such as **Cirrus** and **Plus.** You can use your bank card at ATMs away from home to withdraw money from your checking account and get cash advances on a credit-card account (providing your card has been programmed with a personal identification number, or PIN). Check in advance for limits on withdrawals and cash advances within specified periods. Remember that finance charges apply on credit-card cash advances from ATMs as well as on those from tellers. And note that transaction fees for ATM withdrawals outside your home turf will probably be higher than for withdrawals at home. For specific Cirrus locations in the United States and Canada, call 800/424–7787 (for U.S. Plus locations, 800/843–7587), and press the area code and first three digits of the number you're calling from (or the calling area where you want an ATM).

American Express The company's **Express Cash** system lets you withdraw cash
Cardholder and/or traveler's checks from a worldwide network of 57,000
Services American Express dispensers and participating bank ATMs. You must *enroll first* (call 800/CASH–NOW for a form and allow two weeks for processing). Withdrawals are charged not to your card but to a designated bank account. You can withdraw up to $1,000 per seven-day period on the basic card, more if your card is gold or platinum. There is a 2% fee (minimum $2.50, maximum $10) for each cash transaction, and a 1% fee for traveler's checks (except for the platinum card), which are available only from American Express dispensers.

At AmEx offices, cardholders can also cash personal checks for up to $1,000 in any seven-day period.

Wiring Money You don't have to be a cardholder to send or receive an **American Express MoneyGram** for up to $10,000. To send one, go to an American Express MoneyGram agent, pay up to $1,000 with a credit card and anything over that in cash, and phone a transaction reference number to your intended recipient, who needs only to present identification and the reference number to the nearest MoneyGram agent to pick up the cash. There are MoneyGram agents in more than 60 countries (call 800/543–4080 for locations). Fees range from 5% to 10%, depending on the amount and how you pay. You can't use American Express—only Discover, MasterCard, and Visa credit cards.

You can also use **Western Union.** To wire money, take either cash or a check to the nearest office. (Or you can order money sent by phone, using a credit card.) Money sent from the United States or Canada will be available for pick up at agent locations in Boston within minutes, and fees are roughly 5% to 10%. (Note that once the money is in the system it can be picked up at *any* location.) There are approximately 20,000 agents worldwide (call 800/325–6000 for locations).

Traveling with Cameras, Camcorders, and Laptops

About Film and Cameras If your camera is new or if you haven't used it for a while, shoot and develop a few rolls of film before leaving home. Pack some lens tissue and an extra battery for your built-in light meter, and invest in an inexpensive skylight filter, to both protect your lens and provide some definition in hazy shots. Store film in a cool, dry place—never in the car's glove compartment or on the shelf under the rear window.

Films above ISO 400 are more sensitive to damage from airport security X-rays than others; very high speed films, ISO 1,000 and above, are exceedingly vulnerable. To protect your film, carry it with you and ask for a hand inspection. Don't depend on a lead-lined bag to protect film in checked luggage—the airline may very well turn up the dosage of radiation to see what you've got in there. Airport metal detectors do not harm film, although you'll set off the alarm if you walk through one with a roll in your pocket. Call the Kodak Information Center (tel. 800/242–2424) for details.

About Camcorders Before your trip, put new or long-unused camcorders through their paces. Invest in a skylight filter to protect the lens, and check the lithium battery that lights up the LCD (liquid crystal display) modes. As for the rechargeable nickel-cadmium batteries that are the camera's power source, take along an extra pair, so while you're using your camcorder you'll have one battery ready and another recharging.

About Videotape Unlike still-camera film, videotape is not damaged by X-rays. However, it may be harmed by the magnetic field of a walk-through metal detector. Airport security personnel may want you to turn the camcorder on to prove that that's what it is, so be sure the battery is charged when you get to the airport.

About Laptops Security X-rays do not harm hard-disk or floppy-disk storage. Most airlines allow you to use your laptop aloft but request that you turn it off during takeoff and landing so as not to interfere with navigation equipment. Make sure the battery is charged when you arrive at the airport, because you may be asked to turn on the computer at security checkpoints.

Traveling with Children

Publications The *Boston Parents Paper* (Box 1777, Boston, MA 02130, tel. 617/522–1515), a monthly newspaper that has events and resource listings, is available free at such places as libraries, supermarkets, museums, children's shops, and nursery schools. *Family Travel Times,* published 10 times a year by **Travel With Your Children** (TWYCH, 45 W. 18th St., 7th Floor Tower, New York, NY 10011, tel. 212/206–0688; annual subscription $55), covers destinations, types of vacations, and modes of travel; an airline issue comes out every other year (the last one, February/March 1993, is sold to nonsubscribers for $10).

Books In and Out of Boston with (or without) Children, by Bernice Chesler (Globe Pequot Press, Box Q, Chester, CT 06412, tel. 800/243–0495 or 800/962–0973 in CT; 4th edition, $12.95 plus $2 postage) looks at the city from a child's point of view. *Great Vacations with Your Kids,* by Dorothy Jordan and Marjorie Cohen ($13; Penguin USA, 120 Woodbine St., Bergenfield, NJ 07621, tel. 800/253–6476), and *Traveling with Children—And Enjoying It,* by Arlene K. Butler ($11.95 plus $3 shipping per book; Globe Pequot Press, Box 833, Old Saybrook, CT 06475, tel. 800/ 243–0495, or 800/962–0973 in CT).

Tour Operators **GrandTravel** (6900 Wisconsin Ave., Suite 706, Chevy Chase, MD 20815, tel. 301/986–0790 or 800/247–7651) offers international and domestic tours for grandparents traveling with their grandchildren. The catalogue, as charmingly written and illustrated as a children's book, positively invites armchair traveling with lap-sitters aboard.

Hotels *Kids Love Boston* is a pamphlet sold by the Greater Boston Convention & Visitors Bureau (tel. 617/536–4100) with information on seasonal, family hotel packages. **The Four Seasons Hotel Boston** (200 Boylston St., Boston, MA 02116, tel. 617/338–4400) welcomes families with a host of amenities: a family packet of brochures and advice, cookies and milk before bedtime, plush bathrobes, food to feed the ducks in the Public Garden, complimentary movies, and a Toy Box—the toys are for keeps. **The Ritz-Carlton** (15 Arlington St., Boston, MA 02117, tel. 617/ 536–5700) provides family amenities that include an etiquette course and a special junior Presidential Suite (scaled down to child size) with an accompanying room for the parents.

Home Exchange This is obviously an inexpensive solution to the lodging problem, because house-swapping means living rent-free. You find a house, apartment, or other vacation property to exchange for your own by becoming a member of a home-exchange organization, which then sends you its annual directories listing available exchanges and includes your own listing in at least one of them. Arrangements for the actual exchange are made by the two parties to it, not by the organization. Principal clearinghouses include **Intervac U.S./International Home Exchange** (Box 590504, San Francisco, CA 94159, tel. 415/435–3497), the oldest, with thousands of homes for exchange in its three annual directories; membership is $62, or $72 if you want to receive the directories but remain unlisted. The **Vacation Exchange Club** (Box 650, Key West, FL 33041, tel. 800/638–3841), also with thousands of listings, publishes four annual directories plus updates; the $50 membership includes your listing in one book. **Loan-a-Home** (2 Park La., Apt. 6E, Mount Vernon, NY

10552, tel. 914/664–7640) specializes in long-term exchanges; there is no charge to list your home, but the directories cost $35 or $45 depending on the number you receive. **Vacation Exchange Club** (Box 820, Haleiwa, HI 96712, tel. 800/638–3841) specializes in home exchanges. The club publishes four directories a year, in January, March, July, and September, and updated late listings throughout the year.

Getting There On domestic flights, children under two not occupying a seat travel free. Various discounts apply to children 2–12. The FAA recommends the use of safety seats aloft and details approved models in the free leaflet **"Child/Infant Safety Seats Recommended for Use in Aircraft"** (available from the Federal Aviation Administration, APA-200, 800 Independence Ave. SW, Washington, DC 20591, tel. 202/267–3479). Airline policy varies. U.S. carriers must allow FAA-approved models, but because these seats are strapped into a regular passenger seat, they may require that parents buy a ticket even for an infant under 2 who would otherwise ride free.

Baby-sitting Make your child-care arrangements with the hotel concierge or
Services housekeeper. One local agency is **Parents in a Pinch** (45 Bartlett Crescent, Brookline, MA 02146, tel. 617/739–5437).

Hints for Travelers with Disabilities

Several organizations provide travel information for people with disabilities, usually for a membership fee, and some publish newsletters and bulletins. Among them are the **Information Center for Individuals with Disabilities** (Fort Point Pl., 27–43 Wormwood St., Boston, MA 02210, tel. 617/727–5540 or 800/462–5015 in MA between 11 and 4, or leave message; TDD/TTY tel. 617/345–9743); **MossRehab Hospital Travel Information Service** (1200 W. Tabor Rd., Philadelphia, PA 19141, tel. 215/456–9603, TDD tel. 215/456–9602); **The Society for the Advancement of Travel for the Handicapped** (SATH, 347 5th Ave., Suite 610, New York, NY 10016, tel. 212/447–7284, fax 212/725–8253); **The Travel Industry and Disabled Exchange** (TIDE, 5435 Donna Ave., Tarzana, CA 91356, tel. 818/368–5648); and **Travelin' Talk** (Box 3534, Clarksville, TN 37043, tel. 615/552–6670).

Greyhound Lines (tel. 800/752–4841) will carry a disabled person and companion for the price of a single fare. **Amtrak** (tel. 800/USA–RAIL) requests 24-hour notice to provide redcap service and special seats. Passengers with disabilities are entitled to a 15% discount on the lowest available fare.

Hints for Older Travelers

Organizations The **American Association of Retired Persons** (AARP, 601 E St. NW, Washington, DC 20049, tel. 202/434–2277) provides independent travelers the Purchase Privilege Program, which offers discounts on hotels, car rentals, and sightseeing, and the AARP Motoring Plan, provided by Amoco, which furnishes domestic trip-routing information and emergency road-service aid for an annual fee of $39.95 per person or couple ($59.95 for a premium version). AARP also arranges group tours, cruises, and apartment living through AARP Travel Experience from American Express (400 Pinnacle Way, Suite 450, Norcross, GA 30071, tel. 800/927–0111); these can be booked through travel agents, except for the cruises, which must be booked directly (tel. 800/745–4567). AARP membership is open to those 50 and over; annual dues are $8 per person or couple.

Two other membership organizations offer discounts on lodgings, car rentals, and other travel products, along with such nontravel perks as magazines and newsletters. The **National Council of Senior Citizens** (1331 F St. NW, Washington, DC 20004, tel. 202/347–8800) is a nonprofit advocacy group with some 5,000 local clubs across the United States; membership costs $12 per person or couple annually. **Mature Outlook** (6001 N. Clark St., Chicago, IL 60660, tel. 800/336–6330), a Sears Roebuck & Co. subsidiary with 800,000 members, charges $9.95 for an annual membership.

Note: When using any senior-citizen identification card for reduced hotel rates, mention it when booking, not when checking out. At restaurants, show your card before you're seated; discounts may be limited to certain menus, days, or hours. If you are renting a car, ask about promotional rates that might improve on your senior-citizen discount.

Tour Operators   **Saga International Holidays** (222 Berkeley St., Boston, MA 02116, tel. 800/343–0273), which specializes in group travel for people over 60, offers a selection of variously priced tours and cruises covering five continents.

Further Reading

Some classic Boston books are Louisa May Alcott's *Little Women*, Henry James's *The Europeans* and *The Bostonians*, William Dean Howells's *A Modern Instance* and *The Rise of Silas Lapham*, and George Santayana's *The Last Puritan*.

Individual histories are told in Gerald Green's *The Last Angry Man*, Edwin O'Connor's *The Last Hurrah*, Sylvia Plath's *The Bell Jar*, May Sarton's *Faithful Are the Wounds*, Anthony J. Lukas's *Common Ground*, and Scott Turow's *One L*.

Several other good reads are Alice Adams's *Superior Women*, James Carroll's *Mortal Friends*, Jean Stafford's *Boston Adventure*, and John Updike's *Couples*.

The mystery writers Jane Langton and Robert B. Parker locate the action of their novels in the Boston area.

Arriving and Departing

By Plane

Flights are either nonstop, direct, or connecting. A **nonstop** flight requires no change of plane and makes no stops. A **direct** flight stops at least once and can involve a change of plane, although the flight number remains the same; if the first leg is late, the second waits. This is not the case with a **connecting** flight, which involves a different plane and a different flight number.

More than 50 major airlines fly to Boston's Logan International Airport from principal cities in North America and around the world. In addition, several regional airlines link the Boston area with smaller cities and vacation areas throughout New

England. Many of these regional airlines come and go with each season, so it's best to consult a local travel agent, but **Continental Express** (tel. 617/569–8400) is one carrier.

Smoking Since February 1990, smoking has been banned on all domestic flights of less than six hours duration. A seat in a no-smoking section must be provided for every passenger who requests one, and the section must be enlarged to accommodate such passengers if necessary as long as they have complied with the airline's deadline for check-in and seat assignment. If smoking bothers you, request a seat far from the smoking section.

From the Airport to Downtown Boston Only three miles—and Boston Harbor—separate Logan International Airport from downtown, yet it can seem like 20 miles when you're caught in one of the many daily traffic jams at the two tunnels that go under the harbor. Boston traffic is almost always heavy, and the worst conditions prevail during the morning (6:30–9) and evening (3:30–7) rush hours.

A 24-hour toll-free ground transport number provides information on parking and bicycle access, as well as schedules for Logan Express and Logan Link buses, the subway, and the Airport Water Shuttle (tel. 800/235–6426). A call between 9 AM and 5 PM will receive personalized ground transportation assistance.

By Taxi Cabs can be hired outside each terminal. Fares should average about $15, including tip, assuming that the driver follows the direct Sumner Tunnel route, there are no major traffic jams, and you go no farther than the downtown business district. Call MASSPORT (tel. 617/561–1769) for cab information.

By Water Shuttle **The Airport Water Shuttle** (tel. 800/235–6426) operates year-round and takes approximately seven minutes to cross Boston Harbor. It goes from Logan Airport to Rowes Wharf every 15 minutes, Monday through Friday, 6 AM–8 PM. On Sunday it leaves every 30 minutes, noon–8 PM. A free shuttle bus operates between the airport ferry dock and all airline terminals. Connecting boats are available from Boston to Hingham (tel. 617/740–1253), and Hull (tel. 617/723–7800). The shuttle leaves Rowes Wharf for Logan Airport Monday through Friday (except major holidays), every 15 minutes, 6 AM–8 PM. On Sunday it leaves every 30 minutes, noon–8 PM. The one-way fare is $8 for adults, children under 12 ride free when accompanied by an adult, $4 for senior citizens.

By Subway The **MBTA Blue Line** to Airport Station is one of the fastest ways to reach downtown from the airport. Free shuttle buses connect the subway station with all airline terminals (tel. 800/235–6426).

By Bus The **Logan Link Service** connects all airport terminals to train and subway services at South Station. A one-way shuttle bus ticket is $5 per adult and free for children under 12. Buses depart from the airport every half hour on the half hour 7 AM–9 AM and 3:30 PM–6 PM and from South Station 6:30 AM–9 AM and 3 PM–7 PM weekdays only (tel. 800/23–LOGAN).

By Car If you are driving from Logan to downtown Boston, the most direct route is by way of the Sumner Tunnel ($1 toll inbound; no toll outbound). When there is a serious traffic delay in the tunnel, one alternative is to take Route 1A north to Route 16, then to the Tobin Bridge and into Boston.

The Airport Handicapped Van (tel. 617/561–1769) provides free service between terminals daily, on request.

By Car

New England's major highways are spokes leading to the hub of Boston. I–95 connects New York with Boston and continues north into New Hampshire and Maine. I–93, reached by I–89, is the major feeder from Canada and northwestern New England. The Massachusetts Turnpike (toll) runs east-west across the state and links up with the New York Thruway south of Albany.

Car Rentals

Boston's public transportation system is fine for reaching all historic and entertainment sites in the city, but renting a car gives you easy access to the North Shore, Lexington, Concord, Plymouth, and Cape Cod. Major rental companies with airport and downtown locations include Hertz (tel. 800/654–3131), Avis (tel. 800/331–1212), Budget (tel. 800/527–0700), and Thrifty (tel. 800/367–2277). American International (tel. 617/569–3550), at the airport, and Rent-A-Wreck (tel. 617/282–8200), in Somerville, offer some of the city's lowest rates; you might also check the local budget companies advertising in the weekly *Boston Phoenix*. The major rental companies charge $35–$50 per day for a subcompact, often with a daily allowance of just 75 free miles.

Extra Charges Picking up the car in one city and leaving it in another may entail drop-off charges or one-way service fees, which can be substantial. The cost of a collision or loss-damage waiver (*see below*) can be high, also.

Cutting Costs If you know you will want a car for more than a day or two, you can save by planning ahead. Major international companies have programs that discount their standard rates by 15%–30% if you make the reservation before departure (anywhere from two to 14 days), rent for a minimum number of days (typically three or four), and prepay the rental. Ask about these advance-purchase schemes when you call for information. More economical rentals are those that come as part of fly/drive or other packages, even those as bare-bones as the rental plus an airline ticket (*see* Tours and Packages, *above*).

Other sources of savings are the several companies that operate as wholesalers—companies that do not own their own fleets but rent in bulk from those that do and offer advantageous rates to their customers. Rentals through such companies must be arranged and paid for in advance. Among them are **Auto Europe** (Box 1097, Camden, ME 04843, tel. 207/236–8235 or 800/223–5555, 800/458–9503 in Canada) and **Connex International** (23 N. Division St., Peekskill, NY 10566, tel. 914/739–0066, 800/333–3949, 800/843–5416 in Canada). You won't see these wholesalers' deals advertised; they're even better in summer, when business travel is down. Always ask whether the prices are guaranteed and if unlimited mileage is available. Find out about any required deposits, cancellation penalties, and drop-off charges, and confirm the cost of the CDW.

One last tip: Remember to fill the tank when you turn in the vehicle, to avoid being charged for refueling at what you'll swear is the most expensive pump in town.

Insurance and Collision Damage Waiver The standard rental contract includes liability coverage (for damage to public property, injury to pedestrians, etc.) and coverage for the car against fire, theft (not included in certain countries), and collision damage with a deductible—most commonly $2,000–$3,000, occasionally more. In the case of an accident, you are responsible for the deductible amount unless you've purchased the collision damage waiver (CDW), which costs an average $12 a day, although this varies depending on what you've rented, where, and from whom.

Because this adds up quickly, you may be inclined to say "no thanks"—and that's certainly your option, although the rental agent may not tell you so. Planning ahead will help you make the right decision. By all means, find out if your own insurance covers damage to a rental car while traveling (not simply a car to drive when yours is in for repairs). And check whether charging car rentals to any of your credit cards will get you a CDW at no charge. Note before you decline that deductibles are occasionally high enough that totaling a car would make you responsible for its full value.

More than in any other eastern city, looking at a map *first* and having one with you at all times is essential in Boston. "We have lots of one-way streets and streets with the same names," a city spokesperson admitted cheerfully. "It's not an easy city to drive in, but it's worth it."

By Train

Boston is the northern terminus of **Amtrak**'s (tel. 617/482–3660 or 800/872–7245) Northeast Corridor. **South Station** (Atlantic Ave. and Summer St., tel. 617/345–7451) sees frequent trains arriving from and departing for New York, Philadelphia, and Washington, DC, with connections to all points in the nationwide Amtrak system. South Station is also the eastern terminus of Amtrak's Lake Shore Limited, which travels daily between Boston and Chicago by way of Albany, Rochester, Buffalo, and Cleveland. Amtrak's new New England Express, serving Boston to New York twice daily departs from here; reservations are required and travel time is just under 4 hours.

Boston's **North Station** (Causeway and Friend Sts., tel. 617/722–3200) is used by commuter trains serving points in Massachusetts north and west of the city.

By Bus

Greyhound (at South Station, tel. 617/423–5810) serves Boston with direct trips or connections to all major cities in North America. **Peter Pan Bus Lines** (555 Atlantic Ave., opposite South Station, tel. 617/426–7838) connects Boston with cities elsewhere in Massachusetts, Connecticut, New Hampshire, and New York. **Plymouth & Brockton Buses** (at the Peter Pan Terminal, tel. 508/746–0378) serve towns on Cape Cod. Connections with other modes of public transportation are now easier than ever with the completion of the new multilevel bus deck at South Station.

Staying in Boston

Important Addresses and Numbers

Tourist Information

Boston Common Information Kiosk. A multilingual staff provides maps, brochures, and information about ongoing events. *Tremont St., where the Freedom Trail begins, tel. 617/426–3115. Open Mon.–Sat. 8:30–5, Sun. 9–5.*

Greater Boston Convention & Visitors Bureau. Maps and foreign-language informational materials are available here. *800 Boylston St., Prudential Plaza, tel. 617/536–4100. Open daily 8:30–5.*

Massachusetts Tourism Office. The state tourism office has information on all Massachusetts cities and towns and on day trips. *Saltonstall Bldg., 13th floor, 100 Cambridge St., tel. 617/727–3201. Open weekdays 8:45–5.*

National Park Service Visitor Center. The center shows an eight-minute slide show on Boston's historic sites and provides maps and directions. *15 State St., across from the Old State House, tel. 617/242–5642. Open daily 9–5 in winter; daily 9–6 in summer. Closed major holidays.*

Traveler's Aid Society (17 East St., tel. 617/542–7286) will help to solve the problems of the distressed traveler, weekdays 8:45–4:45. The society has several "outreach booths" (manned by volunteers, so the hours vary): South Station (tel. 617/345–7460), Logan Airport Terminal A (tel. 617/569–6284), and Logan Airport Terminal E (tel. 617/567–5385); Mayor's 24-hour hotline (tel. 617/635–4500).

Emergencies

Police, fire, ambulance (tel. 911). Massachusetts General Hospital (tel. 617/726–2000). Physician Referral Service (weekdays 9–5; tel. 617/726–5800). Dental emergency (tel. 508/651–3521). Poison control (tel. 617/232–2120). Rape crisis center (tel. 617/492–7273).

24-Hour Pharmacies

CVS (Porter Square Shopping Plaza, Massachusetts Ave., Cambridge, tel. 617/876–5519); **Walgreens** (Gallivan Blvd., Dorchester, tel. 617/282–5246).

Getting Around

Boston is a walker's city. You are likely to move faster, and see more, anywhere in downtown, the North End, Beacon Hill, and the Back Bay when you stay on foot. Should you tire, the MBTA's bus, trolley, and subway system is efficient and economical.

By Bus

Bus, trolley, and subway service in Boston and surrounding cities and towns is provided by the Massachusetts Bay Transportation Authority (MBTA). The MBTA bus routes crisscross the metropolitan area and extend farther into the suburbs than those of the subways and trolleys. (Some suburban schedules are designed primarily for commuters.) Current fares on MBTA local buses are 60¢ for adults, 30¢ children 5–11, free under 5. An extra fare is required for the longer suburban bus trips. For general travel information, tel. 617/722–3200 or 800/392–6100 or TDD 617/722–5146, weekdays 6:30 AM–11 PM, weekends 9–6; for 24-hour recorded service information, tel. 617/722–5050; for customer relations, tel. 617/722–5125; for specific

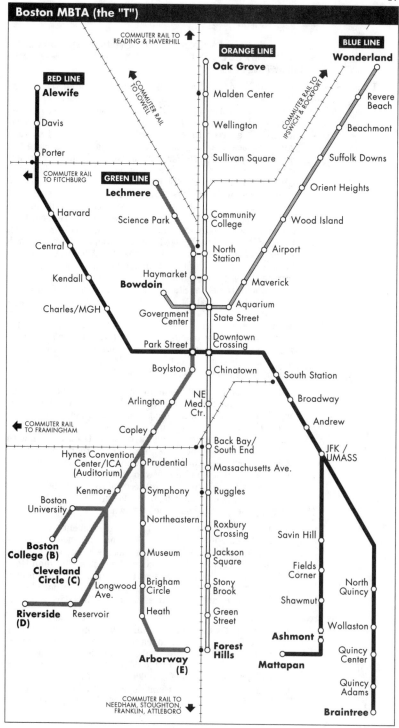

bus route information, tel. 617/722–5000; for MBTA police emergency, tel. 617/722–5151.

A free map of the entire public transportation system is available at the Park Street Station information stand (street level), open daily 7 AM–10 PM.

By Subway and Trolley The MBTA, or "T," operates subways, elevated trains, and trolleys along four connecting lines. The **Red Line** has points of origin at Braintree and Mattapan to the south; the routes join near South Boston and proceed to Harvard and to suburban Arlington. The **Green Line** is a combined underground and elevated surface line, originating at Cambridge's Lechmere and heading south through Park Street to divide into four major routes: Boston College (Commonwealth Avenue), Cleveland Circle (Beacon Street), Riverside, and Arborway. Green Line trains are actually trolleys that travel major streets south and west of Kenmore Square and operate underground in the central city. The **Blue Line** runs from Bowdoin Square (near Government Center) to the Wonderland Racetrack in Revere, north of Boston. The **Orange Line** runs from Oak Grove in north suburban Malden to Forest Hills near the Arnold Arboretum. Park Street Station (on the Common) is the major downtown transfer point for Red and Green Line trains; the Orange and Blue Lines intersect at State Street. Trains operate from about 5:30 AM to about 12:30 AM. Current fares on subways and trolleys are 85¢ for adults, 40¢ for children 5–11, free under 5. An extra fare is required for the distant Green and Red Line stops. Visitor travel passes ($5 for one day, $9 for 3 days, $18 for 7 days) are available at the Boston Common Information Kiosk, Airport station, Back Bay station, Bostix, Out-of-Town News in Cambridge, and the Quincy Market information booth.

By Car Those who cannot avoid bringing a car into Boston should be able to minimize their frustration by keeping to the main thoroughfares and by parking in lots—no matter how expensive—rather than on the street. Parking on Boston streets is a tricky business. Some neighborhoods have residents-only rules, with just a handful of two-hour visitor's spaces; others have meters (25¢ for 15 minutes, two hours maximum). The meter maids are ruthless, and repeat offenders who don't pay fines may find the boot (an immovable steel clamp) secured to one of their wheels by the police. In other words, if you do get parking tickets, pay them if you expect to come back to town.

The major public parking lots are at Government Center and Quincy Market; beneath Boston Common (entrance on Charles Street); beneath Post Office Square; at the Prudential Center; at Copley Place; and off Clarendon Street near the John Hancock Tower. Smaller lots are scattered through the downtown area. Most are expensive, especially the small outdoor lots; a few city garages are a bargain at about $6–$10 a day.

By Taxi Cabs are not easily hailed on the street, except at the airport; if you need to get somewhere in a hurry, use a hotel taxi stand or telephone for a cab. Companies offering 24-hour service include **Checker** (tel. 617/536–7000), **Independent Taxi Operators Association** or ITOA (tel. 617/426–8700), **Green Cab Association** (tel. 617/628–0600 or 617/623–6000), **Town Taxi** (tel. 617/536–5000), and, in Cambridge, **Cambridge Taxi** (tel. 617/876–5000). The current rate is about $1.60 per mile; traffic patterns (one-way streets) often make circuitous routes necessary and add to the cost.

By Limousine The **Airways Transportation Company** (160 Ipswich St., tel. 617/267–2981) takes passengers from any airport terminal to any downtown hotel for $7.50. Minibuses operate daily on the half hour from 7 AM to 7 PM and on the hour from 7 PM to 10 PM. Call for reservations.

By Train The MBTA runs commuter trains to points south, west, and north of Boston. Trains to Framingham, Needham, Franklin, Providence (RI), and Stoughton leave from **South Station** (tel. 617/722–3200). Trains to Fitchburg, Lowell, Haverhill, Ipswich, and Rockport operate out of **North Station** (tel. 800/392–6099).

By Commuter **Mass Bay Lines** (60 Rowes Wharf, tel. 617/542–8000) and **Bos-**
Boat **ton Harbor Commuter Service** (349 Lincoln St., Hingham, tel. 617/740-1253) operate commuter service between Rowes Wharf in downtown Boston and Hewitt's Cove, off Route 3A in Hingham on the South Shore. Schedules change seasonally; call ahead for the current departure times.

Opening and Closing Times

Banks are generally open weekdays 9–4. Some branches are open Sat. 9–noon or 9–1. **Museums** are generally open Mon.–Sat. 9 (or 10)–5 (or 6), Sun. noon–5. Many are closed Mon. **Post Office** hours vary. Most are open weekdays 8–5, Sat. 9–12, and some close Thurs. afternoon; the General Post Office (25 Dorchester Ave., behind South Station, tel. 617/654–5225) is open weekdays 8–8, Sat. 8–5. A self-service machine is available 24 hours. **Public buildings** are open weekdays 9–5. The main branch of the **Boston Public Library** (Copley Sq., tel. 617/536–5400) is open Mon.–Thur. 9–9, Fri.–Sat. 9–5. **Shops** and stores are generally open Mon.–Sat. 9 (or 9:30)–6 (or 7). Many stay open later toward the end of the week. Some, particularly those in malls or tourist areas, are open Sun. noon–5.

Guided Tours

When it comes to touring Boston and environs, today's visitor has the same two options the British had when they struck out at the Middlesex hinterland; by land or by sea. There are several good bus and harbor boat tours, any one of which will whet your appetite for further exploration.

Orientation Tours A guided bus tour is an excellent way for visitors to get their
By Land bearings, both historically and geographically. The in-depth Brush Hill and Gray Line tours are specifically designed for first-time visitors.

Brush Hill Transportation Company (439 High St., Randolph, tel. 617/986–6100). Buses leave from several downtown hotels twice daily from late April to early November for 3½-hour "Boston Adventure" tours of Boston and Cambridge, with stops at the USS *Constitution* and the Tea Party Ship. Winter tours are pared down and leave once a day. Brush Hill also offers tours of Lexington and Concord, as well as Plymouth.
The Gray Line (275 Tremont St., tel. 617/426–8805). A three-hour tour of Greater Boston on a double-decker bus, departing from several downtown hotels, includes the Freedom Trail, the

USS *Constitution*, and the Boston Tea Party ship. Another three-hour tour takes in Lexington, Concord, and Cambridge. A seven-hour tour combines the two tours with a visit to Sudbury. For those who want to explore further, there are trips to Plymouth, Cape Cod, Salem, Gloucester, Martha's Vineyard, and Old Sturbridge Village. In autumn the fall foliage tours take passengers along the coast, to western Massachusetts, and to northern New England. There are no tours offered from December through early spring.

Old Town Trolley (329 W. 2nd St., tel. 617/269–7010). The trolley takes you on a 1½-hour narrated tour of Boston or an hour-long tour of Cambridge. You can catch the trolley at major hotels, Boston Common, Copley Place, or in front of the New England Aquarium on Atlantic Avenue.

By Water **AC Cruise Line** (148 Northern Ave., tel. 617/426–8419). From Memorial Day through Labor Day, the cruise to Gloucester departs daily at 10 AM from their pier on Northern Avenue. Departure times are subject to change; call ahead.

Boston Harbor Cruises (1 Long Wharf, tel. 617/227–4320). Harbor sightseeing tours operate from mid-April through October.

Bay State Cruise Co. (ticket office at 67 Long Wharf, tel. 617/723–7800). Harbor trips to Georges Island are scheduled on the hour: weekdays 10–3, weekends 10–6.

Charles River Boat Co. (100 Cambridgeside Pl., Suite 320, Cambridge, tel. 617/621–3001) offers a 50-minute narrated tour of the Charles River Basin. It departs from the Galleria and Museum of Science dock on the hour from noon–5 daily June–Sept., and on weekends in April, May, and October. A 3-hour dinner cruise on the river and into Boston harbor through the locks departs from the Galleria at 7 PM nightly May–Oct. River cruise is $6 adults, $5 senior citizens, $4 children; dinner cruise is $39 per person.

Special-Interest Tours **Beacon Hill Garden Club Tours** (Box 302, Charles St. Station, tel. 617/227–4392). Every year, on a day in mid-May, the Garden Club sponsors a tour of Beacon Hill's hidden gardens. Tickets may be purchased (in advance or on the day of the tour) at several locations on Beacon Hill and in the Back Bay. Ticket proceeds go toward civic improvements.

Boston Garden Tours and History Center (Boston Garden, Causeway St., tel. 617/720–1002). Visitors take a 45-minute tour of the Garden, which was built in 1928. A new arena is under construction behind the current one, scheduled to open in September 1995. Until then, get a glimpse of the Celtics and Bruins memorabilia, banners hanging from the rafters, and the parquet floors or ice where the games are played; tour the visiting team's locker rooms too. Tours are given every half hour. Admission: $5 adults, $4 senior citizens, $3.50 children under 12. Open daily 10–3:30.

The Boston Globe (135 Wm. T. Morrissey Blvd., tel. 617/929–2652). The city's largest newspaper gives tours, by appointment, Tuesday and Thursday. Tours are free, but participants must be at least 12 years old. Call a few days in advance.

Boston Park Rangers (Parks and Recreation Dept., tel. 617/522–2639) lead nature walks throughout the city's almost 200 parks. All programs are free but a few require reservations; call ahead for current program information.

Commonwealth Brewing Company (138 Portland St., tel. 617/523–8383). This tiny brewery, which began operations in 1986, makes English-style ales and stouts by traditional methods.

The brewery tour is Saturday at 3:30 and Sunday at noon. After the tour, you might want to have a sandwich or a light entrée and sample one of the many beers at the brewery restaurant.

Federal Reserve Bank (600 Atlantic Ave., tel. 617/973–3451). Tours are scheduled every Friday at 10:30 AM, and reservations should be made one week in advance. Visitors will see money counted, checks processed, the computer and currency departments, and a slide program on the function and purpose of the Federal Reserve Bank.

Make Way for Ducklings Tours (Historic Neighborhoods Foundation, 2 Boylston St., tel. 617/426–1885). Tours for children five and older, accompanied by adults, are held on Saturday in late spring, on Friday and Saturday from July 4 to Labor Day. The path begins at Boston Common and follows the route taken by the ducks in Robert McCloskey's popular children's book, *Make Way for Ducklings*.

Samuel Adams Lager Brewery (Boston Beer Company, Jamaica Plain, tel. 617/522–9080) offers 90-minute tours with a tasting at the end, on Thurday at 2 PM and Saturday at noon and 2. Made in small batches, the beer has won more awards than any other American beer. It's also the only beer to pass Germany's strict beer purity law, and to be imported for sale there.

Whale Watches. *A. C. Cruise Company* (148 Northern Ave., tel. 617/426–8419) has whale-watch cruises Wednesday to Sunday at 10:30, mid-April to mid-October ($15 adults, $10 children). The *New England Aquarium* (Central Wharf, off Atlantic Ave., tel. 617/973–5277) sponsors five-hour cruises weekdays at 10 and weekends at 8:30 and 2, May to early October ($23 adults, $18.50 senior citizens and students, $16 children 4–15).

Walking Tours   **Bay Colony Historical Tours** (Box 9186, JFK Post Office, Boston 02144, tel. 617/523–7303). The motorcoach tours of historic areas of Boston are narrated in English and other languages. Custom-designed itineraries, walking tours of the Freedom Trail geared to high school students, and senior citizen tours are available.

Black Heritage Trail (tel. 617/742–5415). A 90-minute walk explores the history of Boston's 19th-century black community. The route passes 14 sites of historical importance on Beacon Hill, including the African Meeting House and the Robert Gould Shaw and 54th Regiment Memorial honoring the North's first black regiment. Guided tours are available by appointment in the winter, and from April–Oct. at 10, noon, and 2 daily from the Shaw Memorial in front of the State House on Beacon Street. Maps and brochures can be obtained for self-guided tours.

Boston by Foot (77 North Washington St., tel. 617/367–2345 or 617/367–3766 for recorded information). A variety of guided walks, available from May to October, includes the Freedom Trail, Copley Square, Beacon Hill, and the North End. Special tours are given once a month. "Boston By Little Feet," an hour-long tour for children 6–12 accompanied by an adult, is held weekly.

Boston Center for Adult Education (5 Commonwealth Ave., tel. 617/267–4430). The BCAE offers perhaps more walking tours than anyone else in Boston. Among the walks are Gallery Hopping on Newbury Street, Contemporary Art on South Street, a tour of Jewish Boston, Back Bay Mansions, the Emerald Necklace, the artsy and elegant South End, and development along the waterfront. You may register over the phone, but there is a limit on the number of people permitted on each tour. It's best to call for a catalogue prior to your visit. Tours average $30 per person.

Boston Walkabouts. A dramatized 64-minute cassette tape tour of the Freedom Trail, in English, French, German, and Japanese versions, is available for $8.95 from Uncommon Boston (437 Boylston St., Boston 02116, tel. 617/731–5854). You must write or phone ahead to have a tape mailed to you.

Freedom Trail. The mile-and-a-half Freedom Trail is marked in the sidewalk by a red line that winds its way past 16 of Boston's most important historic sites. The walk begins at the Freedom Trail Information Center on the Tremont Street side of Boston Common, not far from the MBTA Park Street station. Sites along the Freedom Trail include the State House, Park Street Church, Old Granary Burial Ground, King's Chapel and burying ground, Globe Corner Bookstore, Old State House, Boston Massacre Site, Faneuil Hall, Paul Revere House, Old North Church, Copp's Hill Burying Ground, and the USS *Constitution*, with a side trip to the Bunker Hill Monument.

Harborwalk. Maps are available at the Boston Common Information kiosk for a self-guided tour that traces Boston's maritime history. The walk begins at the Old State House (206 Washington St.) and ends on the Congress Street Bridge near the Boston Tea Party ship and museum.

Historic Neighborhoods Foundation (2 Boylston St., tel. 617/426–1885) is a nonprofit educational foundation that offers a variety of informal and informative guided walking tours, from April through November, covering the North End, Chinatown, Beacon Hill, and the waterfront. A Sunset Stroll through Beacon Hill takes place on Thursday from late April to late August. Tours are Wednesday–Saturday, one neighborhood a day, on a rotating schedule. Ticket prices average $5, and groups are limited to 15 people. Call for the schedule.

Uncommon Boston (437 Boylston St., 5th floor, Boston 02116, tel. 617/731–5854) will make all arrangements for a specific tour or for your entire stay in the city, including meeting you at the airport. The group acts as meeting planners and convention coordinators and coordinates scheduled tours throughout the year—such as "Graveyards and Goodies" at Halloween.

Victorian Society in America (Gibson House Museum, 137 Beacon St., tel. 617/267–6338). This organization sponsors a number of walking tours centered on specific Boston sites, neighborhoods, and architecture representative of the Victorian era.

Women's Heritage Trail (tel. 617/731–5597). Celebrating the lives of 20 women who have made significant contributions to Boston and the nation, this walking trail includes 12 downtown sites. Take a self-guided tour or join a guided tour given on weekends in the summer for a donation. Stop by the National Park Service office next to the Old State House, or the Old South Meeting House for a map; call for weekend reservations.

2 Portraits of Boston

Lobster, Clams, Beans, and Other Favorite Viands of Boston

By Kay Howe Scheller

A freelance writer, Kay Howe Scheller serves also as an advertising consultant specializing in small businesses.

My moment of truth came not in a bullring in Madrid but at a restaurant in Boston. At the stolidly self-righteous age of 12 I had just become a full-fledged vegetarian when, on a family outing to Anthony's Pier 4, my uncle ordered me my first lobster.

It came artfully arranged on a large platter, its tail jutting playfully in the air, its eyes practically level with mine. And, oh, those eyes. Small, hard, as black as the ocean floor at 300 feet, they stared right into my soul, mutely challenging my every humanitarian conviction.

My uncle reached over, cracked open the tail, tore out an enormous chunk of white meat, dredged it in a bowl of hot melted butter, and popped it into my mouth. I knew then that the battle was lost.

After that, whenever we journeyed to Boston from our little landlocked town to the west, I would head for the nearest restaurant that served lobster. It took me years to explore its many variations: baked stuffed lobster, lobster thermidor, lobster pie, lazy man lobster, lobster newburg. I went to Chinatown to sample lobster Cantonese and to the North End to find lobster *fra diavolo*. I ate lobster boiled in seawater, lobster boiled in beer, lobster boiled in champagne.

When I moved to Boston to attend Boston University, I had time to visit the piers along Atlantic Avenue and to see the incredible variety of fish that were hauled in from the Atlantic Ocean by commercial fishermen every day: tuna, bluefish, flounder, haddock, squid, striped bass, tilefish, monkfish, sand dab, mako shark, and of course the sacred cod, a source of great debate among locals and great confusion to tourists. (Schrod, or scrod, denotes a filet taken from the large-flake, white-meat, mildly flavored young cod or haddock.) I discovered that in Boston, while everyone seems to have a different opinion about which fish is the tastiest, most people agree on the best way to cook it: broiled. If you want to go to hell with yourself, add a dab of butter. The theory is that fresh fish needs no disguise (and if it's not fresh, don't eat it).

Once I had sampled every kind of fish available, I became a connoisseur of the clam, a New England food that dates back to the Indians. I learned that there are two kinds of clams: soft-shell or steamer, named for the way they are generally served, steamed until their soft, brittle shells open to expose the meat (overcooking will make them tough), and hard-shell or quahog (pronounced *co-hog),* which come in two sizes, littleneck (the smallest) and cherrystone. I made a pilgrimage to Woodman's in Essex, where the fried clam was invented, to taste them fried lightly in batter with their bellies intact, and I realized that the clam strips at Howard Johnson's were a poor imitation indeed.

I bought a clam rake and went out on the mud flats of the Parker River to dig up some of the littlenecks for which the river is famous. After steaming them just until they opened, I removed the meat from its shell, peeled away the dark, inedible membrane, swished the clam in hot clam broth to wash away the sand, dipped it in melted butter, and let 'er slide. I can describe the taste only as what it must be like to eat a candied ocean wave on a hot summer day. The holy lobster had at last found some competition. The larger quahogs from Cape Cod tasted brinier; with the addition of light cream, salt pork, and potatoes, they made the most wonderful chowder imaginable.

It took me some time to try a raw clam. When I looked at one, shimmering pristinely in its half shell, I understood the saying that "the bravest man in the world is the one who ate the first raw clam." Nevertheless, ever committed, I mustered my courage, dabbed the clam with lemon and Tabasco, scooped it from its shell with my teeth, and let it slide down my throat—and it was good!

Oysters are not as popular in Boston as clams, but I bought them whenever I saw them, and I am hard pressed to say which makes the tastier meal.

Small, delicate, sweet scallops from Cape Cod Bay, broiled to perfection or marinated in lime juice and added to a summer salad; sea scallops, harvested from the cold waters off Gloucester, fried to a golden brown and served with homemade tartar sauce; tiny sweet shrimp or fresh mussels from Maine, sauteed with white wine, garlic, and parsley: Exploring the variations and complexities of New England seafood took me right through my college years.

At the same time, I was fascinated with other specialties of the Boston area. I learned about baked beans from my neighbor, Allie Taylor, a died-in-the-wool Yankee who, like her mother before her, has been cooking them in her special stone crock every Friday night for 50 years. She explained that salt pork, molasses, and hours of slow cooking give the beans their distinctive smoky flavor and rich, sweet taste. (I also learned that very few restaurants make their own; the Ritz, Locke-Ober's, and Durgin-Park are three that still do.) When Allie brought over a pot of beans, she would bring along a big chunk of brown bread "to chase 'em down." Brown bread is made with cornmeal, sour milk or buttermilk, and dark molasses; like the beans, it cooks for hours. Baked beans and brown bread have been a tradition-al Boston dinner since the pilgrims learned how to grow corn, and judging by the way the two go together, I expect they'll be a New England favorite for generations to come.

Another bread that has been around since the days of the pilgrims—and is a popular staple at traditional New En-gland restaurants such as Durgin-Park and the Union Oys-ter House—is cornbread. Aficionados can rave for hours about the delicious grainy texture and the sweet, nutty taste. Those, like myself, who are less enthusiastic are con-vinced that one of its main ingredients is sawdust.

Cornmeal is the principal ingredient in one of the re-gion's most popular desserts, Indian pudding. Corn-meal, molasses, sugar, butter, milk, eggs, and spices are baked in a stone crock for hours, until the sugar caramelizes, the cornmeal swells, and the pudding takes on the density of a foggy night on the coast of Maine. This is another of those dishes that inspires either great loyalty or a loud raspberry. Yet it's easy to understand how the Pil-grims, fortified with a meal of baked beans, brown bread, and Indian pudding, were able to clear the wilderness with-out chain saws or Rototillers. (Or perhaps it's difficult to understand how they could stand up after such a repast.) I much prefer to finish my meal with another New England tradition, the apple pandowdy, a cobbler made with spiced apples in a biscuit dough crust.

When you come to Boston in search of traditional New En-gland fare, look for me at the nearest restaurant that's hold-ing a clambake over an open wood fire. You can't be more traditional than steamers, broth and butter, lobster, corn on the cob, hot dogs, and watermelon. Or perhaps I'll be trying to find the perfect Yankee pot roast or scouring the lobster pounds of Rockport for a four-pounder. The one sure bet is that I won't be out shopping for vegetarian hot dogs.

The Buildings of Boston

By Jane Holtz Kay

Architecture critic for The Nation and a contributor to Progressive Architecture and the Boston Globe, Jane Holtz Kay is the author of Lost Boston and Preserving New England.

The "destination" building, the star of picture post-cards, the familiar structure that draws pilgrims and makes architects' lists, is not a common feature in Boston. The buildings of Boston are less renowned for their solo performance than for their place in a corps. It is the city's overall urban design—the relationship of splendid but neighborly buildings to their community—that gives Boston and its architecture a remarkable identity.

Boston's architecture of ensemble came about almost naturally as the city coped with the features of the landscape in its need to grow. The city founded by the Puritan John Winthrop in 1630 was a place of wetlands and mud flats crowned by three hills. Much smaller than Boston today, the original Boston of 783 acres soon seemed too small. The expansion that followed over three centuries demanded the cutting down of the hills to fill in the coves, a heroic process of transforming topography that called on an army of planners and builders, excavators and architects. Beacon Hill was shaved, the Back Bay formed on the mud flats, and Boston architecture became necessarily a product of collaboration.

Even the city's most renowned architects, Charles Bulfinch and H. H. Richardson, contributed more than their solitary masterpieces. Bulfinch, the city's Federalist architect-hero, not only redesigned the handsome State House and Faneuil Hall but shaped entire architectural enclaves and framed the city's parks. Richardson, America's most famous architect in the 19th century, created America's best known building in that century, Trinity Church, and also designed bridges on a vast park system from the city to the suburbs.

The city-making—the ultimate act of architecture—began slowly. A town whose economy was dependent on seafaring commerce, Boston needed more land to dock its sailing ships and warehouse the goods of its merchants. Moving outward from the crowded shores of the Shawmut peninsula, the city's builders "wharfed out" the town: Layer upon layer of fill topped by brick wharf buildings gradually fingered out to the sea in the 17th and 18th centuries. The North End, with its compact, medieval configuration of houses and streets, became the commercial end of the town. As time passed, builders filled the space between these digits of commerce to create the fist of the 19th century.

At the close of the Revolution, the once slumbering Colonial city again needed to expand, and the city fathers accelerated the ruthless enterprise of growth. The first Boston had grown up around its three hills, Beacon, Copp's, and Fort—the peaks of the old "Tramount" or "Tri-mountain," remembered in today's Tremont Street. (Early portraits depict the three hills serenely overlooking the rocky landscape and watery prospect of Boston.) As the population of postrevolutionary Boston swelled, land-hungry Bostonians simply carved their peaks. The earth from Copp's and Beacon was used to fill the North End's mill pond. Atop the pared down Beacon Hill, the grand dome of Bulfinch's State House was constructed. Copp's Hill became a burying ground. Fort Hill was leveled altogether; today's High Street in the downtown business district is the memento of its vanished height, just as Dock Square commemorates the first life of today's landlocked site.

More than filling in marshy soil to increase the land mass, the planners soon made a distinctly architectural move: They fitted in new structures on the land between isolated buildings. Where lone mansions had sat atop Beacon Hill, builders began to join them, first into duplexes and then into rows. Soon the single homes stretched into streets of row houses, and a new manner of building was born.

C harles Bulfinch oversaw the construction not only as architect but as ranking politician and planner. Beginning late in the 18th century, the master architect brought the look of Georgian London to an expanding Boston. His own row house projects have not survived—the Tontine Crescent, a semicircular enclave of 1793, was flattened into the Victorian buildings on Franklin Street, and the Pemberton Square row houses, carved around a park, were replaced by the grandiose courthouse that stands there today—yet the influence of this row house world endured. While Faneuil Hall and the Harrison Gray Otis houses are prominent among the works of Bulfinch that we see today, the row houses that line Beacon and Park streets reflect his design. And the curving collections of brick buildings around parks, emulated in Louisburg Square and throughout the city, show how he imported the urban style and elegant line of Robert Adam's England to create Boston's distinctive architecture of place.

The heyday of the seemly row lasted for a century. Varying in detail, the rows dominate the architectural landscape of the inner city to this day. The graceful conformity of the Beacon Street houses of this period—"the sunny street that holds the sifted few," in the words of Oliver Wendell Holmes—created a handsome bank of masonry. With their swelling fronts, their elegant wrought-iron trim, and their symmetrical entries, they set the style. Looser and more flowing than the row houses of other cities, rolling over the streets of the hilly peninsula, they became an orderly procession of residences built individually for the merchant princes of the 19th century. Made of brick and stone for the most part, their simple dignity could be copied by architects who lacked Bulfinch's finesse. If the carpenter-builders of Boston could not quite replicate the sweep of the master architect's staircase, the oval dining rooms, the Adamesque details, or the purity and balance of Bulfinch's poised facades, they might nevertheless stamp civilized copies across the Federalist landscape.

The bowfront, that curving bay on the face of the building, added to the elegance of the row house design. Pinched and narrow a row house might appear beside a single house, yet this swell in the facade would expand the view and enlarge the sense of space. Sometimes limited to a mere bay or a one-story oriel window, the projections did more than animate the exterior; they also enlivened the interior, releasing residents from the confines of a constricted space by giving them a more ample outlook. The expanded views to east and west widened the prospect from within and caught the sun as it moved across the sky. From the outside, too, the bow relieved architectural tedium. However relentless the long masonry wall of a row house street, the bowfront made a shifting surface that caught the light and created a chiaroscuro across the row.

Further stylistic variations appeared as the Victorians who followed Bulfinch textured every inch of the face of their houses, applying ornament from a pastry cart of styles as the city became more affluent.

Yet the significance of the row house went beyond style: The upstairs-downstairs mode of the row house came to dominate the city's larger urban development. Able to accommodate more people in a more compact space, Boston could become a walkable city, it could add mass transit, it could shape the rowlike forms around its parks and promenades to come.

As the 19th century advanced, Boston felt again the press of its mounting numbers, and again a crowded city looked beyond its core, this time to the south. City planners saw a new space for the burgeoning population in the South End. By 1850 the old narrow neck to the south of Boston had become the viaduct to a new and splendid zone of row-house architecture.

Once again, no single architect of stature but countless carpenter-builders and designers shaped America's largest Victorian district. As the tree-shaded Louisburg Square on Beacon Hill had determined the arrangement of the rows of mansions framing it, so the centerpieces of the South End's Rutland and Concord squares dictated the design of the curved brick enclaves of row houses around them. Nameless architects and builders brought high stoops and handsome bowfronts to fill in the new blocks. More renowned designers added the churches, schools, and hospitals that enriched the community with landmark buildings.

One more site, the "mournful and inodorous Lake Asphaltics—Back Bay, with its mud, its creeks, and its occasionally good shooting," needed tending to, and by the time the

Civil War had ended, the work on the Back Bay was at hand. Because Boston was now a more cosmopolitan city, France, not Bulfinch's England, provided the model.

Following the design of Baron Haussmann's Paris, Boston planners fashioned a ribbon of greenery, a mall 200 feet wide, along Commonwealth Avenue. Vistas or long corridors of row houses (rather than the South End's organic cluster of parks and buildings) lined this space. As the new railroad carried in dirt from suburban Needham to fill the mud flats, Boston architects drew up the specifications. In 1857 Arthur Gilman set the district's spatial limits and the buildings' setbacks and design silhouettes. Architects as renowned as Richardson and as humble as the carpenter-builder placed their row houses within these frames.

Notching their buildings westward from the newly planted Public Garden, the architects shaped bays, designed the proportions of windows, and chose masonry materials to dictates as orderly as the alphabetical street names of the Back Bay's grid from A (Arlington) to H (Hereford). The embroidery they attached to their facades was high style; in the five decades that followed, the flamboyant work of such architects as Peabody and Stearns, Sturgis and Brigham, and Charles Follen McKim was affixed to the basic row house. The details of the designs record the chronology of shifting styles as construction moved west.

The architects made certain that the interiors of their five-story Back Bay mansions displayed the utmost elegance. Within the row house's 25-foot width, the carved handrails swept upward, the ornate ceilings topped elegant chambers studded with carved fireplaces and laid with parquet floors. The exteriors, too, boasted rich designs. Whether of brownstone or brick, trimmed in limestone or tile, lidded by steeply pitched mansard roofs of slate or hooded by elaborate doorways, they were the ultimate in fashion, the trendsetters of their time.

Copley Square, a distinctly nonsquare space created on the southern edge of the Back Bay, filled slowly with stately buildings to transform the old wasteland of railroad tracks between the South End and the Back Bay. At its eastern end, the new Trinity Church gave a 34-year-old architect with good connections the chance to prove himself the genius of his time. Winning a competition to design the church, Henry Hobson Richardson created a superb work of Victorian architecture. The powerful stone building beneath the peaked red tile roof incorporated the arts of the stained-glass maker John La Farge and the sculptor Augustus Saint-Gaudens into a model of the Cathedral of Salamanca. Atop the piles sunk into the fresh soil of the old Back Bay, the Romanesque masterpiece broadcast to the nation a new style and provided a handsome focus for the infant square.

The closing in of Copley Square with buildings of majesty and diversity culminated in the completion of the Boston Public Library in 1895. McKim, Mead and White created Boston's "people's palace," with murals by John Singer Sargent and bronze doors by Daniel Chester French. The Boston Public Library was the most substantial building of the latest mode, the Classical Revival; its imposing symmetries and the grandeur of its cool white facade helped stamp the Beaux Arts style on late 19th-century America.

Boston would undergo one more topographical transformation, and H. H. Richardson and McKim, Mead and White would share in the final act of city-making only a mile or so from Copley Square. Boston's "Emerald Necklace," beginning at the western border of the Back Bay, was the consequence of the same ecological urgency that gave rise to the Back Bay: the "noxious" condition of the Fens. Again, a single planner determined the layout of the new land and individual architects created major buildings. Yet this time the planner had a somewhat different outlook.

Frederick Law Olmsted was the first to bear the title of landscape architect. The inventor of the term and the creator of parks from Central Park to Yosemite, Olmsted came to Boston at Richardson's behest and spent much of his life in the city shaping just such space. America's greatest parkmaker took the polluted backwaters of the Fens and transformed them into an ordered ring of greenery punctuated by Richardson's handsome bridges and enriched by a chain of plantings along its waterway. Stretching from the edge of the Back Bay Fens to Franklin Park in West Roxbury, punctuated with small waterways and the Arnold Arboretum, the Emerald Necklace became the site for the city's last great architecture of the late 19th and early 20th centuries: the Museum of Fine Arts, the Isabella Stewart Gardner Museum, Harvard Medical School, and nearby residential structures.

Until World War II Boston conditioned its development with respect for the previous 100 years of construction: Architecture and surroundings remained intact. Even as fashions changed, and architects designed replacements in Deco or other modern modes along the stately rows of the Back Bay's Commonwealth Avenue and Newbury, Beacon, and Marlborough streets, the basic context stayed the same. Then, after World War II, the scope of change expanded. Copley Square lost its civilized height of 90 feet to a gargantuan invader, the 890-foot sleek glass tower of the John Hancock, which not only broke through the height barrier but shook Trinity Church to its foundations. In the inner city, the medieval contours of downtown established in the first wharfing out of the city crumbled under the onslaught of asphalt-wrapped towers; at the outer limits, Olmsted's landscape languished.

Finally, preservationists began to be heard. In residential areas of the city, historic or architecturally significant districts appeared; first in the Back Bay and Beacon Hill and later in the South End, the city established rules to guarantee that the style and scale of Boston's row-house world would survive. No more would such intrusions as the New Brutalist concrete Boston Architectural Center of the 1960s be allowed. Copley Square supporters held another competition to shape the ungainly space into a more civilized enclave. The state provided funds to restore Olmsted's neglected ring of greenery.

Elsewhere in the city the building boom had greater consequence for the work of Boston's early placemakers. The medieval street pattern of downtown succumbed to glass and stone monoliths. Starting in 1962 with the Prudential Center, the city's efforts to rouse itself from an economic depression saw the replacement of congenial low-scale buildings and carefully contoured streets by isolated towers and wraparound roads. The old brick West End was flattened for luxury apartments and the filing-cabinet architecture of Government Center. Fine neighborhoods were reduced to rubble, to be succeeded by structures of less considerate design.

Today the urban renewal of the late 1950s and the onrush of oversize modern architecture has abated somewhat. Gridded slabs no longer rise on windy plazas, and Boston's architects have begun to look to their heritage. Some 7,000 of the city's 120,000 buildings have been designated historic landmarks by the city. Architects have learned to excel at clinging to historic form by mastering the art of recycling; they have refurbished old architecture, and born-again buildings abound throughout the city. Adapting the old city to new ways, architects have placed enough fern and butcher block inside renovated buildings to qualify them for certification as the official state flora.

Quincy Market sets the national standard for transformations of this kind. Designed in a Greek Revival style by Alexander Parris in 1826, the market was long a Boston landmark. Then it declined in the 20th century, and by the 1970s the threat of the bulldozer was at hand. But the city rallied, and the vintage marketplace was remade in 1976 as the first of the festival markets that now stud the continent. Renamed Faneuil Hall Marketplace, the three buildings are now a contemporary food emporium in a zone of gentrification, the epitome of a new architecture of recreation.

The reclaimed architecture of Lewis and Commercial wharves and the updated Charlestown Navy Yard with its new buildings typify a trend that has extended to Salem and Newburyport and moved across the country. Recycling is the city's latest architectural solution. An Institute of Contemporary Art springs up in a police station. Alarm clocks now awaken commuters who make their homes in the recycled churches, schools, and mills where bells once signaled the start of services, classes, and work. But modern architectecture in Boston has not found all its solutions in recycling the old and traditional. The controversial, modern Hynes Convention Center, for example, designed by the same architects who gave Boston City Hall, counters 1950's enthusiasm for unmanageable open spaces with a definitively 90s idea that cities are made for people. The Convention Center closes the space that was created by the Massachusetts Turnpike that runs through the city, while the large building gracefully steps in to create a new corridor of sidewalk for pedestrians.

Bullfinch and Richardson also left their marks across the Charles River. But MIT and Harvard have also attracted some of the 20th Century's finest architects. At MIT is Finnish architects Alvar Aalto's Baker House (1947) and Eero Saarinen's Kresge Auditorium (1953) and MIT Chapel (1954), all hallmarks of modern architecture. Adjacent to the fine urban open space of Harvard Yard sits Le Corbusier's remarkable Carpenter Center (1961), the only American work by the Swiss architect.

Back in Boston, new attention is being paid to the city's open spaces. Designers have recognized that they are as essential to the quality of Boston architecture as the green parks and corridors that gave definition to the row house. Thus the spaces-in-between have become new oases. From small and singular vest-pocket parks to larger swaths of space, planners and landscape architects are recouping the amenities. Harborwalk, which will edge 45 miles of the inner city, has already shaped a pedestrian path along the waterfront; inching by the old wharves and new buildings, the thoroughfare has begun to bring the architecture into the ensemble in which Boston has always excelled. At Post Office Square downtown, on the site of a former multistory garage, replacement parking has been built below ground, creating a spacious new park above. And by 2001, Boston's elevated highway—the Central Artery—will be put underground, allowing new urban open spaces to reconnect the city to its historic waterfront.

Architects and planners have become adroit at maximizing minimal environments. Find a fragment of leftover land— at Central Wharf, Winthrop Square, or Union Street—and you find an exercise in the artistry of shaping elegant outdoor space.

The public art of architecture that transformed a few muddy acres crowded with hills endures. Three hundred fifty years after John Winthrop sought to establish his community of souls, the best of Boston's architects still strive for that sense of community in the linking of today's architecture with that of the past.

3 Exploring Boston

Boston can be seen as a series of concentric circles, with the oldest and most famous attractions clustered within easy walking distance of the State House. Many attractions are on the well-marked Freedom Trail; none is far off the track. You might draw an arbitrary line across the peninsula, stretching from, say, the Arthur Fiedler Footbridge (at the Charles River near Beacon and Arlington streets) to South Station, explore everything north of it—with a side trip west into the Back Bay—and truthfully say that you had "seen Boston." In fact, that is all many visitors ever see. This remarkable compactness is a boon to the pedestrian explorer (in central Boston there should be no other kind), and it assures a virtually complete education in the earliest history of the town. But just as Boston outgrew its cramped peninsular quarters, so too must the serious traveler's curiosity extend beyond our random demarcation. We begin our tour at the heart of things, in Boston Common, and follow the circles outward to Charlestown, the Back Bay, and beyond.

Highlights for First-time Visitors

Faneuil Hall, Tour 5
Freedom Trail, Tours 1 and 3–5
Louisburg Square, Tour 1
Museum of Fine Arts, Tour 8
Old North Church, Tour 3
Public Garden, Tour 6

Tour 1: Boston Common and Beacon Hill

Numbers in the margin correspond to points of interest on the Boston Common and Beacon Hill map.

❶ Nothing is more central to Boston than the **Boston Common,** the oldest public park in the United States and undoubtedly the largest and most famous of the town commons around which all New England settlements were once arranged. Boston Common is not "made land," like the adjacent Public Garden; nor is it the result of 19th-century park planning, as is Olmsted's Fens and Franklin Park. It is simply the Common: 50 acres where the freemen of Boston could graze their cattle. It is as old as the city around it. No building of substance ever stood here, and until such time as codfish walk and the Red Sox move to Phoenix, it is safe to say that none ever will.

Start your walk at the **Park Street Station,** on the corner of Park and Tremont streets. This is the original eastern terminus of the first subway in America, opened in 1897 against the warnings of those who believed it would make the buildings along Tremont Street collapse. The copper-roof kiosks are national historic landmarks. The line originally ran only as far as the present-day Boylston stop. The area around the two subway kiosks is noisy with the hustle of commuters, newspaper and fruit vendors, street musicians, and partisans of causes and beliefs ranging from Irish nationalism to Krishna Consciousness. The general dither—and, sad to say, a considerable amount of litter—are more characteristic of the Common's Tremont Street borders than they are of the Beacon Street side.

As you stand at the Park Street Station, you are within a few steps of two historic churches and a burying ground. The

Boston Common and Beacon Hill

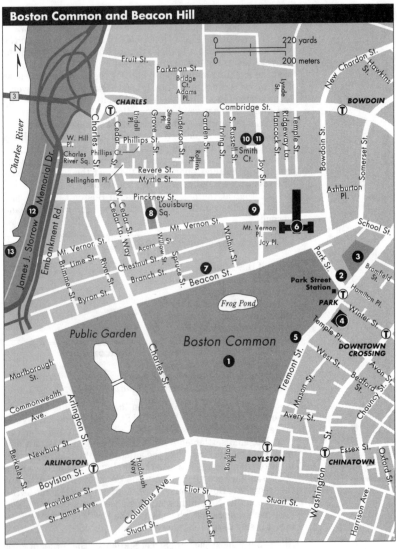

African Meeting House, **10**

Appleton Mansions, **7**

Boston Common, **1**

Esplanade, **12**

Hatch Memorial Shell, **13**

Louisburg Square, **8**

Museum of Afro-American History, **11**

Nichols House, **9**

Old Granary Burial Ground, **3**

Park Street Church, **2**

State House, **6**

St. Paul's Cathedral, **4**

Visitor Information Booth (Boston Common), **5**

❷ Congregationalist **Park Street Church,** designed by Peter Banner and erected in 1809–1810, occupies the corner of Tremont and Park streets. The date may seem incongruous with the architecture, for the church is Georgian in character, perhaps the last major Georgian church built in the area before the Colonial revival of the early 20th century. Here, on July 4, 1831, Samuel Smith's hymn "America" was first sung, and here in 1829 William Lloyd Garrison began his long public campaign for the abolition of slavery. *Tel. 617/523–3383. Open to visitors last week in June–third week in Aug., Tues.–Sat. 9:30–3:30. Year-round Sun. services at 9, 10:45, and 6. Closed July 4.*

❸ Next to the church is the **Old Granary Burial Ground,** named after the public granary that stood on the church site in the 1700s (the sails of the USS *Constitution* were made in the granary loft). Note the winged hourglasses carved into the stone gateway of the burial ground; they are a 19th-century addition, made more than 150 years after this small plot began receiving the remains of Colonial Bostonians. The most famous individuals interred here are heroes of the Revolution: Samuel Adams, John Hancock (the precise location of his grave is not certain), James Otis, and Paul Revere. Here, too, are the graves of the philanthropist Peter Faneuil, Benjamin Franklin's parents (Franklin is buried in Philadelphia), and the victims of the Boston Massacre. *Open daily 8–4:30.*

❹ **St. Paul's Cathedral** (Episcopal), the massive and severe Greek Revival structure on your right as you cross Tremont Street, was built 10 years after the Park Street Church. Even a cursory comparison of the two churches underscores the difference between 18th and early 19th century architectural aesthetics as they applied to large public buildings. Notice the uncarved entablature above St. Paul's pillars; as with New York's Metropolitan Museum of Art, similarly adorned with uncut blocks of stone, the money ran out before carvers could be employed. *Tel. 617/482–5800. Open Sun.–Fri. noon–5. Sun. services at 9 and 11; daily services at 12:15 and 5; Holy Eucharist in Chinese at noon.*

Across Tremont Street from St. Paul's and a little to your left is
❺ a **visitor information booth,** adjacent to the Common's **Parkman Plaza** with its bronzes extolling study, toil, and prayer. The monuments to the Puritan ethic make an ironic contrast to the seedy indolence of many of the characters who frequent this part of the Common. The information booth serves as the starting point for the **Freedom Trail;** guide booklets are available at no charge. For now, we'll head in the opposite direction from the trail and walk past the **Parkman Bandstand.**

The once handsome bandstand is seldom used and has been left to the care of spray-paint vandals. Musical events on the Common (apart from the buskers who work near Park Street Station) are now held within a stockade-like wooden enclosure erected near here each summer for the Concerts on the Common series, which features big-name acts and paid admission.

The **Central Burying Ground** may seem an odd feature for a public park, but remember that in 1756, when it was set aside, this was a lonely corner of the Common. Here are buried Gilbert Stuart, the portraitist most famous for his paintings of George and Martha Washington, and scores of British casualties of the Battle of Bunker Hill.

Walk back toward the bandstand, turn left, and head for the Common's highest ground, once called **Flagstaff Hill** and now surmounted by the **Soldiers and Sailors Monument** honoring those who fought in the Civil War. It was along the slope between the monument and Charles Street that thousands gathered for Pope John Paul II's outdoor mass in October 1979. A granite marker near Charles Street commemorates the event.

Immediately below and to the north is the **Frog Pond,** a tame and frogless concrete depression used as a children's wading pool during the summer and as a skating rink in winter. The site is that of an original pond after which Edgar Allan Poe called Bostonians "Frogpondians" and which was the focal point for the inauguration of Boston's municipal water system in 1848, when a gushing fountain of piped-in water was arranged for the occasion.

From the Frog Pond, walk uphill to the Joy Street steps. Head toward the State House (again, uphill) on the Common side of Beacon Street to reach the splendidly restored **Robert Gould Shaw Memorial,** executed in deep-relief bronze by Augustus Saint-Gaudens. It commemorates the 54th Massachusetts Regiment, a Civil War unit made up of free blacks led by the young Brahmin Robert Gould Shaw. Colonel Shaw died with nearly half of his troops in an assault on South Carolina's Fort Wagner. The monument figures in works by the modern poets John Berryman and Robert Lowell, both of whom lived on the north slope of Beacon Hill in the 1940s.

Here at the corner of Beacon and Park streets is where Beacon Hill, the Common, and downtown Boston converge. If you head down Park Street along the Common, you will pass the **Ticknor Mansion,** a much altered structure of 1804 designed by Charles Bulfinch that now houses an antiques shop and offices, the exclusive **Union Club,** and the Roman Catholic **Paulist Center.** The block ends at the Park Street Church.

❻ Charles Bulfinch's magnificent **State House** stands at the summit of Beacon Hill, which over the years has been vastly reduced from its original height. Beacon Hill, the seat of the Commonwealth's government and of Brahmin Boston itself, was called "Tremont" or "Trimount" by the early colonists. It had three summits, Cotton Hill, Beacon Hill, and Mount Vernon. Beacon, the highest, was named for the warning light (at first an iron skillet filled with tallow and suspended from a mast) set on its peak in 1634. The location of the old beacon was directly behind the State House, on land now occupied by the building's 19th-century additions. In 1790 it was replaced by a brick and stone column, designed by Bulfinch to commemorate American independence.

Neither monument nor hill was destined to stand for long. In 1793 the state bought the summit and the surrounding lands for the new State House. Much of the parcel had been pasture belonging to the estate of John Hancock, whose fine stone mansions stood until 1864 just to the west of the State House. Construction of Bulfinch's masterpiece began in 1795, accompanied by the carving away of Beacon Hill. By 1820 its summit was some 60 feet lower. The soil and gravel removed (and carried off by one of America's first "railroads," run by gravity and horsepower) was used not to fill the Back Bay but to fill the area where Charles Street now stands and to make dry land in the old North Cove (near present-day North Station). To visualize the original terrain, try to think of the Common sloping north to a knoll just behind the State House and reaching just as high as its dome.

While civic expansiveness leveled Beacon Hill, private entrepreneurship tamed and flattened Mount Vernon. Much of this land once belonged to the painter John Singleton Copley, who followed his Tory sympathies and removed himself to Britain as the Revolution approached. After the war, his estate was purchased by a syndicate called the Mount Vernon Proprietors and made the site of the planned suburban development that evolved into today's Beacon Hill neighborhood. As we will see when we walk the streets of the hill, little remains of the original plans for freestanding mansions and grassy squares, for even at the beginning of the 19th century the pressures of population density made row houses inevitable. Mount Vernon, too, was flattened by about 60 feet, the displaced earth being used to push the shores of the Charles even farther back. (Cotton Hill was leveled after 1835, and Pemberton Square replaced it.)

The **State House** is arguably the most architecturally distinguished of American seats of state government; it was built well before the trend toward designs based on the Capitol in Washington. (Charles Bulfinch later held the position of architect of the U.S. Capitol.) The design is neoclassical, poised between Georgian and Federal; its finest features are the delicate Corinthian columns of the portico, the graceful pediment and window arches, and the vast yet visually weightless golden dome. The dome is sheathed in copper from the foundry of Paul Revere; the gilding was added in 1874. During World War II, the entire dome was painted gray so that it would not reflect moonlight during blackouts and offer a target to the Axis bombers (that never showed up).

Bulfinch's work would have stood splendidly on its own, but the growth of the state bureaucracy necessitated additions. The yellow brick annex extending to the rear is clumsily ostentatious, but at least it is invisible from Beacon Street. The light stone wings added to either side of the original early in this century serve no aesthetic purpose.

Inside the State House are Doric Hall, with its statuary and portraits, a part of the original structure; the chambers of the General Court (legislature) and Senate, including the carved wooden *Sacred Cod* that symbolizes the state's maritime wealth; and the Hall of Flags. *Tel. 617/727-3676. Admission free. Open weekdays for tours 10–4. Research library (free) open weekdays 11–5.*

Take the traditional path of retiring governors down the front steps of the State House (to your left, note the statue of a youthful-looking President John F. Kennedy in full stride) and onto Beacon Street, turning right to explore Beacon Hill. The walk can take between two hours and an entire day, depending on one's thoroughness and powers of resistance to the shops on and around Charles Street. Since a specific itinerary would require a complex retracing of steps, we'll concentrate instead on the gaslit highlights of the Hill, clustered in the several small but distinct neighborhoods that quilt its slopes.

Beacon Hill is the area bounded by Cambridge Street on the north, Beacon Street on the south, the Charles River Esplanade on the west, and Bowdoin Street on the east. Within these borders, residents distinguish three informal districts: the flat side (the area west of Charles Street), the south side (the area east of Charles Street and south of Pinckney Street), and the north side (the area east of Charles Street and north of Pinckney Street).

No sooner do you put the State House behind you than you encounter the classic face of Beacon Hill: brick row houses, nearly all built between 1800 and 1850 in a style never far divergent from the early Federal norm. Even the sidewalks are brick, and they shall remain so; in the 1940s, residents staged an uncharacteristic sit-in to prevent conventional paving. Since then, public law, the Beacon Hill Civic Association, and the Beacon Hill Architectural Commision have maintained tight controls over everything from the gas lamps to the color of front doors. Beacon Hill was finished quite nicely a century and a quarter ago, and as the Yankees say, "If it ain't broke, don't fix it."

At the corner of Beacon and Joy streets is the headquarters of **Little, Brown,** a venerable mainstay of Boston's publishing trade. Farther down Beacon, past Walnut Street, are the twin **Appleton Mansions** built by the pioneer textile family. Taking a tour will give you the rare opportunity to look out through the famed purple panes of Beacon Hill; only a few buildings have them, and they are as valuable as an ancestor in the China Trade. The color was the result of the action of sunlight on the imperfections in a shipment of glass sent to Boston around 1820. *39 and 40 Beacon St., tel. 617/227–3550. Admission free. Tours of 40 Beacon St. by appointment.*

Adjacent to the mansions is the private **Somerset Club** (42 Beacon St.). The older of the two buildings (the newer was built to match) was erected in 1819 by David Sears to a design by Alexander Parris, the architect of Quincy Market. It represents a rare intrusion of the granite Greek Revival into Beacon Hill.

The American Meteorological Society occupies 45 Beacon Street, the last of three houses built by Charles Bulfinch for Harrison Gray Otis, who was one of the Mount Vernon Proprietors, a Boston mayor, and a U.S. senator. The **Second Otis House,** built in 1802 at 85 Mount Vernon Street, is today a private home. Tour 2 stops in at the **First Otis House,** on Cambridge Street. Otis moved into the **Third Otis House** at 45 Beacon Street in 1805 and stayed until his death in 1848. His tenure thus extended from the first days of Beacon Hill's residential development almost to the time when many of the Hill's prominent families decamped for the Back Bay, which was just beginning to be filled at the time of Otis's death.

Not all the families left; enough remained that the south slope of the Hill—where you are now—never lost its Brahmin character and at worst fell into a dowdy yet respectable eclipse. By the middle of the present century natives and newcomers alike began to realize that here was prime territory for the new urban gentry. In what other city can one live so elegantly within 10 minutes' walk from the central office district? Thus the unchanged facades of Beacon Hill are more and more likely to conceal condominiums and expensive apartments rather than four-story, single-family dwellings. They survive, too, but at prices in excess of a million dollars. Similarly, the people who live here are more likely to be young stockbrokers married to lawyers than DAR matrons whose fathers knew Justice Holmes.

One old family that stayed was that of Admiral Samuel Eliot Morison, the sailor-historian who lived his entire life at 44 Brimmer Street on the "flat side" of the Hill, the part separated from the slope by Charles Street. (This was land reclaimed with fill from the State House excavation; the oldest houses here are in the granite-faced 1828 block on Beacon between Charles and Brimmer streets.) Morison's family home was nearly new when he was born there in 1887, and the river bank was across the street. When he died in 1976, the river was on the other side of Storrow Drive and the Esplanade. His house has since been divided into condos.

Morison, the quintessential Boston gentleman scholar, did not have to look far to find the material for his Harvard dissertation; the papers of a prominent ancestor had been stashed at 44 Brimmer. The ancestor's name was Harrison Gray Otis. In Boston, that is known as being well-connected.

Chestnut and **Mt. Vernon,** two of the loveliest streets in America, are distinguished not only for the history and style of their individual houses but for their general atmosphere and character as well. **Mt. Vernon Street** is the grander of the two, its houses set back farther and rising taller; it even has a free-standing mansion, the Second Otis House. Mt. Vernon opens
❽ out on **Louisburg Square,** an 1840s model for town-house development that was never repeated on the Hill because of space restrictions. The little green belongs collectively to the owners of the homes facing it. The statue at the north end of the green is of Columbus; the one at the south end is of Aristides the Just; both were a gift in 1850 of a Greek merchant in Boston, who lived on the square. The houses, most of which are now divided into apartments and condominiums, have seen their share of famous tenants: William Dean Howells at 4 and 16; the Alcotts at 10; and in 1852 the singer Jenny Lind was married in the parlor of 20.

There is no water in Louisburg Square today, and the ground level is some 60 feet below the height of the original hill, yet the legend long persisted that this was the location of the Rev. William Blackstone's spring. Blackstone was the original Bostonian, having come here to live with his books and his apple trees four or five years before the arrival of the Puritans in 1630. It was he who invited them to leave Charlestown and come to where the water was purer, he who sold them all but six acres of the peninsula he had bought from the Indians. He left for Rhode Island not long after, seeking greater seclusion; a plaque at 50 Beacon Street commemorates him. (The name "Boston" given by the Puritans comes from Boston, England, originally St. Botolph's Town.)

❾ At 55 Mt. Vernon Street is the **Nichols House,** an early side-entrance home built in 1804 and attributed to Bulfinch. This was the lifelong residence of Rose Standish Nichols, a philanthropist, peace advocate, and one of the first women to practice the profession of landscape gardening. Although Nichols's life spanned the latter years of the 19th and the first half of the 20th centuries, few of the furnishings in her home date from later than the mid-Victorian era. The deep window seat with a view down Mt. Vernon Street is straight out of a Henry James novel.

The house gives a pervasive impression of how a Brahmin lady of means and modesty lived among the rich and comfortably aging possessions of her forebears. Nichols arranged in her will for her home to become a museum, and visitors have been calling since her death more than a quarter of a century ago. *55 Mt. Vernon St., tel. 617/227–6993. Admission: $3. Open Tues.– Sat. 1–5 (summer); Wed. and Sat. 1–5 (spring and fall); Sat. 1–5 (winter).*

Around the corner at 5 Joy Street, in a later bowfront mansion, is the headquarters of the **Appalachian Mountain Club,** a source of useful information on outdoor recreation, both nearby and in New England's North Country. *Tel. 617/523–0636. Open weekdays 8:30–5:15.*

Chestnut Street is more modest than Mt. Vernon, yet in its trimness and minuteness of detail it is perhaps even more fine. Delicacy and grace characterize virtually every structure, from the fanlights above the entryways to the wrought-iron boot scrapers on the steps. Francis Parkman lived here, as did Julia Ward Howe, Richard Henry Dana, and Edwin Booth. Booth's sometime residence at 29A, dating to 1800, is the oldest home on the south slope of the Hill.

Running parallel to Chestnut and Mt. Vernon streets, half a block down Willow Street from Louisburg Square, is **Acorn Street,** a narrow span of cobblestones lined on one side with almost toylike row houses and on the other with the doors to Mt. Vernon's hidden gardens. These were once the houses of artisans and small tradesmen; today they are every bit as prestigious as their larger neighbors. Acorn Street may be the most photographed street of its size in Boston.

There is another side to Beacon Hill: the north slope. Until just a few years ago it was not uncommon to hear the south slope called "the good side," with obvious connotations for the streets north of Pinckney. There are still a fair number of relatively low-cost apartments here in turn-of-the-century apartment buildings popular with students, new young professionals, and a handful of older blue-collar families. (There are also blocks and cul-de-sacs that would be perfectly at home in the vicinity of Chestnut and Mt. Vernon.) But gentrification is setting in, and yesterday's modest apartments are today's condos.

The north slope of the Hill was built up long before the Mount Vernon Proprietors set to work, although almost all its old wooden houses are gone now. Exceptions may be found at 5 and 7 Pinckney, near the corner of Joy, where a structure of 1791 stands. Joy Street beyond this point was a black neighborhood during the late 18th and early 19th centuries. The **African Meeting House** at 8 Smith Court (near Joy and Myrtle), built in 1806, is the oldest black church building still standing in the United States. It was constructed almost entirely with black labor, using funds raised in both the white and the black communities. The facade is an adaptation of a design for a town house published by the Boston architect Asher Benjamin. The school for colored children moved into the basement in 1808. In 1832 the New England Anti-Slavery Society was formed here under the leadership of William Lloyd Garrison. Daily tours are offered by the staff of the Museum of Afro-American History, which is located across the street. Inquire at the museum.

Opposite the Meeting House is the home (1799) of **William Nell,** a black crusader for school integration active in Garrison's circle. These sites and others are part of a **Black Heritage Trail,** a walking tour that explores the history of the city's black community during the 19th century. The recently established ⑪ **Museum of Afro-American History** provides information on the trail and on black history throughout Boston. *46 Joy St., tel. 617/742–1854. Admission to gallery: $3 adults, $1.50 senior citizens. Open weekdays 10–4. Information on the Trail can also be obtained from the National Park Service Visitor Center, 15 State St., tel. 617/742–5415. Tours Apr.–Oct., daily 10, noon, and 2; Nov.–Mar. by appointment.*

A visit to the north slope of the Hill should include a walk down Revere Street and glances into Rollins Place, Phillips Street, and Bellingham Place. These trim residential courts all dead-end at a hidden cliff; the shuttered white clapboard house at the blind end of Rollins Place is not a house at all but a false front masking a small precipice.

Head west on Revere Street to **Charles Street.** With a few exceptions, other streets in the area lack commercial establishments, and Charles Street makes up for it. Here is Boston's antiques district (the side streets on the flat side have some good shops, too) and an assortment of bookstores, leather goods shops, small restaurants, and vintage clothing boutiques. Dollhouse furniture, Italian ice cream, fresh fruit, and hardware are within steps of one another. The activity would be a curious sight to the elder Oliver Wendell Holmes, the publisher James T. Fields, and others who lived here when the neighborhood belonged to the establishment literati. Charles Street sparkles at dusk from gas street lamps, making it a romantic place for an evening stroll.

At the northern end of Charles Street is the footbridge cross-⑫ ⑬ ing Storrow Drive to the **Esplanade** and the **Hatch Memorial Shell.** The Boston Pops, made immensely popular by its former maestro, the late Arthur Fiedler, gives free concerts here during the summer. Bostonians haul lawn chairs and blankets to the lawn in front of the shell; bring a picnic, find an empty spot, and you'll feel right at home, too. More than a pleasant place for a stroll, a run, or a picnic, the Esplanade is home port for the fleet of small sailboats that dot the Charles River Basin. They belong to Community Boating, which offers membership on a monthly or seasonal basis. Here, too, is the **Union Boat Club Boathouse,** private headquarters for the country's oldest rowing club. The boathouse was built at the turn of the century. If you come here with children, bring a few leftover rolls from breakfast; the ducks are always hungry.

Tour 2: The Old West End

Numbers in the margin correspond to points of interest on The Old West End map.

Cambridge Street draws the line between Beacon Hill proper and the old West End. Little remains of the West End—a few brick tenements, nothing more—since blocks of old structures were razed in the 1960s to make way for the Charles River Park apartment and retail development. The only survivors in this area having any real history are two public institutions, ❶ ❷ **Massachusetts General Hospital** and the **Suffolk County (or**

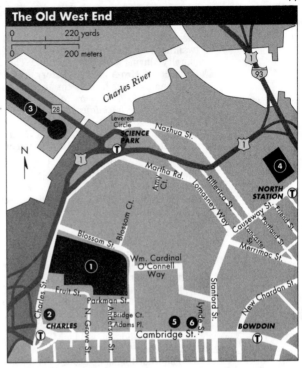

The Old West End

0   220 yards

0   200 meters

Charles Street) Jail. Both are near the Charles Street Circle, where the Longfellow Bridge (called the Salt and Pepper Shaker Bridge for obvious reasons) begins its reach across the Charles to Cambridge. The jail is interesting chiefly for its central building of 1849, designed by Gridley Bryant at the close of Boston's Granite Age. That makes it terribly old for a jail and all the more crowded and miserable; the courts have been trying for years to get the county to close it. The new Nashua Street Jail was constructed in 1991, and a year later the hospital purchased the Charles Street Jail; it remains to be seen what it will do with this historic building.

Far more humanitarian associations are attached to the nearly adjacent hospital, usually called **Mass General,** which was incorporated in 1811. Seven years later work began on the domed granite **Bulfinch Pavilion,** which today stands at the center of a complex of modern buildings. The amphitheater beneath the dome was for many years the hospital's main operating room, where scholarly audiences learned the latest surgical techniques. It was here, on October 16, 1846, that Dr. John Collins Warren first performed an operation on a patient rendered senseless to pain by ether. You may visit the amphitheater today (use the hospital's North Grove Street entrance) and see a display describing this discovery that made modern surgery possible. *Admission free. Open 9–5 when no meeting is in session.*

Mass General was once the home of the Harvard Medical School, and it was in a laboratory here around Thanksgiving 1849 that one of Boston's most celebrated murders took place.

Dr. George Parkman, a wealthy landlord and Harvard benefactor, was bludgeoned to death by Dr. John Webster, a Harvard medical professor and friend who supposedly became exasperated by demands that he repay a personal loan. After several days of mystery over Parkman's disappearance, Webster's doom was sealed when part of the victim's jaw was discovered in the laboratory stove. Other grisly evidence turned up in the cesspool beneath Webster's privy. The professor was hanged and buried in an unmarked grave on Copp's Hill in the North End.

Boston's original science museum, the Society of Natural History, was located in the spacious mansionlike structure at Berkeley and Newbury streets. Its successor institution, the ❸ **Museum of Science,** occupies the modern compound of buildings that stand north of Mass General, on a site astride the Charles River Dam and its boat locks. The museum's collections date to 1830; its development as a tremendously successful educational resource was largely accomplished under the recent directorship of the explorer, mountaineer, and mapmaker Bradford Washburn. More than 400 exhibits cover astronomy, astrophysics, anthropology, progress in medicine, computers, the organic and inorganic earth sciences, and much more. Washburn and his curators made the Museum of Science a leader in hands-on education; many exhibits invite the participation of children and adults. The Transparent Woman's organs light up as their functions are described, newborn chicks hatch in an incubator, and a powerful generator produces controlled indoor lightning flashes. The museum has three restaurants and a gift shop. *Tel. 617/723–2500 or 617/523–6664. Admission: $6.50 adults, $4.50 students, children 4–14, and senior citizens. Open Tues.–Sun. 9–5, Fri. until 9. Closed Mon., Thanksgiving, and Christmas; free Wed. 1–5 Nov.–Apr.*

The **Charles Hayden Planetarium,** located in the Museum of Science, features the $2 million Zeiss planetarium projector and New England's most sophisticated multi-image system that combine to produce exciting programs on astronomical discoveries. Laser light shows, using a new visual technology complete with brilliant laser graphics and computer animation, are scheduled Friday–Sunday evenings. *Tel. 617/523–6664. Admission for each: $6.50 adults, $4.50 children and senior citizens.*

The **Mugar Omni Theater** in the Museum of Science features state-of-the-art film projection and sound systems. The 76-foot, four-story domed screen wraps around and over you, and 27,000 watts of power drive the sound system's 84 loudspeakers. *Tel. 617/523–6664. Admission: $6.50 adults, $4.50 senior citizens and children 4–14, under 4 free when seated on an adult's lap. Shows from 11 AM; tickets must be purchased a day in advance. Reduced price combination tickets are available for the museum, planetarium, and Omni Theater.*

Behind Mass General and the sprawling Charles River Park apartment complex is a small grid of streets recalling an older Boston. Here are furniture and electric supply stores, a good discount camping supply house (Hilton's, on Friend Street), and the Commonwealth Brewery and Tavern on Portland Street (*see* Special-Interest Tours, *above*). The main drag here ❹ is Causeway Street, home of the **Boston Garden,** where the Celtics (basketball) and the Bruins (hockey) play their home games. For the past few years there has been talk of either modernizing the old Garden or razing it (a new federal office building has already risen next to the Garden). We can proba- bly expect another decade of debate; meanwhile, trains to the North Shore still run out of **North Station,** behind the Garden.

If you head up Cambridge Street, away from Charles Street Circle and the river, you will pass on your left the first **Harrison Gray Otis House,** now the headquarters of the Society for the Preservation of New England Antiquities (SPNEA), an orga- nization that owns and maintains dozens of historic properties throughout the region. The society has restored the Otis House and opened two floors of it as a museum. The furniture, tex- tiles, wall coverings, and even the interior paint, specially mixed to match old samples, are faithful to the Federalist era, c. 1790–1810. Visitors will be surprised to see how bright and vivid were the colors favored in those days and to learn that closets had not quite made their appearance. The dining room is laid out as though Harry Otis were about to come in and have a glass of Madeira; one gets the feeling he would have been good company. *141 Cambridge St., tel. 617/227–3956. Admission: $4 adults, $2 children, $3.50, senior citizens. Open Tues.–Fri. for tours at noon, 1, 2, 3, and 4; Sat. tours hourly 10–4.*

Built in 1806 to a design of the great builder and architect Ash- er Benjamin, the **Old West Church** next door stands along with Otis's house as a reminder of the days when the West End near Bowdoin Square was a fashionable district. Forty years ago, when the Church served as a public library and polling place, Congressman John F. Kennedy voted here. *Open Mon.–Sat. 9–4:30. Sun. service at 11.*

Tour 3: Government Center and the North End

Numbers in the margin correspond to points of interest on the Government Center and the North End map.

Just where the old West End meets downtown Boston stands **Government Center,** one of the most ambitious of the city's self- transformations of the 1960s. It completely obliterated the raffish, down-at-heels Scollay Square, a bawdy, raucous place where sailors would go when they came into port, famous for its burlesque houses and the sort of ambience that is always re- membered more fondly as the years go by. (A small plaque in the square behind the Crescent Building marks the site of the Howard Theater's stage.) The **Center Plaza,** only six stories high, separates Tremont Street (Cambridge becomes Tremont here) from the higher ground of Pemberton Square, site of the old and "new" courthouses. Across Tremont stands the much older **Sears Crescent,** a curving commercial block that the new building sought to imitate.

The single most arresting structure in Government Center is **City Hall,** an upside-down ziggurat set within a vast sloping plaza of red brick. The design by Kallman, McKinnell, and Knowles relegates administrative functions to the upper floors and places offices that deal with the public on street level. De- spite the democratic intentions, the building is not much loved, though that may have less to do with its architecture than with its being the place you can't fight. And there has been criticism of the absence of intimacy and verdure in the surrounding 10 acres of brick.

Government Center and the North End

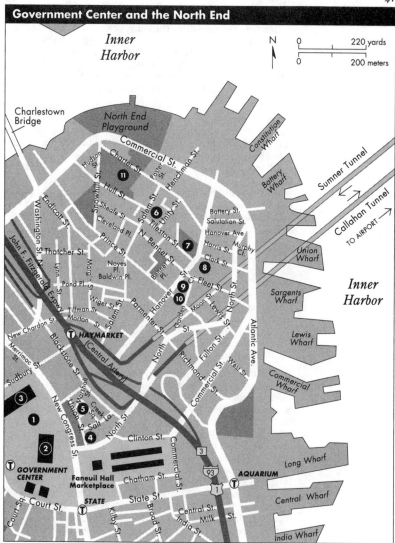

Inner Harbor

N

0   220 yards
0   200 meters

Charlestown Bridge

North End Playground

Commercial St.

Constitution Wharf

Sumner Tunnel

Callahan Tunnel
TO AIRPORT

Charter St.

Hudson St.

Illinois St.

Foster St.

Henchman St.

Battery Wharf

Hull St.

⑪

Sheafe St.

Cleveland Pl.

Salem St.

Unity St.

Tileston St.

N. Bennet St.

⑥

Battery St.

Salutation St.

Hanover Ave

Union Wharf

Endicott St.

Washington St.

Prince St.

⑦

Harris St.

Murphy Ct.

Clark St.

Inner Harbor

Thatcher St.

Noyes Pl.

Baldwin Pl.

Margin St.

Bennet St.

⑧

Fleet St.

John F. Fitzgerald Expwy

Lynn St.

Pond Pl.

Wiget St.

Salem St.

Parmenter St.

Hanover St.

⑨
⑩

Cooper St.

Moon St.

Garden Ct.

North St.

N. Lewis St.

Atlantic Ave.

Sargents Wharf

New Chardon St.

Tillman St.

Morton St.

🚇 HAYMARKET

(Central Artery)

North St.

Richmond St.

Fulton St.

Commercial St.

West St.

Lewis Wharf

Commercial Wharf

Merrimac St.

Blackstone St.

Hanover St.

Union St.

Creek Sq.

Salt St.

Clinton St.

Commercial St.

3

93

Sudbury St.

③

①

New Congress St.

⑤

④

North St.

🚇 AQUARIUM

Long Wharf

②

🚇 GOVERNMENT CENTER

Faneuil Hall Marketplace

Chatham St.

Central Wharf

🚇 STATE

Court St.

Court Sq.

State St.

Kilby St.

Broad St.

India St.

Central St.

Milk St.

India Wharf

Boston Stone, **5**
City Hall, **2**
Copp's Hill Burying Ground, **11**
Government Center, **1**
John F. Kennedy Federal Office Building, **3**
Old North Church, **6**

Paul Revere House, **9**
Paul Revere Mall (Prado), **7**
Pierce-Hichborn House, **10**
St. Stephen's Church, **8**
Union Oyster House, **4**

❸ The twin towers adjacent to City Hall Plaza constitute the **John F. Kennedy Federal Office Building,** designed by the Bauhaus founder Walter Gropius, who lived and taught in the Boston area toward the end of his life. Gropius's home, which he designed in textbook Bauhaus style, is in nearby suburban Lincoln; it is on the property roster of SPNEA and is open to visitors (inquire at SPNEA, 141 Cambridge St.).

Behind City Hall, past a small thatch of streets that survived urban renewal and an overhead expressway that will not, stands the oldest neighborhood in Boston and one of the oldest in the New World. Men and women walked the narrow streets of the North End when Shakespeare was not yet 20 years dead and Louis XIV was new to the throne of France. The town of Boston bustled and grew rich here for a century and a half before American independence. In the 17th century the North End *was* Boston, for much of the rest of the peninsula was still under water or had yet to be cleared of brush.

The North End visible to us today is almost entirely a creature of the late 19th century, when brick tenements began to fill with European immigrants. The Irish and the Jews both had their day here, but the Italians, more recent arrivals, have stayed. For more than 60 years the North End has been Italian Boston, so much so that one wonders whether the Puritan shades might scowl at the Mediterraneans' verve, volubility, and Roman Catholicism. This is not only a district of Italian restaurants (there are dozens) but of Italian groceries, bakeries, churches, social clubs, cafés, festivals honoring saints and food, and street-corner debates over soccer games.

Since the mid-1970s, change has been in the air. The conversion of wharves along the nearby waterfront to apartments, condos, and boutiques has brought pressures that have breached the boundaries of this neighborhood in which it was once hard to find an apartment unless you knew someone. Now it is a rare block in which one or more tenements have not gotten the exposed brick and track-lighting treatment; "gentrification" is a word that makes some of the old guard nervous (the others sell). It is unlikely that the North End will soon fall to being Italian in name and menu only; the people with Abruzzese accents that you see on Salem and Hanover streets are not paid actors, and they are not all going to move away tomorrow. However, the Italian population here is aging, and a recent estimate indicates that its numbers have dwindled to about half of the neighborhood total.

To get to the North End, walk down the steps at the rear of City Hall Plaza and cross New Congress Street. Faneuil Hall and the statue of Samuel Adams are off to your right. Closer at hand, in the vest-pocket park framed by New Congress Street and Dock Square, are two less conventional bronze statues, one seated on a bench and the other standing eye to eye with passersby. Both represent James Michael Curley, mayor, governor, congressman, and model for all urban bosses. It is well that he has no pedestal; he was much more a man than an idol.

❹ Turn left and walk past the **Union Oyster House.** The building was first the residence and shop of Hopestill Capen in 1714, and in 1771–1775 Isaiah Thomas published the *Massachusetts Spy* here. The city's oldest restaurant, the Union Oyster House has been operating on this site since 1826. Follow Marshall Street

⑤ behind the Oyster House and past the **Boston Stone,** set into the brick wall of the gift shop of the same name. This was a paint-mixing stone, older than the 1737 date the inscription suggests, that was long used as milepost zero in measuring distances from Boston. Marshall Street leads into Blackstone Street, where on Fridays and Saturdays pushcart vendors sell fish, fruit, and vegetables. This is commonly called the Haymarket, though the Haymarket Square bus and subway stop is farther down New Congress Street, behind the big parking garage.

As you cross Blackstone Street on your way to the passage beneath the Fitzgerald Expressway (named for John Kennedy's grandfather, Mayor John "Honey Fitz" Fitzgerald), look down at the bronze sculptures of everyday garbage embedded in the pavement. This was done in 1976 in whimsical reproduction of a typical afternoon's debris. The work of Mags Harries, *Asaroton* takes its name from the Greek word for unswept floors.

The **Fitzgerald Expressway** appears to be not long for this earth. After years of wrangling, federal funding has been approved for replacing the structure with an underground central artery that will carry a larger volume of traffic. Along with the third harbor tunnel to Logan Airport, the project is expected to take until 2001 to complete. In the meantime we may expect traffic tie-ups as the job proceeds.

Opposite the pedestrian tunnel beneath the expressway is the beginning of Salem Street, an ancient and constricted thoroughfare of meat markets, kitchen-supply shops, barrels of olives and *baccala* (salt cod), and one or two stores selling furniture that makes the late Rococo look staid. It is an agreeable old street filled with fine smells, especially as you reach the coffee and spice shop at the corner of Parmenter Street. A few steps to the right on Parmenter will take you to the North End branch of the **Boston Public Library,** where a bust of Dante acknowledges local cultural pride. (There is no corresponding bust of Yeats or Joyce in the South Boston branch.)

Time Out If you continue on Salem Street to Cooper Street, make a left, and then a right on Margin Street, you'll stumble upon **Pizzeria Regina** (11½ Thacher St.) and what some consider the best pizza in Boston: It's thin-crusted, oily, and wonderful. There are other branches, but this is the one to go to. **Galleria Umberto** (289 Hanover St.) turns out pizza that rivals Regina's, but you have to sample its slices standing up and get here before 2 PM. Ask for directions; the North End can be a maze.

Return to Salem Street and continue beyond the point where the stores thin out; up ahead is the church famous for two lanterns that glimmered from its steeple on the night of April 18, **⑥** 1775. Christ Church, the **Old North Church** (1723), the oldest church building in Boston, was designed by William Price from a study of Christopher Wren's London churches. It is best known for the tower from which the signal lanterns of Paul Revere flashed warning to Charlestown of British troop movements. (The original tower blew down in 1804; the present one was put up in 1954 after yet another gale). But the Old North, still the home of an active Episcopal congregation (including members of the Revere family), is an impressive building in its own right. Inside, note the graceful layout of pews (reserved in Colonial times for the families that rented them) and gallery; the bust of George Washington, pronounced by the Marquis de Lafayette to be the best likeness of the general he ever saw; the brass chandeliers, made in Amsterdam in 1700 and installed here in 1724; and the clock, the oldest still running in an American public building. Try to visit when changes on the bells are scheduled to be rung; recently restored and rehung, they bear the inscription, "We are the first ring of bells cast for the British Empire in North America." The work of the English bell foundry of Abel Rudhall, the bells today sound as sweet as when the boy Paul Revere rang them on Sabbath mornings. A small museum next to the church houses such artifacts as a musket from the battle of Lexington and a vial of tea decanted from the boots of a participant in the Boston Tea Party. *Tel. 617/523-6676. Open daily 9-5. Sun. services at 9, 11, and 4. Closed Thanksgiving.*

Immediately behind the Old North Church and across Unity
❼ Street is the **Prado,** or **Paul Revere Mall,** lined with bronze plaques that tell the stories of famous North Enders and centering on Cyrus Dallin's equestrian statue of Paul Revere. It may surprise visitors who are largely familiar with Revere through Longfellow's "Midnight Ride" and statues such as this to know that the man was stocky and of medium height; whatever dash he possessed was in his eyes rather than his physique. That physique served him well enough, for he lived to be 83 and buried nearly all his revolutionary comrades.

The **Ebenezer Clough House** (not open to the public), built in 1712 and now the only local survivor of its era aside from the Old North, stands at 21 Unity Street. This spot requires an exercise in imagination: Picture the streets lined with houses such as this, with an occasional grander Georgian mansion and modest wooden survivors of old Boston's many fires, and you will come to an approximation of what the North End looked like when Paul Revere was young.

The Prado opens onto Hanover Street, named for the ruling dynasty of 18th-century England. Almost directly opposite is
❽ **St. Stephen's,** the only Bulfinch church still standing in Boston. A rebuilding in 1802 of an earlier structure, it has served as a Catholic parish since 1862. *Open daily 8:30-5. Sun. services at 8:30 and 11; weekday services 7:30 AM; Sat. and holidays 9 AM.*

A left turn at St. Stephen's will take you to the harbor end of Hanover Street and the Boston headquarters of the U.S. Coast Guard (not open to visitors); a right turn at the Coast Guard Station takes you to the Christopher Columbus Waterfront Park, with a lovely rose garden, and the restored wharves off Atlantic Avenue. A right turn at the church takes you through the business blocks of Hanover Street, thick with pastry shops and Italian espresso houses.

Time Out **Caffe Vittoria** (296 Hanover St.) specializes in cappuccino and special coffee drinks; its Old World cafe ambience makes it a great spot at any hour. Next door, **Mike's Pastry** (300 Hanover St.) has fresh ricotta, cannoli, and other Italian pastries.

Beyond Hanover Street, by way of Fleet Street and Garden Court, is North Square. Here is the oldest house in Boston, the
❾ **Paul Revere House,** built nearly a hundred years before Re-

vere's 1775 midnight ride through Middlesex County. He owned it from 1770 until 1800, although he and his wife (Rachel Revere, for whom the facing park is named) rented it out during the later part of that period. The house was restored about 1905, after a century of disrepair; pre-1900 photographs show it as a shabby warren of storefronts and apartments. The clapboard sheathing is a replacement, but 90% of the framework is original. The downstairs is furnished as it would have been in the 17th century, while the second floor reflects the time of Revere's occupancy (although few of the articles are his own). The self-guided tour makes use of explanatory notes mounted on the railings that extend through the rooms. Attendants are available to answer questions. *19 North Sq., tel. 617/523–1676. Admission: $2 adults, 75¢ children 5–17, $1.50 senior citizens and college students. Open Apr. 15–Oct. 31, daily 9:30–5:15; other times until 4:15. Closed holidays and Mon. Jan–Mar.*

⑩ Next door is the brick **Pierce-Hichborn** (or Hitchborn) **House,** one of the city's oldest brick buildings, once owned by relatives of Revere's mother. *29 North Sq., tel. 617/523–1676. Admission: $2 adults, 75¢ children 5–18, $1.50 senior citizens and college students. Combined admission for the Paul Revere and Pierce-Hichborn houses: $3.25 adults, $1 children 5–18, $2.25 senior citizens and college students. Open daily for guided tours only at 12:30 and 2:30.*

Most of the North End's historic sites are to be found east of Salem Street in the area we have just been exploring, and we must backtrack across Salem into the steep and narrow residential streets to savor the old Italian flavor of the neighbor-
⑪ hood. Keep walking uphill and you will reach the **Copp's Hill Burying Ground,** which incorporates four cemeteries established between 1660 and 1819. Near the Charter Street gate is the tomb of the Mather family, the dynasty of divines (Cotton and Increase were the most famous sons) who held sway in Boston during the heyday of the old theocracy. Many headstones were chipped by practice shots fired by British soldiers during the occupation of Boston, and a number of the musketball pockmarks can still be seen. Of all Boston's early cemeteries, Copp's Hill seems most to preserve an ancient and melancholic air. *Open daily 9–4.*

Tour 4: Charlestown

Numbers in the margin correspond to points of interest on the Charlestown map.

The view from Copp's Hill to the north encompasses the mouth of the Charles and much of Charlestown, and it is dominated by the spars and rigging of the USS *Constitution* and the spare granite obelisk of the Bunker Hill Monument. Both ship and monument, and the Charlestown neighborhoods that adjoin them, can be reached via the Charlestown Bridge; from Copp's Hill, turn left on Charter Street, descend to Commercial Street, and turn left again to reach the bridge. A more interesting way to get to the *Constitution* might be to take the water shuttle operated by **Boston Harbor Cruise** (tel. 617/227–4320); it costs $1 each way and runs year-round every 15 or 30 minutes, weekdays 6:30 AM–8 PM, weekends 10 AM–6 PM.

The USS *Constitution*, nicknamed Old Ironsides for the strength of its oaken hull, not because of any iron plating, is the oldest commissioned ship in the U.S. Navy. As such, the men and women who look after her are regular Navy personnel. She is moored at a national historic site, the **Charlestown Navy Yard,** one of six established to build warships. For 174 years, as wooden hulls and muzzle-loading cannon gave way to steel ships and sophisticated electronics, the yard evolved to meet the changing needs of a changing navy.

You come upon the entrance almost immediately after alighting from the Charlestown Bridge (the No. 93 bus from Haymarket Square, Boston, stops three blocks from the entrance, and in summer there are boats from Long Wharf, Boston). In addition to the *Constitution,* visitors may tour the USS *Cassin Young,* a World War II destroyer typical of the ships built here during that era; the museum; the commandant's house; and the collections of the Boston Marine Society. The Yard itself is a virtual museum of American shipbuilding for almost her entire history. Here are early 19th-century barracks, workshops, and officers' quarters; a ropewalk (an elongated building for making rope) designed in 1834 by the Greek Revival architect Alexander Parris and used by the Navy to turn out cordage for more than 125 years; and one of the two oldest dry docks (the one nearer the entrance) in the United States. The *Constitution* was first to use this dry dock (in 1833).

The USS *Constitution* was launched in Boston, where Constitution Wharf now stands, in 1797. Her principal service was during Thomas Jefferson's campaign against the Barbary pirates, off the coast of North Africa, and in the War of 1812. She never lost an engagement. Sailors show visitors around the ship, taking them below decks to see the impossibly cramped living quarters and the places at the guns where the desperate and difficult work of naval warfare under sail was carried out. *Tel. 617/426–1812. Admission free to* Constitution. *Admission to museum: $3 adults, $2 senior citizens, $1 children 6–16. Open daily 9–5 in winter, 9–6 in summer. The ship will be in dry dock through early 1994 for repairs. During this time two decks will be open for tours and a film of the tour will be shown at the adjacent museum.*

The phrase "Battle of Bunker Hill" is one of America's most famous misnomers. The battle was fought on Breed's Hill, and that is where Solomon Willard's 220-foot shaft of Quincy granite stands. The monument, for which the Marquis de Lafayette laid the cornerstone in 1825, rises from the spot occupied by the southeast corner of the American redoubt on the hot afternoon of June 17, 1775. That was the day on which a citizen's militia, commanded by Colonel William Prescott not to fire "till you see the whites of their eyes," inflicted more than 1,100 casualties on the British regulars (who eventually seized the hill). It was a Pyrrhic victory for the British; the brave American defense greatly boosted Colonial morale. Among the dead were the brilliant young American doctor and political activist Joseph Warren, recently commissioned as a major general but fighting as a private, and the British Major Pitcairn, who two months before had led the redcoats into Lexington. Pitcairn is buried in the crypt of the Old North. Warren lay in a shallow grave on Breed's Hill until the British evacuation of Boston, when his remains were disinterred and buried ceremoniously in the Old Granary. How was the body identified? Warren's dentist recognized his handiwork in a pair of false teeth secured with silver

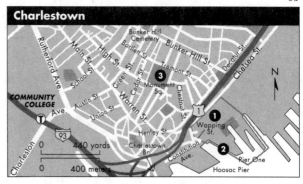

wire. The "dentist" was Paul Revere, a jack and master of many trades, who made the teeth's silver springs.

3 Ascend the **Bunker Hill Monument** (Main Street to Monument Street, then straight uphill) by a flight of 294 steps. There is no elevator, but the views from the observatory are worth the climb. At the base, four dioramas tell the story of the battle; ranger programs are given hourly. (Another Bunker Hill presentation, the multimedia show "Whites of Their Eyes," is shown in a pavilion near the Navy Yard entrance.) If you are in Boston on June 17, go to the hill to see a full-scale historical demonstration of the battle; it's quite a production. *Tel. 617/ 242–5641. Admission free. Lodge open daily 9–5, monument until 4:30. Closed Thanksgiving, Christmas, and New Year's Day.*

Time Out   Built in 1780, the **Warren Tavern** (2 Pleasant St.) is a restored Colonial neighborhood pub once frequented by George Washington and Paul Revere. Stop in for a drink or some American food with an international twist.

The blocks around the Bunker Hill Monument are a good illustration of a neighborhood in flux. Elegantly restored Federal and mid-19th-century town houses stand cheek by jowl with working-class quarters of similar vintage but more modest recent pasts. Nearby Winthrop Square also has its share of interesting houses. Farther north along Main Street is City Square, Charlestown's main commercial district. On Phipps Street you'll find the grave of John Harvard, a young minister who in 1638 bequeathed his small library to the fledgling Cambridge College, which was to be renamed in his honor. The precise location of the grave is uncertain, but a monument of 1828 marks its approximate site. John Harvard is also commemorated in the nearby Harvard Mall, a vest-pocket park.

Tour 5: Downtown Boston

Numbers in the margin correspond to points of interest on the Downtown Boston map.

The financial district—what Bostonians usually refer to as "downtown"—is off the beaten track for visitors who are concentrating on following the Freedom Trail, yet there is much to see in a walk of an hour or two. There is little logic to the streets here; they are, after all, village lanes that only happen to be lined with 40-story office towers. Just as the great fire of 1872 swept the old financial district clear, the downtown construction of the past two decades has obliterated many of the buildings where Boston businessmen of Silas Lapham's day sat at their rolltop desks.

The area is anchored at one end by Faneuil Hall and Quincy Market, at the other by South Station and Chinatown. It is bordered by Tremont Street and the Common on the west, by the harbor wharves on the east. Natives may be able to navigate the tangle of thoroughfares in between, but few of them manage to give intelligible directions when asked, and you will be better off trusting to a map. The area may be confusing, but it is mercifully small.

Just south of Government Center, at the corner of Tremont and ● School streets, stands **King's Chapel,** built in 1754 and never topped with the steeple that the architect Peter Harrison had planned. The first chapel on this site was erected in 1688, when Sir Edmund Andros, the royal governor whose authority temporarily replaced the original Colonial charter, appropriated the land for the establishment of an Anglican place of worship. This rankled the Puritans, who had left England to escape Anglicanism and had until then kept it out of the colony. (In the 1780s King's Chapel became the first American church to embrace a new threat to congregationalist orthodoxy called Unitarianism.)

It took five years to build the solid Quincy granite structure. As construction proceeded, the old church continued to stand within the walls of the new, to be removed in pieces when the stone chapel was completed. The builders then went to work on the interior, which remains essentially as they finished it, a masterpiece of elegant proportions and Georgian calm. The chapel's bell is Paul Revere's largest and, in his opinion, his sweetest-sounding. *Open Tues.–Fri. 10–2, Sat. 10–4. Sun. service at 11. Music program Tues. 12:15–12:45.*

The adjacent **King's Chapel Burying Ground,** the oldest in the city, contains the remains of the first Massachusetts governor, John Winthrop, and several generations of his descendants. Here, too, are many other tombs of Boston worthies of three centuries ago. Two markers recall individuals famous for less conventional reasons. Take the path to the right from the entrance and then left by the chapel to the gravestone (1704) of Elizabeth Pain, the model for Hester Prynne in Hawthorne's *The Scarlet Letter.* The prominent slate monument near the entrance to the yard tells (in French) the story of the Chevalier de Saint-Sauveur, a young officer who was part of the first French contingent that arrived to help the rebel Americans in 1778. He was killed in a riot that began when hungry Bostonians were told they could not buy the bread the French were baking for their men with their own wheat—an awkward situation made worse by the language barrier. The chevalier's internment here was probably the occasion for the first Catholic mass in what has since become a predominantly Catholic city.

Time Out   **Rebecca's Café** (18 Tremont St.), with an array of fresh salads, sandwiches, and homemade pastries, is a comfortable place to stop for a casual lunch.

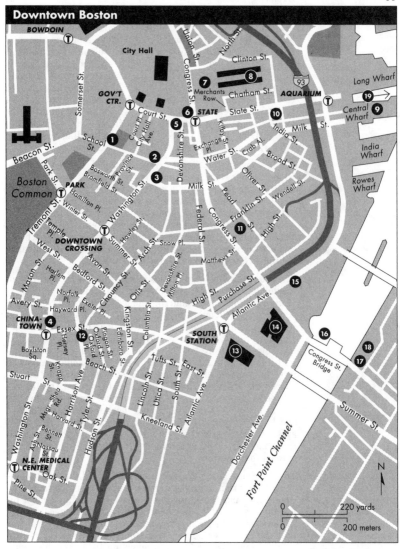

Downtown Boston

Beaver II, **16**
Boston Children's Museum, **17**
Boston Massacre Site, **6**
Boston Tea Party Site, **15**
Chinatown, **12**
Combat Zone, **4**
Computer Museum, **18**

Faneuil Hall, **7**
Federal Reserve Tower, **14**
Globe Corner Bookstore, **2**
Harbor Islands, **19**
King's Chapel, **1**
New England Aquarium, **9**

New England Telephone Building, **11**
Old South Meeting House, **3**
Old State House, **5**
Quincy Market, **8**
South Station, **13**
U.S. Custom House, **10**

Follow School Street down from King's Chapel (away from Tremont, with the Parker House Hotel on your right) and pass the **old City Hall,** with Richard S. Greenough's bronze statue of **Benjamin Franklin** (1855), which was Boston's first portrait sculpture. Franklin was born (1706) a few blocks from here on Milk Street and attended the Boston Latin School, founded near the City Hall site in 1635. (The school has long since moved to the avenue Louis Pasteur, near the Fenway.) Franklin, as a young man, went to Philadelphia, where he lived most of his long life. Boston's municipal government moved to the new City Hall in 1969, and the old Second Empire building now houses offices and Maison Robert, a French restaurant.

At the Washington Street corner of School Street stands the ❷ **Globe Corner Bookstore,** until recently a museum of old editions and now once again a working bookstore. It was built in 1718, and throughout most of the 19th century it counted among its clientele the leading lights of literary society—Emerson, Holmes, Longfellow, Lowell. The seminally important Boston publishers Ticknor and Fields also had offices here. Among the store's specialties are books about New England, books by New England authors, and travel titles.

❸ The **Old South Meeting House** is a short block to the right down Washington Street, at the corner of Milk. Built in 1729, it is Boston's second oldest church. Unlike the older Old North, the Old South is no longer the seat of an active congregation. And its principal associations have always been more secular than religious. Some of the fieriest of the town meetings that led to the Revolution were held here, culminating in the tumultuous gathering of December 16, 1773, called by Samuel Adams to face the problem of three ships, laden with dutiable tea, anchored at Griffin's Wharf. The activists wanted the tea returned to England, the governor would not permit it—and the rest is history. To cries of "Boston harbor a tea-pot tonight" and John Hancock's "Let every man do what is right in his own eyes," the protestors poured out of the Old South, headed to the wharf with waiting comrades, and dumped £18,000 worth of tea into the water.

The Old South suffered no small amount of indignity in the ensuing Revolution. Its pews were ripped out by occupying British troops, and the interior was used as a riding school by Burgoyne's light dragoons. A century later it escaped destruction in the Great Fire of 1872, only to be threatened with demolition by developers. Aside from the windows and doors, the only original interior features surviving today are the tiered galleries above the main floor. The pulpit is a reproduction of the one used by colonial divines and secular firebrands. Public contributions saved the church, and it remains open to visitors today. *Tel. 617/482-6439. Admission: $2.50 adults, $1 children 6–18, $2 students and senior citizens. Open Apr. 1–Oct. 31, daily 9:30–5; Nov. 1–Mar. 31, weekdays 10–4, weekends 10–5. Lecture-concert series (free with admission) Oct.-Apr., Thurs. 12:15.*

Washington Street is the main commercial street of downtown Boston. Turning left on leaving the Old South, you follow a pedestrian mall and pass many of the area's major retail establishments (don't overlook the side streets). Soon you reach the two venerable anchors of Boston's mercantile district, Filene's and Jordan Marsh (*see* Shopping). William Filene founded his Boston store in 1881 near the site of the present eight-story building (1912). The famous automatic bargain basement was an innovation of his son, Edward Filene. Jordan Marsh was the creation of Eben Jordan, who arrived in Boston from Maine around 1840 with $1.25 in his pocket and opened Jordan Marsh (Marsh was a partner) in 1851. The huge store has been expanding on its Washington Street site since 1871, most recently with a spacious addition in the late 1970s.

❹ Just beyond Jordan Marsh is the **Combat Zone** on lower Washington Street, a two-block area of nude-dancing bars, peep shows, "adult" bookstores, and "adult" movie houses. The Combat Zone was an early 1970s experiment that concentrated these establishments and their clientele in a small, easily circumscribed area following the demolition of Scollay Square. The Combat Zone occasionally lives up to its name; while it is not particularly dangerous during the daytime, it is not recommended to the casual stroller at night.

Pressing on the Combat Zone from the other direction (on and about Stuart Street) are the Tufts New England Medical Center, Chinatown (which also perceives a threat from Tufts' expansion), and Boston's theater district. The theater district is small: The Wilbur, Shubert, Emerson Majestic, and Colonial theaters and the Wang Center for the Performing Arts all cluster near the intersection of Tremont and Stuart streets. Yet the area does an increasingly lively business booking Broadway tryouts, road shows, and big-name recitals.

A right turn onto Washington Street from the doorstep of the Old South will take you past the Globe Corner Bookstore once again, past Pi Alley (named after the loose type, or "pi," spilled from the pockets of printers when upper Washington Street was Boston's newspaper row—or after colonial pie shops, depending on the story you believe), and to the rear of the Old State House near the intersection of Court Street.

❺ The **Old State House** was the seat of the Colonial government from 1713 until the Revolution, and after the evacuation of the British from Boston in 1776 it served the independent Commonwealth until the new State House on Beacon Hill was completed. John Hancock was inaugurated here as the first governor under the new state constitution. Like many Colonial-era landmarks, it fared poorly in the years that followed. Mid-19th century photos show the old building clumsily chimnied and mansarded, with signs in the windows advertising a variety of businesses. In the 1830s the Old State House served as Boston City Hall. When demolition was threatened in the name of improving the traffic flow, the Bostonian Society organized a restoration, completed in 1882. After a two-year, $4-million federal preservation and renovation project, the Old State House has reopened and changed the focus of its exhibits. The permanent collection traces Boston's Revolutionary War history, while changing exhibits on the second floor address such contemporary issues as "Urban Renewal and Boston's West End." *206 Washington St., tel. 617/720–3290. Admission: $2 adults, 75¢ children 6–18, $1.50 senior citizens and college students, free to Massachusetts schoolchildren. Open daily 9:30–5. Closed Thanksgiving, Christmas, and New Year's Day.*

A brightly colored lion and unicorn, symbols of British imperial power, appear at the gable ends of the State Street facade of the Old State House. The originals were pulled down in 1776. For proof that bygones are bygones, we may look not only to the restoration of the sculptures but to the fact that Queen Elizabeth II stood on the Old State House balcony and addressed a cheering crowd during the U.S. bicentennial celebration in 1976.

Directly in front of the Old State House is a circle of cobblestones marking a far more sober juncture in the relations between Great Britain and its erstwhile colonies. The stones (now **❻** located in a traffic island) mark the site of the **Boston Massacre,** which occurred on the snowy evening of March 5, 1770, when a small contingent of British regulars fired in panic upon a taunting mob of Bostonians. Five townsmen died. In the legal action that followed, the defense of the accused soldiers was undertaken by John Adams and Josiah Quincy, both of whom vehemently opposed British oppression but who were devoted to the principle of fair trial. All but two of the nine regulars charged were acquitted; the others were branded on the hand for manslaughter.

We head down State Street, known before the Revolution as King Street and even then a nascent center of finance. In the 19th century State Street was headquarters for banks, brokerages, and insurance firms; while these businesses have now spread throughout the downtown district, "State Street" retains much the same connotation in Boston that "Wall Street" has elsewhere. The early commercial hegemony of State Street was symbolized by Long Wharf, built originally in 1710 and extending some 1,700 feet into the harbor. If today's Long Wharf does not appear to be that long, it is not because it has been shortened but because the land has expanded around it. State Street once met the water at Kilby Street on the south and Merchants Row on the north. Landfill operations were pursued relentlessly through the years, and the old coastline is now as much a memory as such Colonial State Street landmarks as Governor Winthrop's 1630 house and the revolutionary-era Bunch of Grapes Tavern, where Bostonians met to drink and wax indignant at their treatment by the British.

Turning left off State Street onto Merchants Row, we leave the old financial marketplace and encounter, first, an historic marketplace of ideas and, second, an old provisions market reborn as the emblem of downtown revitalization. Faneuil Hall ("the Cradle of Liberty") and the Quincy Market (also known as Faneuil Hall Marketplace) face each other across a small square thronged with people at all but the smallest hours.

❼ Like so many other Boston landmarks, **Faneuil Hall** (pronounced "Fan'l") has evolved over the years. The original structure was erected in 1742, the gift of Peter Faneuil, whose intention was that the hall serve as both a place for town meetings and a public market. It burned in 1761 and was immediately rebuilt according to the original plan of its designer, the Scottish portrait painter John Smibert.

In 1772 Samuel Adams stood here and first suggested that Massachusetts and the other colonies organize a Committee of Correspondence to maintain semiclandestine lines of communication in the face of hardening British repression. Nine years earlier, James Otis had helped inaugurate the era that culminated in American independence when he dedicated the rebuilt hall to the "cause of liberty." In later years the hall lived up to Otis's dedication when Wendell Phillips and Charles Sumner pleaded the abolitionist cause from its podium.

Faneuil Hall was substantially enlarged and remodeled in 1805 according to the design of Charles Bulfinch, and this is the building we see today. Its purpose remains the same; the great balconied hall is made available to citizens' groups on presentation of a request signed by a required number of responsible parties. In national election years the hall is usually host to debates featuring contenders in the Massachusetts presidential primary.

At ground level the mercantile purposes Faneuil had in mind are still served. But instead of the meats and produce available in timeworn stalls until a dozen years ago, today's visitor finds shops more in keeping with the tone of the nearby Quincy Market restoration.

Inside Faneuil Hall is the great mural *Webster's Reply to Hayne*, Stuart's portrait of Washington at Dorchester Heights, and dozens of other paintings of famous Americans. On the top floors are the headquarters and museum of the **Ancient and Honorable Artillery Company of Massachusetts,** the oldest militia in the nation (1638). Its status is now ceremonial, but it is justly proud of the arms, uniforms, and other artifacts on display.

Why is there a weathervane in the shape of a grasshopper atop Faneuil Hall? One story has it that Sir Thomas Gresham, founder of the Royal Exchange in London, was found as an abandoned baby in a field in 1519 by children chasing grasshoppers. Gresham put a grasshopper weathervane atop the Exchange, of which Peter Faneuil became a member years later, and Faneuil liked the symbol and had one placed on Faneuil Hall. Today it is the symbol of the entire Quincy Market development. *Open daily 9–5. Closed Thanksgiving, Christmas, and New Year's Day.*

❽ Quincy Market consists of three structures, 535 feet in length, built to the design of Alexander Parris in 1826. The market is named after Boston mayor Josiah Quincy (not the Josiah Quincy who helped to defend the Boston Massacre soldiers), who promoted the project and the massive landfill operations that accompanied it to alleviate the cramped retailers' conditions in Faneuil Hall. The center building is of granite, with a Doric colonnade at either end and a classical dome and rotunda at the center; the north and south market buildings are predominantly brick.

Quincy Market served its purpose as a retail and wholesale distribution center for meat and produce for a century and a half. By the 1970s, though, the market area had become seedy. Some of the old tenants—the famous Durgin-Park restaurant and a few butchers and grocers in the central building—had hung on through the years, but the old vitality had disappeared. Buildings were in disrepair and demolition was a distinct possibility. Fortunately, the old notions of urban renewal as something that had to be done with a bulldozer were beginning to yield to the idea of "recycling" buildings to new uses. With the participation of the Boston Redevelopment Authority, the architect Benjamin Thompson planned the renovation of all three Quincy Market buildings. The central structure has kept its traditional market-stall layout, but most of the new businesses on the first floor offer international and specialty foods (raw shellfish, cold pasta salads, sausages on sticks, cheesecake, baklava—you name it). Interspersed with these temptations are the updated stalls of provisioners who have been in the market since before you were born. Doe, Sullivan, the cheese seller, settled here in 1829.

Upstairs in the central building are sit-down restaurants, and along the arcades on either side are vendors selling photographs of Boston, silkscreened aprons, and boutique chocolate chip cookies. Nor is there a shortage of bars.

The north and south market buildings, separated from the central market by attractive pedestrian malls with trees and benches, house more substantial retail establishments, offices, and additional restaurants. There may be more restaurants in Quincy Market than existed in all of downtown Boston before World War II. Abundance and variety, albeit of an ephemeral sort, have been the watchwords of Quincy Market since its reopening in 1976. Some people consider it all hopelessly trendy; 50,000 visitors a day rather enjoy the extravaganza. You'll want to decide for yourself. *Open Mon.–Sat. 10–9, Sun. noon–6. Restaurants and bars generally open daily 11 AM–2 AM.*

At the end of Quincy Market opposite Faneuil Hall, the newly constructed **Marketplace Center,** between the market buildings and the expressway is filled with shops and boutiques. Beyond is Columbus Park, bordering on the harbor and on several of Boston's restored wharves. **Lewis Wharf** and **Commercial Wharf,** which long lay nearly derelict, had by the mid-1970s been transformed into condominiums, apartments, restaurants, and upscale shops. **Long Wharf's** Marriott hotel was designed to be compatible with the old seaside warehouses. Sailboats and power yachts ride here at anchor; Boston's workaday waterfront is now located along the docks of South Boston, in East Boston (directly opposite Columbus Park), and in the huge containerized shipping facilities at the mouth of the Mystic.

Central Wharf, immediately to the right of Long Wharf as you face the harbor, is the home of one of Boston's most popular ❾ attractions, the **New England Aquarium.** Here you'll find seals, penguins, a variety of sharks and other sea creatures—more than 2,000 species in all, some of which make their home in the aquarium's four-story, 187,000-gallon observation tank, the largest of its kind in the world. Ramps wind around the tank, leading to the top and allowing visitors to view the inhabitants from many vantage points. Feeding time should not be missed; since it happens five times a day, you'll probably catch it at least once. The procedure lasts nearly an hour and takes divers 23 feet into the tank. There are also dolphin and sea lion shows aboard *Discovery,* a floating marine mammal pavilion, and whale watch cruises. The aquarium was for many years the winter home of the late André the Seal, made famous in a popular children's book. André summered in the Gulf of Maine and returned to the Aquarium each fall; having lived a full seal lifetime, André passed away in Maine in 1986, and all New England mourned him. *Tel. 617/973–5200 (whale watch informa-*

tion, 617/973–5277). Admission: $7.50 adults, $3.50 children 3–11, $6.50 senior citizens; free Thurs. after 3 PM, Oct.–Mar. Open weekdays 9–5, Thurs. until 8, weekends and holidays 9–6. Closed Thanksgiving, Christmas, and New Year's Day.

If you backtrack on Central Wharf and along Milk Street beneath the expressway, you will soon arrive at an open square dominated by a Greek Revival temple that appears to have ❿ sprouted a tower. That is just what it is. This is the **U.S. Custom House** (1847), the work of the architects Ammi Young and Isaiah Rogers. That is, the bottom part is their work. The tower (would skyscrapers have looked like this if they were built in the 1840s?) was added in 1915, making the Custom House the city's tallest building. Note the grafting job that was done on the great rotunda, surmounted by its handsome dome; the dome's outer surface was once the roof of the building, and now it is imbedded in the base of the tower.

The U.S. Customs Service having moved into more modern quarters, the Custom House has been sold to the city of Boston, which is considering how the distinctive structure might best be used. We should hope that any renovation will include a reopening of the 25th-floor observatory, which offers a fine panorama of downtown Boston and the harbor.

Virtually all tangible historical associations in the Government Center area were obliterated in the demolition of Scollay Square and the surrounding streets. It was in a garret on one of these streets that Alexander Graham Bell first transmitted a human voice—his own—by telephone. When the building where Bell had his workshop was torn down in the 1920s, the phone company had the room dismantled and reassembled in ⓫ the headquarters lobby of the **New England Telephone Building.** There the room looks just as it did on June 3, 1875, when Bell first coaxed his voice across a wire. (His famous call to Thomas Watson, "Come here, I want you," was made nearly a year later in another part of town.) Telephone memorabilia and a 160-foot mural tell the story of the phone. *185 Franklin St. Admission free. Open weekdays 8:30–5.*

One corner of downtown that has been relatively untouched by high-rise development is the old **leather district,** which is nestled into the angle formed by Kneeland Street and Atlantic Avenue opposite South Station. This was the wholesale supply area for raw materials in the days when the shoe industry was a regional economic mainstay, and a few leather firms are still located here. The leather district is probably the best place in downtown Boston to get an idea of what the city's business blocks looked like in the late 19th century.

⓬ The leather district directly abuts **Chinatown,** which is also bordered by the Combat Zone and the buildings of the Tufts New England Medical Center. The Massachusetts Turnpike and its junction with the Southeast Expressway are another presence here, serving to isolate Chinatown from the South End in much the same way the Fitzgerald Expressway isolates the North End from downtown.

Chinatown's borders may be constrained, yet it remains one of the larger concentrations of Chinese-Americans in the United States, and it is a vibrant center for both the private and the public aspects of local Chinese culture. As in most American Chinatowns, it is the concentration of restaurants that attracts the visitors, and today the numerous Chinese establishments are interspersed with a handful of Vietnamese eateries—a reflection of the latest wave of immigration into Boston.

Most Chinese restaurants, food stores, and retail businesses are located along Beach and Tyler streets and Harrison Avenue. The area around the intersection of Kneeland Street and Harrison Avenue is the center of Boston's textile and garment industry, and a number of shops here specialize in discount yard goods (*see* Shopping).

Time Out It's a special treat to sample the Chinese baked goods in shops along Beach Street. Many visitors familiar with Cantonese and even Szechuan cookery will still be surprised and delighted with moon cakes, steamed cakes made with rice flour, and other sweets that seldom turn up on restaurant menus.

⓭ **South Station,** the colonnaded granite structure at the intersection of Atlantic Avenue and Summer Street, is the terminal for all Amtrak trains (and now Greyhound buses) in and out of Boston. Behind the station's grand 1900s facade, a major renovation project has converted the terminal into a modern, intermodal transit center. As the Dewey Square area is one of Boston's most active renewal districts (witness the new Dewey Square Tower and the multistructure International Place, dominated by a cylindrical tower punctuated by hundreds of postmodern Palladian windows), it is appropriate that the old station was made over into an arrival-and-departure point worthy of a great city.

Walk down Atlantic Avenue from South Station, past the
⓮ strikingly designed **Federal Reserve Tower.** *600 Atlantic Ave., tel. 617/973–3451. Tours given Fri. at 10:30 AM; reservations should be made a week in advance.*

Farther on along Atlantic Avenue, at the foot of Pearl Street, a plaque set into the wall of a commercial building marks the site
⓯ of the **Boston Tea Party.** That this was the site of Griffin's Wharf is only further evidence of Boston's relentless expansion into its harbor: The narrow Fort Point Channel is now all that separates the old Shawmut Peninsula from the once-distant neck of land that became South Boston.

When you cross Fort Point Channel on the Congress Street Bridge, you encounter—on a pier at the middle of the bridge—
⓰ the *Beaver II,* a faithful replica of one of the Tea Party ships that was forcibly boarded and unloaded on the night Boston Harbor became a teapot. It anchored here as a part of the bicentennial festivities in 1976 and has stayed on. The interpretive center on the adjacent pier contains exhibits explaining what happened on that cold evening and what led up to it. Visitors receive a complimentary cup of tea. *Tel. 617/338–1773. Admission: $6 adults, $3 children 5–14, $5 senior citizens and students. Open daily 9–4 in winter, 9–6 in summer; closed Dec.–Feb.*

At the opposite end of the bridge—you are now in the Fort Point Channel area of South Boston, not the residential part—
⓱ is Museum Wharf, home of the popular **Boston Children's Museum.** The multitude of hands-on exhibits designed with kids in mind includes a petting zoo of small animals, computers, video cameras, and exhibits designed to help children understand

cultural diversity, their bodies, and disabilities. Don't miss Grandmother's Attic, where kids can dress up in old clothing. The museum shops are a good source of children's books and gifts. Check local listings or call for a schedule of special exhibits, festivals, and performances. *300 Congress St., tel. 617/426–6500 (617/426–8855 for recorded information). Admission: $7 adults, $6 children 2–15 and senior citizens, $2 1-year-olds; $1 Fri. 5–9. Open Tues.–Sun. 10–5, Fri. until 9. Closed Mon. except during Boston school vacations and holidays, Thanksgiving, Christmas, and New Year's Day.*

⑱ Museum Wharf is also the home of the world's only **Computer Museum,** housing exhibits chronicling the spectacular development of machines that calculate and process information. There are more than 75 exhibits, including the two-story, Walk-Through Computer.™ Computer-animated films are shown daily. Given the importance of high technology to the local economy, the establishment of this institution is an act akin to the hanging of the sacred cod in the State House. *300 Congress St., tel. 617/426–2800 or 617/423–6758 for talking computer. Admission: $7 adults, $5 children 5–18, senior citizens, and students; ½ price Sun. 3–5. Open Tues.–Sun. 10–5, Fri. until 9. Closed Mon. except during Boston school vacations and holidays; closed Fri. evenings in winter.*

At the Northern Avenue crossing of Fort Point Channel, one block up from Congress Street where the channel meets the harbor, is a vast empty space currently used for parking. This is the Fan Pier, proposed site of a city within a city that could be the largest Boston public works project since the filling of the Back Bay. Plans for the area are in limbo.

Head back to Long Wharf and, in summer, you can board a boat that will take you to one of the most scenic and historically interesting, yet perhaps most consistently overlooked of Boston
⑲ attractions: the **Harbor Islands.** There are more than two dozen islands in the inner and outer harbors, most of them incorporated into **Harbor Islands State Park.** Some of the islands housed military installations during World War II; others were the sites of hospitals, prisons, even raffish resort hotels. Most have now reverted to a seminatural state. The focal point of the park is 30-acre Georges Island, on which the pre–Civil War **Fort Warren** stands, partially restored and partially in ruins. Confederate prisoners were once housed here. Until the advent of modern long-range electronic defenses, coastal installations such as this were vital to the nation's security. Georges Island is reached in summer by pedestrian-only ferries from Long Wharf. *Bay State Cruises, tel. 617/723–7800. Boats operate May 1–Oct. 11.*

July 1—Labor Day, visitors can take free water taxis from Georges to Gallups, Lovells, Peddocks, Grape, and Bumpkin islands. Bumpkin and Gallups are small islands, easily explored within an hour or so; Lovells and Grape each cover about 60 acres. Peddocks Island's 185 acres are dotted with the ruins of Fort Andrews; guided tours are recommended. All the harbor islands are accessible by private boat, with the exception of Thompson's Island, an education center. Activities on the islands include picnicking, hiking (there are plenty of ruins to explore and beautiful views), and fishing; swimming is permitted on Lovells (*see* Sports, Fitness, Beaches in Chapter 6).

Tour 6: The Back Bay

Numbers in the margin correspond to points of interest on the Back Bay, the South End, and the Fens map.

In the folklore of American neighborhoods, the Back Bay stands with New York's Park Avenue and San Francisco's Nob Hill as a symbol of propriety and high social standing. You will still occasionally hear someone described as coming from "an old Back Bay family," as though the Back Bay were hundreds of years old and its stone mansions the feudal bastions of the Puritan settlers from the time they got off the boat.

Nothing could be further from the truth. The Back Bay is one of Boston's new neighborhoods, scarcely 125 years old. Before the 1850s it *was* a bay, a tidal flat that formed the south bank of a distended Charles River. Remember, Boston since time immemorial has been a pear-shaped peninsula joined to the mainland by an isthmus (the Neck) so narrow that in early Colonial times a single gate and guardhouse were sufficient for its defenses. Today's Washington Street, as it leaves downtown and heads toward the South End, follows the old Neck.

Filling along the Neck began in 1850 and resulted in the creation of the South End neighborhood we will look at later. To the north, a narrow causeway called the Mill Dam (later Beacon Street) was built in 1814 to separate the Back Bay from the Charles. Bostonians began to fill in the shallows in 1858, using gravel brought from West Needham by railroad at a rate of up to 3,500 carloads per day. It took 30 years to complete the filling as far as the Fens. When the work was finished, the old 783-acre peninsula had been expanded by approximately 450 acres.

Thus the actual Back Bay became the neighborhood of Back Bay. Almost immediately, fashionable families began to decamp from Beacon Hill and the recently developed South End and to establish themselves in the brick and brownstone row houses they built upon the man-made land. Churches and cultural institutions followed, until by 1900 the streets between the Public Garden and Massachusetts Avenue had become unquestionably the smartest, most desirable neighborhood in all Boston. An air of permanence and respectability drifted in as surely as the tides once had; the Back Bay mystique was born.

❶ A walk through the Back Bay properly begins with the **Boston Public Garden,** the oldest botanical garden in the United States. Its establishment marked the first phase of the Back Bay reclamation project. Although the Garden is often lumped together with the Common, even in the minds of natives, the two are separate entities with different histories and purposes and a distinct boundary at Charles Street. The Common, as we have seen, has been public land since Boston was founded in 1630. The Public Garden belongs to a newer Boston; it occupies what had been salt marshes on the edge of the Common's dry land. The marshes supported rope-manufacturing enterprises in the early 1800s, and by 1837 the tract was covered with an abundance of ornamental plantings donated by a private citizen. The area was fully defined in 1856 by the building of Arlington Street, and in 1860 (after the final wrangling over the development of this choice acreage) the architect George Meacham was commissioned to plan the park that survives to this day. The central feature of the Public Garden is its irregularly designed pond, intended to appear, from any vantage point along its banks, much larger than its nearly four acres. The pond has been famous since 1877 for its **swan boats,** which make leisurely cruises during the warm months of the year. Like the Esplanade, the Public Garden pond is favored by ducks, and for the price of a few boat rides and a stale loaf of bread you can amuse children here for a good hour or more. The bridge over the pond has been described as the world's smallest suspension bridge.

The Public Garden boasts the finest formal plantings to be seen in central Boston. They line the beds along the main walkways and are changed with the seasons. The spring planting of tulips is especially colorful. And there is a good sampling of native and European tree species.

The dominant work among the park's statuary is Thomas Ball's equestrian George Washington (1869), which faces the head of Commonwealth Avenue at the Arlington Street gate. This is Washington in a triumphant pose as liberator, surveying a scene that, from where he stood with his cannons at Dorchester Heights, would have comprised an immense stretch of blue water. A few yards to the north of Washington (to the right if you're facing Commonwealth Avenue) is the granite and red marble Ether Monument, donated in 1866 by Thomas Lee to commemorate the first use of anesthesia 20 years earlier at Massachusetts General Hospital. Other Public Garden monuments include statues of the pioneer Unitarian preacher and transcendentalist William Ellery Channing, at the corner opposite his Arlington Street church; the author (*The Man Without a Country*) and philanthropist Edward Everett Hale, at the Charles Street Gate; and the abolitionist senator Charles Sumner and the Civil War hero Colonel Thomas Cass, along Boylston Street. *Tel. 617/635–4505. Open dawn–10 PM. Not recommended for strolling after dark, even if you find a gate open. Swan boats: $1 adults, 75¢ children, mid-Apr.–late Sept.*

The mall that extends down the middle of Commonwealth Avenue also has its share of statuary. The most interesting memorial here is the newest one, the portrayal of Samuel Eliot Morison seated on a rock as if he were peering out to sea. The statue is at the Exeter Street intersection.

Time Out Top Boston-area chefs have each submitted one recipe to the kitchen of the **Parish Cafe** (361 Boylston St.). The sandwiches are great here, and the café stays open until 1 AM.

If a walk in the Public Garden has left you in a mood more for verdure than for bricks and mortar, take the Arthur Fiedler Footbridge (corner of Beacon and Arlington) to the **Esplanade,** which continues along the Charles River for the entire length of the Back Bay (*see* Tour 1, *above*). The best place to begin exploring the streets of the Back Bay is at the corner of Commonwealth Avenue and Arlington Street, with Washington and his horse looking over your shoulder. The grand design of the district is dramatically and immediately apparent here. The planners of the Back Bay were able to do something that had never before been possible in Boston: to lay out an entire neighborhood of arrow-straight streets. The planners were heavily influenced by the recent rebuilding of Paris according to the plans of Baron Haussmann. While other parts of Boston may be

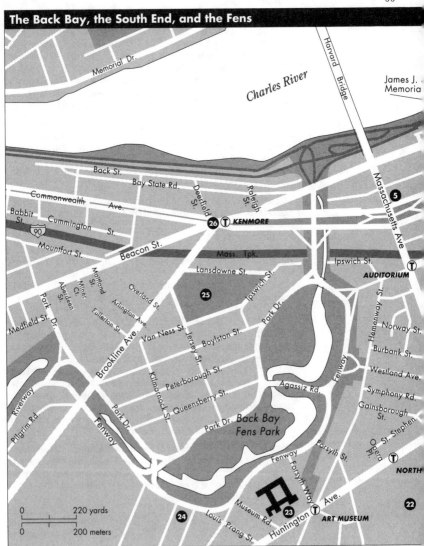

Charles River

Memorial Dr.

Harvard Bridge

James J. Memoria

Massachusetts Ave.

5

Back St.

Bay State Rd.

Deerfield St.

Raleigh St.

Commonwealth Ave.

Babbit St.

Cummington St.

90

26 T KENMORE

Mountfort St.

Beacon St.

Mass. Tpk.

Ipswich St.

Lansdowne St.

Ipswich St.

AUDITORIUM

Hemenway St.

Norway St.

Medfield St.

Park Dr.

Aberdeen St.

Fullerton St.

Highland St.

Miner Cir.

Overland St.

Arlington Ave.

Van Ness St.

25

Park Dr.

Boylston St.

Jersey St.

Burbank St.

Westland Ave.

Symphony Rd.

Fenway

Riverway

Pilgrim Rd.

Brookline Ave.

Kilmarnock St.

Peterborough St.

Queensberry St.

Agassiz Rd.

Gainsborough St.

Opera

St. Stephen

T NORTH

Park Dr.

Back Bay Fens Park

Fenway

Forsyth Way

Forsyth St.

Fenway

22

0   220 yards

0   200 meters

24

Louis Prang St.

Museum Rd.

23 T ART MUSEUM

Huntington Ave.

Arlington Street Church, **8**	Christian Science Church, **16**	Isabella Stewart Gardner Museum, **24**	Northeastern University, **22**
Bay Village, **21**	Church of the Covenant, **10**	John Hancock Tower, **6**	Oliver Ames Mansion, **5**
Baylies Mansion, **3**	Copley Place, **14**	Kenmore Square, **26**	Prudential Center, **15**
Boston Public Library, **13**	Emmanuel Church, **9**	Museum of Fine Arts, **23**	Public Garden, **1**
Burrage Mansion, **4**	Fenway Park, **25**	"New" Old South Church, **12**	Rutland Square, **19**
Cathedral of the Holy Cross, **18**	First Baptist Church, **11**		Symphony Hall, **17**
	Gibson House, **2**		Trinity Church, **7**
			Union Park, **20**

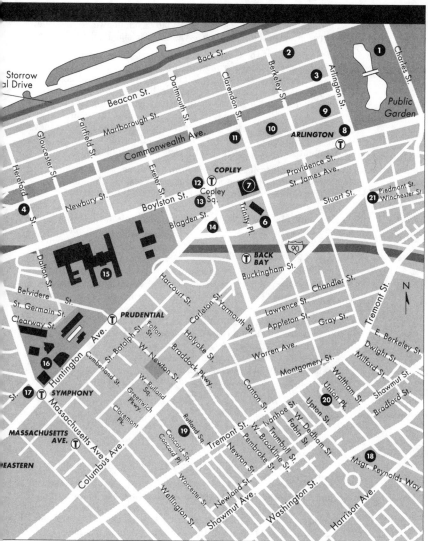

reminiscent of the mews and squares of London, the main thoroughfares of the Back Bay (especially Commonwealth Avenue) resemble nothing so much as they do Parisian boulevards.

Beginning at the Charles, the main east-west streets are Beacon Street, Marlborough Street, Commonwealth Avenue, Newbury Street, and Boylston Street. They are bisected by eight streets named in alphabetical order from Arlington to Hereford, with three-syllable street names alternating with two-syllable names. Service alleys run behind the main streets; though they are used now for garbage pickup and parking, they were built so that delivery wagons could be driven up to basement kitchens. That's how thorough the planning was.

Some aspects of the Back Bay, such as the way households were distributed, became matters more of change than of design. Old families with money congregated on Beacon Street, families with old Boston names but not much money gravitated to shady Marlborough. The nouveau riche tended to build on Commonwealth Avenue. Newbury and Boylston, originally residential rather than commercial streets, were the province of a mix of middle and upper middle class families, as were the side streets.

Back Bay is a living museum of urban Victorian residential architecture. The earliest specimens are nearest to the Public Garden (there are exceptions where showier turn-of-the-century mansions replaced 1860s town houses), and the newer examples are out around the Massachusetts Avenue and Fenway extremes of the district. The height of Back Bay residences and their distance from the street is essentially uniform, as are the interior layouts chosen according to lot width. Yet there is a distinct progression of facades, beginning with French academic and Italianate designs and moving through the various "revivals" of the 19th century. By the time of World War I, when development of the Back Bay was virtually complete, architects and their patrons had come full circle to a revival of the Federal period, which had been out of fashion for only 30 years when the filling began. If the Back Bay architects had not run out of land, they might have gotten around to a revival of Greek Revival.

An outstanding guide to the architecture and history of the Back Bay is Bainbridge Bunting's *Houses of Boston's Back Bay*, which is available in paperback in nearly all Boston bookstores. A reading of this thorough study can be expanded upon only by visits to Back Bay houses. A few are open to the public.

❷ The **Gibson House** offers a representative look at how life was arranged in—and by—these tall, narrow, formal buildings. One of the first Back Bay residences (1859), the Gibson House is relatively modest in comparison with some of the grand mansions built during the decades that followed. Unlike other Back Bay houses, the Gibson family home has been preserved with all its Victorian fixtures and furniture intact—not restored, but preserved; a conservative family scion lived here until the 1950s and left things as they were. Now it serves as the meeting place for the New England chapter of the Victorian Society in America. A stereopticon lies on a table in the study, a butler's pantry has a dumbwaiter and a copper-lined sink (so the dishes wouldn't scratch), the late 19th century basement kitchen is fully equipped, and a China Trade dinner service can be seen in the sumptuous second-floor dining room. Here you will understand why a squad of servants was a necessity in the old Back Bay. *137 Beacon St., tel. 617/267–6338. Admission: $3. Tours May–Oct., Wed.–Sun. at 1, 2, and 3; Nov.–Apr., weekends at 1, 2, and 3.*

Among the grander Back Bay houses, two that now house public institutions can be entered for a view of at least their first-floor common areas. One is the **Baylies Mansion** (5 Commonwealth Ave.) of 1904, now the home of the Boston Center for Adult Education. Another is the **Burrage Mansion** (314 Commonwealth Ave.), built in 1899 in an extravagant French château style, complete with turrets and gargoyles, that reflects a cost-be-damned attitude uncommon even among the wealthiest Back Bay families. The Boston Evening Clinic is now housed in the Burrage house.

Two Back Bay mansions are the homes of organizations that promote foreign language and culture: the **French Library in Boston** (53 Marlborough St.) and the German-oriented **Goethe Institute** (170 Beacon St.) See the *Boston Globe* Calendar section on Thursday for information on lectures, films, and other events in the handsome quarters of these respected institutions.

The largest Back Bay mansion is the **Oliver Ames Mansion** (355 Commonwealth Ave., corner of Massachusetts Ave.). Built in 1882 for a railroad baron and Massachusetts governor, this opulent château was recently renovated and now houses offices and shops.

The Great Depression brought an end to the old Back Bay style of living, and today only a few of the houses serve as single-family residences. Most have been cut up into apartments and, more recently, expensive condominiums. Interior details have experienced a mixed fate, suffering during the years when Victorian fashions were held in low regard and undergoing careful restoration now that the aesthetic pendulum has swung and moneyed condo buyers are demanding period authenticity. The blocks and blocks of original facades have survived on all but Newbury and Boylston streets, so the public face of the Back Bay remains much the same as it has always been. The greatest enemy of the brownstones is the weather; when water gets into cracks in the stones and freezes, it causes the spalling and defacement that is all too noticeable in buildings fronted with this porous material.

The Back Bay's residential streets are protected from incompatible development by strict zoning laws, yet the 20th century has hit hard along Newbury and Boylston streets. Newbury is Boston's Fifth Avenue, with Brooks Brothers, F. A. O. Schwarz, and dozens of specialty shops offering fashion clothing, china, antiques, paintings and prints, and expensive hardware. It is also a street of beauty salons and sidewalk cafés. Boylston Street, similarly busy but a little less posh, boasts elegant apparel shops. Here, too, is the severe pale gray stone mass of **The New England Building,** within which are interesting murals and historical dioramas. Across from the New England's old headquarters (on the right between Berkeley and Clarendon as you face downtown) is the company annex, a huge postmodern structure at 500 Boylston Street.

Time Out The **Harvard Book Store Cafe** (190 Newbury St.) serves meals
or coffee and pastry—outdoors in nice weather. Since it's a real
bookstore, you can browse to your heart's content.

Boylston Street, the southern commercial spine of the Back
Bay, separates the sedate old district (some say not effectively
enough) from the most ambitious developments this side of
downtown. One block south of Boylston, on the corner of St.
James Avenue and Clarendon Street, stands the tallest building in New England: the 62-story **John Hancock Tower,** built in
the early 1970s and notorious in its early years as the building
whose windows fell out. The stark and graceful reflective
rhomboid tower, designed by I. M. Pei, had a problem with the
loosening and dropping of its panes due to the seating of the
glass in the sills and the wind torquing of the entire building.
The problem was corrected: The building's 13 acres of glass
were replaced to more rigorous standards, and the central core
was stiffened. The 60th-floor observatory is one of the three
best vantage points in the city, and the "Boston 1775" exhibit
shows what the city looked like before the great hill-leveling
and landfill operations commenced. *Observatory ticket office,
Trinity Pl. and St. James Ave., tel. 617/247–1977. Admission:
$2.75 adults, $2 children 5–15 and senior citizens. Open Mon.–
Sat. 9 AM–10 PM, Sun. noon–10. Closed Thanksgiving and
Christmas.*

The Hancock Tower stands at the edge of **Copley Square,** a civic
space that is defined by three monumental older buildings. One
is the stately, bowfronted **Copley Plaza Hotel,** which faces the
square on St. James Avenue and serves as a dignified foil to two
of the most important works of architecture in Boston, if not in
the United States. At the left is **Trinity Church,** Henry Hobson
Richardson's masterwork of 1877. In this church Richardson
brought his Romanesque revival to maturity; all the elements
for which Richardson was famous—bold polychromatic masonry, careful arrangement of masses, sumptuously carved interi-
or woodwork—come together magnificently in Trinity.

A full appreciation of the architecture of Trinity Church requires an appreciation of the logistical problems of building it in
this location. Remember, the Back Bay is a reclaimed wetland
with a high water table; bedrock, or at least stable glacial till,
lies far beneath the wet clay near the surface. Like all older
Back Bay buildings, Trinity Church sits on submerged wooden
pilings. But Trinity's central tower weighs 9,500 tons, and most
of the 4,500 pilings beneath the church structure are under that
tremendous central mass. The pilings are checked regularly,
by means of a hatch in the subbasement, to make sure the water
level is high enough to keep them from dry-rotting.

Don't miss the interior of Trinity Church. Richardson engaged
some of the great artists of his day—John LaFarge, William
Morris, and Edward Burne-Jones among them—to execute the
paintings and stained glass that makes this a monument to
everything that was right about the Pre-Raphaelite spirit and
the nascent aesthetic of Morris's arts and crafts movement.
LaFarge's brilliant paintings, including the intricate ornamen-
tation of the vaulted ceilings, have been cleaned only once, in
the late 1950s, and have never been substantially retouched.
Today they look as though the paint were barely dry.

The Back Bay is a great neighborhood for ecclesiastical architecture. Many of the old downtown congregations relocated on the newly filled land and applied their considerable resources to building fine new churches. These experiments in the Gothic and Romanesque revivals have aged well and blend harmoniously with the residential blocks.

❽ The **Arlington Street Church** (1861) is opposite the Park Square corner of the Public Garden. *Enter at 351 Boylston St. Open weekdays 10–5. Sun. service at 11.*

❾ **Emmanuel Church of Boston** (1862), on Newbury Street between Arlington and Berkeley streets, offers free Bach cantatas each Sunday morning (*see* Off the Beaten Track). *Tel. 617/ 536–3355. Open Mon.–Thurs. 10–4 by appointment. Sun. service at 10.*

❿ The **Church of the Covenant** (1867), at the corner of Newbury and Berkeley, has windows by Louis Tiffany. *Open Tues.–Fri. 9–noon. Sun. service at 10.*

⓫ The **First Baptist Church** (1872), at the corner of Clarendon Street and Commonwealth Avenue, is an earlier Richardson creation. *Open weekdays 10–4. Sun. service at 11.*

⓬ The **"New" Old South Church** (1875), successor to the Old South Meeting House of Tea Party fame, is on Copley Square at the corner of Boylston and Dartmouth streets. *Open weekdays 8:30–6, Sat. 9–4. Sun. service at 11.*

Opposite the New Old South and forming, with Trinity Church, **⓭** a bulwark of Copley Square, stands the **Boston Public Library.** When this building was opened in 1895, it confirmed the status of McKim, Mead and White as apostles of the Renaissance Revival and reinforced a Boston commitment to the enlightenment of the citizenry that goes back 350 years to the founding of the Public Latin School.

Enter the older part of the library from the Dartmouth Street side, passing through the enormous bronze doors (they close at 5 PM) by Daniel Chester French, the sculptor of the Lincoln Memorial. Or walk around Boylston Street to Philip Johnson's addition of 1972, built in emulation of the mass and proportion of the original building, though not of its extraordinary detail. This airy, skylit structure houses the library's circulating collections. After passing the turnstiles, follow the hallway to your left to reach the old building, now the reference wing. At the desk near the door between the two buildings you can pick up information on the artwork you will presently see.

The corridor leading from the annex opens onto the courtyard around which the original library is built. A patio furnished with chairs rings a flower garden and fountain; from here the bustle of the city seems miles away. Beyond the courtyard is the main entrance hall of the building of 1895, with its vaulted ceiling, marble staircase, and immense stone lions commemorating Massachusetts regiments in the Civil War. The hall at the top of the stairs leads to Bates Hall, one of Boston's most sumptuous interior spaces. This is the main reference reading room, 218 feet long with a barrel-arch ceiling 50 feet high.

Charles McKim saw to it that the interior of his building was ornamented by several of the finest painters of the day. The murals at the head of the staircase, depicting the nine muses, are the work of the French artist Puvis de Chavannes; those in the book request processing room to the right are Edwin Abbey's interpretations of the Holy Grail legend. Upstairs, in the public areas leading to the fine arts, music, and rare books collections, are John Singer Sargent's mural series on the subject of Judaism and Christianity.

The old library building has been standing for almost 100 years now, and despite its structural soundness and architectural beauty it is showing the effects of age and deferred maintenance. Fortunately, a massive new renovation plan is in the works. Within the next few years McKim's palace of learning will sparkle, and we're promised that it will no longer be necessary to trek all the way to the new wing to visit the rest rooms. *Open Mon.–Thurs. 9–9, Fri. and Sat. 9–5.*

If the John Hancock Tower is a bold intruder on the southeast corner of Copley Square, the southwest corner has to deal with ⑭ an even more assertive modern presence. **Copley Place,** built between 1980 and 1984, comprises two major hotels (the highrise Westin, left, and the Marriott, right) and dozens of shops, restaurants, and offices attractively grouped on several levels around bright, open indoor spaces. The scale of the project bothers some people, as does the fact that so vast a complex of buildings effectively isolates the South End from the Back Bay. *Shopping galleries generally open Mon.–Sat. 10–7, Sun. noon–5.*

⑮ The same complaint might have been made of the **Prudential Center,** which dominates the acreage between Boylston Street and Huntington Avenue two blocks west of the library. But the "Pru" was built almost 25 years ago, when monumental urban redevelopment projects had yet to be called into question; moreover, no love has been lost on the railroad yards the Pru displaced, which also blocked off the South End.

Yet the Pru has its problems. The elevation of its shopping mall from the street, and the ring road that surrounds it, make it less inviting to Boylston Street foot traffic. As for the **Prudential Tower** itself, Bainbridge Bunting made an acute observation when he called it "an apparition so vast in size that it appears to float about the surrounding district without being related to it." Ongoing modifications to the Boylston Street frontage of the Prudential Center will eliminate the ring road and better unite the complex with the urban space around it, but the tower will have to float on, vast as ever. More significantly, the expansion of the adjacent Hynes Auditorium will enable Boston to attract larger conventions, helping to boost its economy.

Not long after Prudential staked its claim in the Boylston-Huntington blocks, it was followed by the headquarters complex of ⑯ the **Christian Science Church.** The mother church of the Christian Science faith was established here by Mary Baker Eddy in 1879. Mrs. Eddy's original granite First Church of Christ, Scientist (1894) has since been enveloped by the domed Renaissance basilica added to the site in 1906, and both church buildings are now surrounded by the offices of the *Christian Science Monitor* and by I. M. Pei's complex of church administration structures completed in 1973. The 670-foot reflecting pool, maintained so that water constantly spills over its inner banks, is a pleasant spot to stroll. *175 Huntington Ave., tel. 617/450–*

3790. Open Tues.–Sat. 9:30–4, Sun. 11:15–2. Free tours on the hour in the church and every ten min. in the maparium (closed Sun.). Services Sun. 10 and 7, Wed. 7:30 PM.

The best views of the pool and the precise, abstract geometry of the entire complex are from the **Prudential Center Skywalk,** a 50th-floor observatory that offers fine views of Boston, Cambridge, and the suburbs to the west and south. *Tel. 617/236–3318. Admission: $2.75 adults, $1.75 children 5–15, students, and senior citizens. Skywalk open Mon.–Sat. 10–9:45, Sun. noon–9:45.*

With commerce and religion accounted for by the Prudential Center and the Christian Science headquarters, the neighborhood still has room for a temple to music. **Symphony Hall,** since 1900 the home of the Boston Symphony Orchestra, stands at the corner of Huntington and Massachusetts avenues, another contribution of McKim, Mead and White to the Boston landscape. Acoustics, rather than exterior design, make this a special place for performers and concertgoers. Acoustical science was a brand new field of research when Professor Wallace Sabine planned Symphony Hall's interior, yet his efforts were so successful that not one of the 2,500 seats is a bad one from which to hear the Symphony, the Boston Pops, or the frequent guest performers. *301 Massachusetts Ave., tel. 617/266–1492. Tours by appointment with the volunteer office.*

Tour 7: The South End

Numbers in the margin correspond to points of interest on The Back Bay, the South End, and the Fens map.

Symphony Hall marks one corner of the Back Bay proper. From here you can walk down Huntington Avenue to the Museum of Fine Arts and the Fens, returning to the Charles River side of the Back Bay by way of Kenmore Square and Beacon Street or Commonwealth Avenue. Or, keeping Symphony Hall on your right, you can follow Massachusetts Avenue to Columbus Avenue, turn left on Columbus, and begin an exploration of the South End. As Kenmore Square and the Fens district properly form a separate area, we'll walk instead toward the South End, a neighborhood eclipsed by the Back Bay more than a century ago but now solidly back in fashion.

As we saw earlier, the filling of the shallows along Boston Neck began nearly a decade before the main expanse of the Back Bay was buried under Needham gravel. Streets were laid out and building commenced immediately; most of the characteristic bowfront houses of the South End (except those built around 1870 between Columbus and Huntington avenues) were constructed between 1851 and 1859. With the Back Bay still under water, the spanking new rows of brick town houses in the South End began to attract upwardly mobile residents of downtown areas that were becoming more commercial, along with a few adventurous residents of Beacon Hill.

The South End is an anomaly of planning and architecture in Boston. It neither grew up haphazardly along cowpaths and village lanes, like the old sections, nor followed a strict, uniform grid like that of the Back Bay. Bainbridge Bunting called its effect "cellular," and it is certainly more a sum of random blocks and park-centered squares than of bold boulevards and long, clear vistas. The observation is usually made that while the Back Bay is French-inspired, the South End is English. The houses, too, are different. In one sense they continue the pattern established on Beacon Hill (in a uniformly bowfronted style), yet they also aspire to a much more florid standard of decoration. Detailing can be a little extravagant in the Back Bay, but there it usually follows some established pattern; in the South End we find windows and entryway embellishments that seem to have been much more fancifully concocted, yet they are repeated so extensively that they must have been shipped by the carload as the new streets developed.

Even if the South End's beginnings were not glamorous, it is an intimate and nicely proportioned neighborhood that deserved a better reputation than it had at the outset. Consider the literary evidence: Howells's Silas Lapham abandoned the South End to build a house on the water side of Beacon as material proof of his arrival in Boston society. In *The Late George Apley*, John P. Marquand's Brahmin hero tells how his father decided, in the early 1870s, to move the family from his South End bowfront to the Back Bay—a consequence of his walking out on the front steps one morning and seeing a man in his shirtsleeves on the porch opposite. One gets the impression that this was a far worse offense than appearing stark naked on a condo balcony today. Regardless of whether Marquand exaggerated Victorian notions of propriety (if that were possible), the fact is that people like the Apleys did decamp for the Back Bay, the South End becoming what a 1913 guidebook called a "faded quarter."

A more practical reason for the relegation of the South End to the social backwaters was that it was literally out of the way. Railroad tracks separated it from the Back Bay, and disunity between state planners in the Back Bay and their city counterparts in the South End left the two districts with conflicting grid patterns that have never comfortably meshed. Ironically, the Prudential and Copley Place developments have only exacerbated the situation.

Whatever the reasons, the South End by 1900 was a neighborhood of lower middle class families and rooming houses. It had not lost its association with upward mobility, however, and blacks, many of them holders of the prestigious Pullman porter jobs on the railroads, began to buy the old bowfronts and establish themselves in the area.

There is still a substantial black presence in the South End, particularly along Columbus Avenue and Massachusetts Avenue, which marks the beginning of the predominantly black neighborhood of Roxbury. The early integration of the South End set the stage for its eventual transformation into a remarkable polyglot of ethnic groups. You are likely to hear Spanish spoken along Tremont Street, and there are Middle Eastern groceries along Shawmut Avenue. At the northeastern extreme of the South End, Harrison Avenue and Washington Street connect the area with Chinatown, and consequently there is a growing Asian influence. Still another minority presence among the neighborhood's ethnic groups, and sometimes belonging to one or more of them, is Boston's largest gay population.

Irish Roman Catholics are no longer well represented here,
which is ironic, since they left behind the enormous Gothic
⓲ Cathedral of the Holy Cross at the corner of Washington Street
and Monsignor Reynolds Way. Although it is now used princi-
pally for such special occasions as the recent investiture of the
new archbishop and the Pope's 1979 visit, it remains the premier church of the Archdiocese of Boston, New England's largest Catholic church. Incorporated in the front vestibule arch
are bricks from a convent burned during anti-Catholic rioting
in nearby Somerville in 1834. *Open weekdays 9–4; Sun. services at 10.*

About 25 years ago, middle-class professionals, mostly white,
began looking at the South End as though it had just been filled
in and built over, and they didn't care who might be walking
around in shirtsleeves. They bought old rooming houses—for
as little as $40,000 15 years ago—and reconverted them to sin-
gle-family occupancy, usually with one rental unit on the
ground floor, below the high-stepped main entrance. Certain
blocks thus became completely gentrified; elsewhere the
house-by-house socioeconomic mix matches the area's ethnic
diversity. That longtime low-income residents are also working
to improve housing conditions can be seen in the sweat-equity
residences of the Frankie O'Day Block on Columbus Avenue
near Clarendon Street. And now that the prices of buildings
have gone way up, condominium development has begun.

Although it would take years to understand the place fully, you
can capture something of the flavor of the South End within a
few hours' walk. To see elegant house restorations, go to
⓳ Rutland Square (between Columbus Avenue and Tremont
⓴ Street) or **Union Park** (between Tremont Street and Shawmut
Avenue). These oases seem miles distant from the city around
them. For upscale galleries and restaurants catering to young
urban professionals, head to **Tremont Street.**

Time Out   **Botolph's on Tremont** (569 Tremont) serves gourmet Italian
cuisine in light and airy yet striking surroundings. There's a
bistro atmosphere, with the high-gloss black and red chairs,
black tables, lush plants, and contemporary paintings hung
high on the white walls. Open daily for lunch and dinner, dishes
range from $6 to $12, and they can be eaten as leisurely or as
quickly as your schedule permits.

You can return to the Back Bay from the South End via Dartmouth, Clarendon, or Berkeley streets. If you have more time,
follow Columbus Avenue almost into Park Square, turn right
on Arlington Street, then left onto one of the narrow streets of
㉑ Bay Village. The neighborhood is a pocket of early 19th-centu-
ry brick row houses that appears to be almost a toylike replica
of Beacon Hill. Edgar Allan Poe once lived here. It seems im-
probable that so fine and serene a neighborhood can exist in the
shadow of busy Park Square—a 1950s developer might easily
have leveled these blocks in an afternoon—yet here it is, another Boston surprise.

Tour 8: The Fens

*Numbers in the margin correspond to points of interest on The
Back Bay, the South End, and the Fens map.*

Return now to the western end of the Back Bay and to Symphony Hall at the intersection of Massachusetts and Huntington avenues. With the front entrance of Symphony Hall on your right, walk down Huntington Avenue (note: this route is not recommended at night). On your left is the New England Conservatory of Music and, on Gainsborough Street, its recital Center, Jordan Hall. Just beyond, also on the left, is the sprawling campus of **Northeastern University** (360 Huntington Ave., tel. 617/373–2000).

Established in 1898, Northeastern has an enrollment of approximately 34,000, including part-time students. It is one of the world's largest cooperative education plan universities, where students in a wide variety of disciplines alternate periods of classroom study with terms of employment in related professions. Northeastern's engineering school is strong, and the university offers important programs in nursing, computers, business administration, pharmacy, criminal justice, marine sciences, and the human development professions. There is even a law school. Northeastern students are largely commuters who keep a low local profile.

The **Museum of Fine Arts,** often called the MFA, opened in this building in 1909 after 33 years at a site (now demolished) in Copley Square. The location of the MFA here, between Huntington Avenue and the Fenway, helped to cap the half-century development of the Back Bay and its linkage with the brackish marshes that marked the old Brookline shore. Here the developers grew expansive; here public institutions such as the Harvard Medical School, long confined to cramped downtown quarters, were relocated in an atmosphere of grandeur previously denied Boston by her geographical and philosophical parameters.

The central topographical feature of this part of Boston is the marshland known as the **Back Bay Fens.** After all the work that had gone into filling in the bay, it would have been little extra trouble to obliterate the Fens with gravel and march row houses straight through to Brookline. But the planners, realizing that enough pavement had been laid between here and the Public Garden, hired none other than Frederick Law Olmsted to make the Fens into a park. Olmsted applied his genius for heightening natural effects while subtly manicuring their surroundings; today's Fens park consists of still, irregular reedbound pools surrounded by broad meadows, trees, and flower gardens.

The Fens mark the beginning of Boston's Emerald Necklace, a loosely connected chain of parks designed by Olmsted that extends along the Fenway, Riverway, and Jamaicaway to Jamaica Pond, the Arnold Arboretum, and Franklin Park. Farther off, at the Boston-Milton line, the vast Blue Hills Reservation offers some of the Boston area's best hiking, scenic views, even a ski lift. (We'll return to the Arboretum and Franklin Park later.)

The Museum of Fine Arts was founded in 1870, and for six years exhibitions of its relatively small collections were held on the upper floors of the Boston Athenaeum. In 1876 it moved to its own quarters in a Gothic structure where the Copley Plaza Hotel now stands in Copley Square. Just as the MFA was beginning to outgrow this space, the Fenway area was becoming fashionable, and in 1909 the move was made to Guy Lowell's somewhat severe BeauxArts building, to which the West Wing designed by I. M. Pei was added in 1981.

When you walk past Cyrus Dallin's *Appeal to the Great Spirit* and into the main entrance, count on staying for a while if you have any hope of even beginning to see what is here.

The connoisseurs who began the MFA collections were as enamored as any cultured Victorians with the great works of European civilizations; nevertheless, their initial acquisition was a work by an American, Washington Allston's *Elijah in the Desert*, and succeeding years have seen its holdings of American art grow to a size that surpasses those of all but two or three U.S. museums. The MFA has more than 50 works by John Singleton Copley alone; it has major paintings by Winslow Homer, John Singer Sargent (whose murals grace the building's grand staircase), Fitz Hugh Lane, Edward Hopper, and a galaxy of American painters ranging from the earliest phase of native New England folk art and colonial portraiture to the Hudson River School, turn-of-the-century realism, and the New York abstract expressionists of the 1950s and 1960s.

American decorative arts are amply represented here, particularly those of New England in the years before the Civil War. Rooms of period furniture, much of it from the matchless Karolik collection, show the progression of taste from the earliest Pilgrim pieces through the 18th-century triumphs of the Queen Anne style and the Hepplewhite, Sheraton, and Empire trends.

The MFA's displays of silver hollow ware and flatware from the Colonial and Federalist eras include pieces by John Coney, a Boston silversmith who flourished in the first decades of the 1700s. Coney took as apprentice a young French Huguenot named Apollos Rivoire, who anglicized his name and taught his craft to his son, Paul Revere. The holdings of the MFA will convince anyone who thinks of Revere simply as a sounder of alarms that the patriot was one of the greatest artists ever to turn his hand to silver.

The museum also boasts the most extensive collection of Asiatic art gathered under one roof anywhere in the world, with Chinese porcelains of the T'ang Dynasty especially well represented. The Egyptian rooms display statuary, mummies, furniture reproductions, and exquisite gold jewelry. The gathering of treasures at the MFA proceeds chronologically through the Hellenistic and Roman eras; the early Roman imperial period is recalled by marble busts, jewelry, and glassware.

European art is represented by works of the 11th through the 20th centuries; among the highlights are Donatello's marble relief *The Madonna of the Clouds* (in the second-floor Renaissance sculpture gallery) and paintings by Fiorentino and Van der Weyden. The French Impressionists are perhaps better represented here than at any New World museum other than the Chicago Art Institute; the 43 Monets, many of them recently cleaned, again vibrate with their original colors, and there are canvases by Renoir, Pissarro, Manet, and the Americans Mary Cassatt and Childe Hassam.

The museum has strong collections of textiles and costumes and prints dating from the 15th century, including a great deal of work by Dürer and Goya. (Many of the prints are kept away from light and may be seen only by appointment.) The museum's collection of antique musical instruments, expanded in 1979 by the acquisition of an important group of early keyboard instruments, is among the best in the world. (The hours for this collection differ from the regular museum hours; call for the schedule.) Frequent concert programs at the MFA use instruments closely modeled after those in the collection.

The museum's new West Wing, a handsome, airy, well-lit space, is used primarily for traveling exhibitions and special temporary shows drawn from the museum's holdings. The West Wing also houses the museum shop, where reproductions of Revere silver and other decorative items may be purchased. The recently renovated and reopened Evans Wing houses American paintings on the first floor and European paintings on the second. The museum has a good restaurant and a less formal cafeteria serving light snacks; both are in the West Wing. *465 Huntington Ave., tel. 617/267-9300 (617/267-9377 for recorded schedule and events information). Admission: $7 adults, $6 senior citizens, $3.50 children 6–17, free under 6; free to all Wed. 4–10. Open Tues.–Sun. 10–4:45, Wed. until 9:45. West Wing open Thurs. and Fri. until 9:45, with admission reduced by $1. 1-hr tours available.*

On the Fenway Park side of the Museum of Fine Arts, the newly constructed **Tenshin Garden**, the "garden at the heart of heaven," allows visitors to experience landscape as a work of art. A stone wall separates the formal garden from the nearby park, and a curved and graceful gate made of Japanese cypress opens onto a path of Mexican river stones that leads to a bench surrounded by white gravel. A combination of Japanese and American trees and shrubs fuse the concept of the Japanese garden with features of the New England landscape. Stone lanterns are placed at intervals, and a bridge at the center links longevity on the one side with prosperity on the other.

Two blocks west of the MFA, on the Fenway, stands the ❷❹ **Isabella Stewart Gardner Museum,** an institution with as idiosyncratic a history as any in Boston. Isabella Stewart, a spirited young society woman, came from New York to Boston in 1860 to marry John Lowell Gardner. The Brahmin and his bride became enthusiastic art collectors, filling their Commonwealth Avenue mansion with treasures brought home from frequent trips to Europe. Gardner died in 1898, and "Mrs. Jack" set about building the Venetian palazzo of her dreams on the newly created Fenway. She called it Fenway Court and filled it with her acquisitions, opening it at a private party on New Year's Day 1903.

Mrs. Gardner lived on the top floor at Fenway Court until her death in 1924. Throughout the two decades of her residence she continued to build her collection under the tutelage of the young Bernard Berenson, who became one of the most respected art connoisseurs and critics of the 20th century. When she died, the terms of her will stipulated that everything in Fenway Court remain exactly as she left it, paintings, furniture, everything down to the last little object of *vertu* in a hall cabinet. (Out of a wish to protect the works from fading while respecting the stringent terms of the bequest, the museum's curators have had to install shades in some windows and on glass cabinet tops.)

Thus the Gardner Museum is a monument to one woman's taste—and a trove of spectacular paintings, sculpture, furniture, and textiles. There is much to see: *The Rape of Europa,* the most important of Titian's works in an American collection; paintings and drawings by Matisse, Whistler, Bellini, Van Dyck, Botticelli, and Rubens; John Singer Sargent's oil portrait of Mrs. Gardner herself, in the Gothic Room. On March 19, 1990, 13 works of art were stolen from Mrs. Jack's collection in one of the country's most talked-about art heists. Vermeer's "The Concert" was the most famous painting taken, and to date, none of the works have been recovered. Because the works of art were irreplaceable under the terms of Mrs. Jack's will, and because of the high cost of insurance, the Gardner Museum chose to go uncovered. Today, with over 2000 works in the collection and insurance rates dramatically lower because of the increase in recovery of stolen art, the Gardner has reevaluated its policy and carries insurance. At the center of the building is the magnificent courtyard, fully enclosed beneath a glass roof, in which there are always fresh flowers—poinsettias at Christmas, lilies at Easter, chrysanthemums in the fall—just as there were when Mrs. Jack lived here. The already renowned Gardner Museum Café has become even more renowned lately with the addition of a new chef who has designed a creative menu with an Italian flair. The intimate restaurant overlooks the courtyard and in the spring and summer tables and chairs spill into the courtyard for even more relaxed dining. *280 The Fenway, tel. 617/566-1401 (617/734-1359 for recorded concert information Sept.–May). Admission: $6 adults, $3 students and senior citizens, children under 12 free, students free on Wed. Open Tues.–Sun. 11–5. Café open Tues.–Fri. 11:30–3, weekends 11–4; tel. 617/566-1088. No reservations.*

Park Drive runs along the opposite side of the Fens from the MFA and the Gardner Museum. If you follow Jersey Street (now Yawkey Way) from Park Drive, you will reach the Boston **㉕** shrine known as **Fenway Park.** This is one of the smallest and oldest baseball parks in the major leagues. It was built in 1912, when the grass on the field was real—and it still is today. Fenway has been a bittersweet place for the Red Sox, with a World Series victory in 1918; pennants in 1946, 1967, 1975, and 1986; and a divisional championship in 1988. Babe Ruth pitched here when the place was new; Ted Williams and Carl Yastrzemski slugged out their entire careers here. Yawkey Way is named for the late Tom Yawkey, who bought the team in 1933 as a 30th-birthday present for himself and spent the next 43 years pursuing his elusive grail. For Red Sox baseball fans, there is a great deal of myth associated with their support of the "Olde Towne Team." Fans are said to believe a "curse" hangs over the club due to their ill-fated trade of a young Babe Ruth to archrivals, the New York Yankees.

㉖ **Kenmore Square,** home to fast-food parlors, new-wave rock clubs, an abundance of university students, and an enormous neon sign advertising Citgo gasoline, is two blocks north of Fenway Park. The neon sign is so thoroughly identified with the area that historic preservationists have fought successfully to save it—proof that Bostonians are an open-minded lot who do not require that their landmarks be identified with the American Revolution.

Kenmore Square is a block east of the Commonwealth Avenue campus of Boston University. You can board one of the Green Line trains at the Square for a surface-level ride through Brookline or out to Boston College, or you can head in the opposite direction for a quick (if it isn't rush hour) underground trip through the Back Bay to downtown.

The "Streetcar Suburbs"

Numbers in the margin correspond to points of interest on The "Streetcar Suburbs" map.

The 19th-century expansion of Boston was not confined to the Back Bay and the South End. Toward the close of the century, as the working population of the downtown district swelled and public transportation (first horsecars, then electric trolleys) linked outlying suburbs with the core city, development of the "streetcar suburbs" began. These areas answered the housing needs of both the rising native middle class and the second-generation immigrant families who were outgrowing the narrow streets of the North and West Ends.

South Boston was a landfill project of the mid-1880s, and as such it is not a true streetcar suburb; its expansion predates the era of commuting. Some of the brick bowfront residences along East Broadway in City Point date from the 1840s and 1850s. But the neighborhood came into its own with the influx of Irish Americans around 1900, and the Irish still hold sway here. "Southie" is a Celtic enclave, as the annual St. Patrick's Day parade attests.

South Boston projects farther into the harbor than any other part of Boston save Logan Airport, and the views of the Harbor Islands from along Day Boulevard or Castle Island are fine. At L Street and Day Boulevard is the L Street Beach, where an intrepid group called the L Street Brownies swims all year long and celebrates New Year's Day with a dip in the icy Atlantic. **Castle Island Park** is no longer on an island, but **Fort Independence,** when it was built here in 1801, was separated from the mainland by water. The circular walk from the fort around Pleasure Bay is delightful on a warm summer day. The statue near the fort is of Donald McKay, whose clipper ships once sped past this point on their way to California and the Orient.

Near the juncture of the South Boston peninsula with the Dorchester mainland, off Telegraph Street, stands the high ground of Thomas Park, where you will find the **Dorchester Heights Monument** and National Historic Site. In 1776 Dorchester Heights commanded a clear view of downtown Boston, where the British had been under siege since the preceding year. Here George Washington set up the cannons that Henry Knox, a Boston bookseller-turned-soldier and later secretary of war, had hauled through the wilderness following their capture at Fort Ticonderoga. The artillery did its job of intimidation, and the British troops left Boston, never to return. *Thomas Park (near G St.), tel. 617/242–5642. Admission free. Grounds open daily; monument closed for restoration through 1994.*

South of the Dorchester Heights Monument, on the other side of Columbus Park, a stark, white, prowlike building at the tip

The "Streetcar Suburbs"

of Columbia Point pays homage to one of Washington's successors as president, a native Irish Bostonian named John F. Kennedy. The **Kennedy Library** is the official repository of his presidential papers. There is also a replica of his desk, and there are screenings of a film on his life. The new Steven M. Smith Wing, dedicated in February 1991, provides more exhibition space for the trove of Kennedy memorabilia. The harborfront site alone is worth a visit, even without the library's interpretive displays. *Columbia Point, tel. 617/929–4523. Admission: $5 adults, $3 students and senior citizens, $1 children 6–16, under 6 free. Open daily 9–5. Free shuttle bus every 20 min. from the T.*

Inland from Columbia Point are Dorchester, Roxbury, and Jamaica Plain, all rural retreats barely more than a century ago, now thick with tenements and the distinctive three-family or six-family triple-decker apartment houses of Boston's streetcar suburbs. Both Dorchester and Roxbury are almost exclusively residential, tricky to navigate by car, and accessible by elevated train (the Red or Orange Lines) only if you know exactly where you are going. The two contiguous neighborhoods border on **Franklin Park,** an Olmsted creation of more than 500 acres noted for its zoo.

The 70-acre **Franklin Park Zoo,** near the Seaver Street–Blue Hill Avenue corner of the park, has been renovated during the past decade and has an especially fine walk-through aviary. The Waterfowl Pond and Children's Zoo are a three-acre facility designed especially for ages two to nine. The new Tropical Forest Pavilion has a gorilla exhibit and 32 other species of mammals, reptiles, birds, and fish. Franklin Park has a golf course and well deserves the daytime attention that offsets its nighttime reputation as a dangerous part of town. The park, 4 miles from downtown, is reached by the #16 bus from Forest Hills (Orange Line) or Andrew (Red Line). *Blue Hill Ave., tel. 617/442–2002 or 617/442–4896. Admission: $5 people over 11, $2.50 children 4–11; free Tues. 9–10. Park gates open Nov.– Feb., daily 9–3:30; Mar.–Oct., daily 9–5. Closed Thanksgiving, Christmas, and New Year's Day.*

During the growing season, no one with an eye for natural beauty and more than a couple of days to spend in Boston should pass up the **Arnold Arboretum.** This 265-acre living laboratory, administered by Harvard University, is open to pedestrians during daylight hours all year long. It can be reached by taking the #39 bus from Copley Square or by taking the Orange Line to Forest Hills and the #16 bus to the Arboretum. The arboretum was established in 1872 according to the terms of a bequest from James Arnold, a New Bedford merchant. The arboretum contains more than 7,000 kinds of trees and shrubs native to the North Temperate Zone, and something is always in season from early April through September. The rhododendrons, azaleas, lilacs, magnolias, and fruit trees are spectacular in bloom. The Bonsai collection has individual specimens that are Japanese imports more than 300 years old. *Rtes. 1 and 203, Arborway, tel. 617/524–1718. Admission free. Grounds open daily dawn–dusk; visitor's center open 10–4. Hour-long guided tours Sun. at 2, May 1–Nov.*

If you have the time and stamina for a jaunt of approximately 3½ miles, it is possible to walk almost the entire distance from the Arnold Arboretum to Kenmore Square within the Emerald

Necklace. Just follow the Jamaicaway north from its beginning at the circle that marks the northern tip of the arboretum. Within one long block you'll reach Jamaica Pond. Continue along the Jamaicaway through Olmsted Park, past Leverett Pond. From a point just north of here, either Brookline Avenue or the Riverway will take you to the Fens and Kenmore Square. Along the way you will pass many of the spacious freestanding mansions built along the park borders of Jamaica Plain around the turn of the century, when this was the choicest of the streetcar suburbs. Not the least of your pleasures as you pass along this stretch will be that you are walking, not driving. The Jamaicaway was one of Boston's first attempts at moving traffic at a pace faster than a walk, and it worked well only for horse-drawn carriages and the slower and narrower early automobiles. If you think that Boston still isn't very good at hurrying cars around, remember that unlike most American cities, it has been inhabited almost exclusively by pedestrians for two-thirds of its history.

From Kenmore Square it's just a few minutes on the MBTA Green Line to Coolidge Corner in Brookline, where a four-block walk north on Harvard Street takes you to the **John Fitzgerald Kennedy National Historic Site.** This was the home of the 35th president of the United States from his birth on May 29, 1917, until 1920, when the family moved to nearby Naples and Abbottsford streets. Mrs. Rose Kennedy provided the furnishings for the restored two-and-a-half-story, wood-frame structure. *83 Beals St., tel. 617/566-7937. Admission: $1 adults, children under 17 and senior citizens free. Open daily 10–4:30 except Thanksgiving, Christmas, and New Year's Day; tours every 45 min. 10:30–3:30.*

Boston for Free

Boston's Travel Planner is available free (tel. 617/536–4100).

Thursday's *Boston Globe Calendar*, the *Boston Phoenix*, and *Tab* are excellent sources for listings of free events taking place in the city that week. *Boston* magazine gives a monthly overview.

Church Concerts Saturday's *Boston Globe* lists that Sunday's music programs, most of which are free.

King's Chapel (School and Tremont Sts., tel. 617/227–2155) hosts a half-hour recital Tuesdays at 12:15.

Concerts **City Hall Plaza Concerts** (Government Center, tel. 617/635–4006 or 242–1775) take place every Wednesday in July and August, 7:30–10 PM, sponsored by the Boston Department of Parks and Recreation.

Federal Reserve Bank of Boston (600 Atlantic Ave., tel. 617/973–3453) hosts musical performances, including opera, plus dance and other cultural programs in its ground-floor auditorium Thursdays at 12:30 PM.

The **Hatch Memorial Shell** on the bank of the Charles River is the site of numerous concerts during the summer months, and the Boston Pops and the Boston Ballet are among the performers.

Festivals **Boston's North End** comes alive during the summer months with a series of Italian *feste* honoring various saints. The programs usually include a blessing, a procession, and lots of robust food and entertainment. For information, tel. 617/536–4100.

Lectures In a city with so many schools and colleges, the most difficult task can be deciding which lecture to attend. Thursday's *Boston Globe* Calendar has a full listing.

The **Arco Forum of Public Affairs** (Kennedy School of Government, 79 JFK St., tel. 617/495–1380) sponsors an impressive list of speakers, including heads of state. Forums, many of which are broadcast on National Public Radio and C-Span, are held several nights a week during the academic year.

The **Ford Hall Forum** (271 Huntington Ave., Suite 240, tel. 617/373–5800) offers a lecture series every spring and fall; the speakers may be political or literary figures. Thursday lectures at 7 in the Old South Meeting House, Sunday lectures at 7 in Blackman Auditorium of Northeastern University (370 Huntington Ave.). Lectures are not held every week; call for the schedule.

Museums While most museums charge admission, several museums schedule a period when admission is free to all: **the Museum of Fine Arts,** Wednesday 4–10; the **Museum of Science,** Wednesday 1–5 November–April; the **Aquarium,** Thursday after 3 October–March; **the Children's Museum,** reduced to $1 Friday 5–9.

Television Show Tickets Shows that are produced locally for television networks often welcome live audiences. Call the stations for specific ticket information.

WBZ (Channel 4, NBC), 1170 Soldiers Field Road, Allston, tel. 617/787–7000.
WCVB (Channel 5, ABC), 5 TV Place, Needham, tel. 617/449–0400.
WGBH (Channel 2) and **WGBX** (Channel 44, PBS) 125 Western Avenue, Allston, tel. 617/492–2777.
WHDH (Channel 7, CBS), 7 Bulfinch Place, tel. 617/725–0777.
WSBK (Channel 38), 83 Leo M. Birmingham Parkway, Brighton, tel. 617/783–3838.

What to See and Do with Children

Kids who are interested in history will find much to enjoy in Boston. The city's historical legacy is vivid and accessible: Youngsters can see just where Paul Revere's lanterns were hung, and they can walk the decks of an undefeated man-of-war. Along with the history, Boston has museums, theaters, and parks to play in. Young readers visiting the Public Garden may recognize such sights as the Pepperpot Bridge from Robert McCloskey's *Make Way for Ducklings*.

Boston Children's Museum has hands-on educational and cultural exhibits for kids of all ages. (Tour 5: Downtown Boston) *T stop, South Station.*
Boston Children's Theatre (93 Massachusetts Ave., tel. 617/424–6634). Students of the Boston Children's Theatre School perform four plays between November and April. Stagemobile, a touring company, performs locally during the summer months.
The ***Boston Parents Paper*** (tel. 617/522–1515), published

monthly and distributed free throughout the city, is an excellent resource for finding out what's happening.

Historic Neighborhoods Foundation (2 Boylston St., tel. 617/426–1885) offers tours geared to children, including "In Search of Grandmother's House," "Kids' Views of the North End," and "Kids' Views of the Waterfront."

Make Way for Ducklings Tours, Boston By Little Feet, and **Historic Neighborhoods Foundation Tours** are all geared toward little ones. (*see* Walking Tours).

Museum of Fine Arts prepares a free guide to help families get the most out of the museum; ask for it as you enter. The **Children's Room** offers free drop-in art classes Wednesday through Friday 3:30–4:45 (except during school vacations) for children 6–12; classes visit different exhibits and then engage in a project. (Tour 8: The Fens) *T stop, Museum.*

The **Museum of Science** has countless exhibits, including an 18-foot dinosaur; a wave machine, and thunder and lightning shows. (Tour 2: The Old West End) *T stop, Lechmere.*

New England Aquarium (Tour 5: Downtown Boston) *T stop, Aquarium.*

Puppet Showplace Theater (*see* Chapter 9, The Arts and Nightlife).

Swan Boats (Public Garden) have carried enchanted visitors of all ages around the pond since 1877. (Tour 6: The Back Bay) *T stop, Arlington.*

USS *Constitution* (Tour 4: Charlestown) *T stop, Haymarket; then MBTA bus 92 or 93 to Charlestown City Sq. or Boston Harbor Cruise water shuttle from Long Wharf.*

Off the Beaten Track

The Catalonian Chapel at the Museum of Fine Arts is easy to overlook and well worth seeking out. The apse was moved from the Church of Santa Maria in Mur, Catalonia, complete with the only series of 12th-century Romanesque frescoes to be found outside Spain. It also houses an excellent collection of 15th-century Spanish altarpieces. *465 Huntington Ave., tel. 617/267–9300.*

Emmanuel Church of Boston, a Back Bay brownstone Gothic Episcopal church, is a popular spot for classical music lovers on Sunday morning at 10, mid-September through mid-May. The service includes a Bach cantata performed by a professional 16-piece orchestra and 16-member chorus. *15 Newbury St., tel. 617/536–3355. Admission free.*

The Maparium is a 30-foot stained-glass globe that gives you the experience of walking through the world on a glass bridge. *Christian Science Church, Massachusetts and Huntington Aves., tel. 617/450–3790. Admission free. Open Tues.–Sat. 9:30–4.*

Sightseeing Checklists

Historical Buildings and Sites

This list of Boston's principal buildings and sites includes both attractions that were covered in the preceding tours and additional attractions that are described here for the first time.

Oliver Ames Mansion, now a private residence, is the Back Bay's largest mansion. (Tour 6: The Back Bay) *T stop, Hynes Center.*

Appleton Mansions provide a rare glimpse of the famous purple-glass window panes of Beacon Hill. (Tour 1: Boston Common and Beacon Hill) *T stop, Park St.*

Baylies Mansion, one of the grander Back Bay mansions, now houses the Boston Center for Adult Education. (Tour 6: The Back Bay) *T stop, Park St.*

Blackstone Block, at the Haymarket, is Boston's oldest commercial block, named for the city's first settler, William Blaxton. Still home to the city's butchers after more than 100 years, it's now also the site for a thriving produce market every Friday and Saturday morning. *T stop, Haymarket.*

Boston Athenaeum, one of the oldest libraries in the country, was founded in 1807 and moved to its present imposing quarters, a national historic landmark building, in 1849. Its collection of more than 600,000 volumes is for the use of members (who pay an annual fee). Accredited researchers in need of materials not available elsewhere may be granted admission. The holdings are impressive: most of George Washington's private library; the King's Chapel Library sent from England in 1698; manuscripts and books associated with the Adams family; a collection of pre-1950 American art and photography. Occasional exhibitions of more recent works are open to the public. Free guided tours Tues. and Thurs. by appointment. *10½ Beacon St., tel. 617/227–0270. Admission free. Open weekdays 9–5:30, Sat. 9–4. Closed Sat. June–Sept., closed holidays and Bunker Hill Day (June 17). T stop, Park St.*

Boston Common is the oldest public park in America. (Tour 1: Boston Common and Beacon Hill) *T stop, Park St.*

Boston Massacre Site, in front of the Old State House, marks the spot where British soldiers fired in panic upon a mob of Bostonians. (Tour 5: Downtown Boston) *T stop, State.*

Boston Public Library on Copley Square was designed by McKim, Mead and White. (Tour 6: The Back Bay) *T stop, Copley.*

Bulfinch Pavilion (Ether Dome), part of Mass General Hospital, has the distinction of being the first place where ether was used on a patient. (Tour 2: The Old West End) *T stop, Charles/ MGH.*

Bunker Hill Monument provides a wonderful view of Boston and marks the site where a citizens militia was commanded not to fire "till you see the whites of their eyes." (Tour 4: Charlestown) *T stop, Community College.*

Burrage Mansion is an extravagant French château–style building with gargoyles and turrets. (Tour 6: The Back Bay) *T stop, Hynes Center.*

Capen House (Union Oyster House), the city's oldest restaurant, dates back to 1826. (Tour 3: Government Center and the North End) *T stop, Government Center.*

Charlestown Navy Yard, a National Historic Site, is home to the USS *Constitution.* (Tour 4: Charlestown) *T stop, Haymarket; then MBTA bus 92 or 93 to Charlestown City Sq. or Boston Harbor Cruise water shuttle from Long Wharf.*

Clough House, built in 1712, gives you an idea of what the exterior of a North End building looked like in Colonial times. (Tour 3: Government Center and the North End) *T stop, Haymarket or North Station.*

Club of Odd Volumes, the second oldest book collectors' club in America, has its headquarters in an early 19th-century residence. *77 Mt. Vernon St., tel. 617/227–7003. Open to the public only for special exhibits. T stop, Park St.*

Commercial Wharf's condominiums and offices occupy the granite building that was part of Granite Wharf until 1868, when Atlantic Avenue was built. *East of Atlantic Ave. T stop, Aquarium.*

Copley Plaza Hotel is a stately, bow-fronted classic. (Tour 6: The Back Bay) *T stop, Copley.*

Custom House is composed of an 1847 Greek Revival temple topped by a tower, which was added in 1915. (Tour 5: Downtown Boston) *T stop, Haymarket.*

Custom House Block, once a storehouse for goods awaiting duty imposition, is now shops and offices. *Long Wharf. T stop, Aquarium.*

Cyclorama (Boston Center for the Arts), the second largest glass dome in the country (after the U.S. Capitol), was built by William Blackall in 1884 to house the painting *Battle of Gettysburg* by Paul Philippoteaux. Alfred Champion later used it as a garage and invented the first spark plug. Now it's used for exhibitions and performances. *539 Tremont St., tel. 617/426–5000. Admission by contribution. Open daily 9–5. T stop, Copley.*

Dorchester Heights Monument is where George Washington set up the cannons that drove the British troops from Boston for good. (The "Streetcar Suburbs") *T stop, Broadway; then City Point bus to G St.*

Emerson College (1929), designed by the architects who built the Ritz-Carlton Hotel, is one of the few Art Deco–style buildings in the Back Bay. *7 Arlington St. at Marlborough St. T stop, Arlington.*

Exeter Theater, Boston's oldest (1914) continually operating movie theater, is now Waterstone's Booksellers. *26 Exeter St. at Newbury St. T stop, Copley.*

Faneuil Hall has served as a place for town meetings since the original structure was built in 1742. (Tour 5: Downtown Boston) *T stop, Haymarket.*

First Public School Site. A plaque marks the site where Benjamin Franklin, John Hancock, and Samuel Adams attended the country's first school. *School St. at Old City Hall. T stop, Park St.*

Fisher Junior College occupies an elegant Victorian mansion (1903) that epitomizes old-world elegance. The marble hanging stairway with its 24K-gold plate balustrade, the Circassian walnut-paneled dining room, and the library with hand-carved rosewood doors and sterling silver knobs are among the genteel touches. *118 Beacon St., tel. 617/262–3240. Admission free. Open weekdays 8:30–4:30, and (Sept.–May) Sat. 9–3. T stop, Arlington.*

Flour and Grain Exchange Building was built in 1889–1892 for the Chamber of Commerce. *177 Milk St. T stop, State.*

44 Hull Street, Boston's narrowest house at 9 feet 6 inches wide, is 200 years old. *T stop, Haymarket or North Station.*

Benjamin Franklin's Birthplace. The Franklins' 15th child (of 17) was born here in 1706; a bronze bust commemorates the spot. *Boston Post Building, 17 Milk St. T stop, State.*

French Library celebrates French culture and language through its films, lectures, and books. (Tour 6: The Back Bay) *T stop, Arlington.*

Gibson House, built in 1859, was one of the Back Bay's first residences. (Tour 6: The Back Bay) *T stop, Arlington.*

Goethe Institute promotes German language and culture through films and other events. (Tour 6: The Back Bay) *T stop, Arlington or Copley.*

Chester Harding House, built in 1808, is a national historic landmark, the residence and studio of Chester Harding, a well-known painter. The Boston Bar Association bought it in the early 1900s and restored it in 1962–1963. *16 Beacon St. Closed to the public. T stop, Park St.*

Horticultural Hall, the headquarters for the Massachusetts Horticultural Society, was built in 1900, and houses the country's oldest and most diverse horticultural library. *300 Massachusetts Ave., tel. 617/536–9280. Admission free. Open weekdays 8:30–4:30, Sat. 10–2. T stop, Symphony.*

Rose Fitzgerald Kennedy Birthplace. Birthplace of John, Robert, and Teddy's mother. The Historic Neighborhoods Foundation's "Kennedy Roots Tour" includes this landmark. *4 Garden Court. Not open to the public. T stop, Haymarket.*

John Fitzgerald Kennedy National Historic Site was JFK's birthplace and home until he was three years old. (The "Streetcar Suburbs") *T stop, Coolidge Corner.*

Lewis Wharf, now a complex housing condos and offices, served originally as home port to the clipper ships of the 1850s. Its buildings were warehouses. *East of Atlantic Ave. near Commercial St. T stop, Aquarium.*

Long Wharf, Boston's oldest existing wharf, is now home port for tour boats. *East of Atlantic Ave. T stop, Aquarium.*

Louisburg Square is a lovely little green surrounded by the 1840s townhouses and cobblestone streets of Beacon Hill. (Tour 1: Boston Common and Beacon Hill) *T stop, Park St.*

Massachusetts State House is a Charles Bulfinch neoclassical masterpiece. (Tour 1: Boston Common and Beacon Hill) *T stop, Park St.*

Mercantile Wharf Building, constructed of Italian granite in 1857 to house the harbor's sailmakers and riggers, was renovated in 1976 for apartments and shops. *Atlantic Ave. between Cross and Richmond streets. T stop, Haymarket.*

George Middleton House, believed to be the oldest house on Beacon Hill, was built in 1797. The original owner was George Middleton, a black jockey and horsebreaker. *5–7 Pinckney St. Not open to the public. T stop, Park St.*

Mt. Vernon Street, in Beacon Hill, is one of the loveliest streets in America. (Tour 1: Boston Common and Beacon Hill) *T stop, Park St.*

New England Conservatory, founded in 1867, is the oldest conservatory in the country. *290 Huntington Ave. T stop, Symphony.*

New England Historic Genealogical Society. New Englanders trace their family trees with the help of the society's collections, which date to the 17th century. The society dates from 1845. *99–101 Newbury St., tel. 617/536–5740. Fee to use the facility. Open Tues.–Sat. 9–5. Wed. and Thurs. until 9. On the first Wed. of each month at 7PM, an introductory lecture is given on how to perform your own genealogical study. T stop, Copley.*

The New England. The first chartered mutual life insurance company in the country houses dioramas of the development of the Back Bay (inside the Newbury Street entrance) and eight historic murals by Charles Hoffbauer (in the front lobby). *501*

Boylston St. Admission free. Open daily 9–9. T stop, Arlington or Copley.

New England Telephone Building contains the reassembled workshop (the actual building housing the workshop at the time was torn down in the 1920s) from which Alexander Graham Bell transmitted his voice across a wire for the first time. (Tour 5: Downtown Boston) *T stop, Government Center.*

Nichols House gives an excellent impression of how a Brahmin lady of means and modesty lived. (Tour 1: Boston Common and Beacon Hill) *T stop, Park St.*

99 Salem Street is the site of the country's oldest bakery; bread was baked here for the Continental Army. Now part of the open market. *T stop, Haymarket.*

Northeastern University, with 34,000 students, is one of the world's largest universities offering a cooperative education plan, allowing students to alternate between classroom learning and on-the-job training. (Tour 8: The Fens) *T stop, Northeastern.*

Old Boston Art Club, a Queen Anne Revival of 1881, was home to the Boston Art Club until 1948; it is now Copley High School. *152 Newbury St. Closed to the public. T stop, Copley.*

Old City Hall, a Second Empire building, is marked by a bronze statue of Ben Franklin—the city's first portrait sculpture. (Tour 5: Downtown Boston) *T stop, Park St.*

Old Corner Bookstore (Globe Corner Bookstore) served the leading literary luminaries for much of the 19th century. (Tour 5: Downtown Boston) *T stop, State.*

Harrison Gray Otis Houses (first, second, and third) (Tour 1: Boston Common and Beacon Hill) *T stop, Charles/MGH or Bowdoin.*

Park Street Station is the original eastern terminus of the first subway in America. (Tour 1: Boston Common and Beacon Hill) *T stop, Park St.*

Phillips School, built in 1824, became one of the city's first integrated schools in 1854. *Anderson and Pinckney Sts. T stop, Park St.*

Piano Craft Guild. When it was new in 1853, the Chickering piano factory was the second largest in the world. In 1972 it was renovated for artists' space. *791 Tremont St. T stop, Ruggles.*

Pierce-Hichborn House is one of the city's oldest brick buildings. (Tour 3: Government Center and the North End) *T stop, Haymarket.*

Quincy Market consists of three buildings filled with specialty shops, food stalls, and restaurants. (Tour 5: Downtown Boston) *T stop, Haymarket.*

Paul Revere House, owned by Paul Revere from 1770 until 1800, is the oldest house in Boston. (Tour 3: Government Center and the North End) *T stop, Haymarket.*

Rollins Place, built in 1843 to house artisans and tradesmen who worked on Beacon Hill, has a *trompe l'oeil* Greek Revival villa at one end. *Revere St. T stop, Haymarket.*

Sears Crescent is a curving commercial block in Government Center. (Tour 3: Government Center and the North End) *T stop, Government Center.*

17 Chestnut Street, a Bulfinch building of 1808, was the home of Julia Ward Howe. *Not open to the public. T stop, Park St.*

70–75 Beacon Street are Greek Revival residences built by Asher Benjamin in 1828. *Not open to the public. T stop, Park St.*

Somerset Club is housed in one of Beacon Hill's only Greek Revival buildings. (Tour 1: Boston Common and Beacon Hill) *T stop, Park St.*

South Station has a grand 1900s facade. (Tour 5: Downtown Boston) *T stop, South Station.*

Symphony Hall, home to the Boston Symphony Orchestra since 1900, is another McKim, Mead and White contribution. (Tour 6: The Back Bay) *T stop, Symphony.*

34 Beacon Street, the former home of *the* Cabots of Boston, is now headquarters for Little, Brown and the New York Graphic Society. *T stop, Park St.*

29A Chestnut Street is the oldest home on the south slope of Beacon Hill. (Tour 1: Boston Common and Beacon Hill) *T stop, Park St.*

Union Wharf was constructed in 1846 and renovated in 1979 for condominiums. *North of Atlantic Ave. and Commercial St. T stop, Haymarket.*

USS *Constitution,* nicknamed Old Ironsides, is the oldest commissioned ship in the U.S. Navy. (Tour 4: Charlestown) *T stop, Haymarket; then MBTA bus 92 or 93 to Charlestown City Sq. or Boston Harbor Cruise water shuttle from Long Wharf.*

Museums

This list of Boston's museums includes both museums that were covered in the preceding tours and museums that are described here for the first time.

Boston Children's Museum (Tour 5: Downtown Boston) *T stop, South Station.*

Boston Tea Party Ship (*Beaver II)* (Tour 5: Downtown Boston) *T stop, South Station.*

Charlestown Navy Yard (Tour 4: Charlestown) *T stop, Haymarket; then MBTA bus 92 or 93 to Charlestown City Sq. or Boston Harbor Cruise water shuttle from Long Wharf.*

Computer Museum (Tour 5: Downtown Boston) *T stop, South Station.*

Isabella Stewart Gardner Museum (Tour 8: The Fens) *T stop, Brigham Circle.*

Institute of Contemporary Art. Housed in a firehouse of 1884, renovated in the early 1970s by Graham Gund, the institute has no permanent collection but shows temporary exhibits by the famous and not-so-famous. *955 Boylston St., tel. 617/266–5152. Admission: $5 adults, $2 children under 16 and senior citizens, $3 students with ID; free Wed. and Thurs. 5–9. Open Wed. 5–9, Thurs. noon–9, Fri.–Sun. noon–5. T stop, Hynes Center.*

Massachusetts Historical Society has paintings and a library of books and manuscripts from 17th-century New England. *1154 Boylston St., tel. 617/536–1608. Admission free. Open weekdays 9–4:45. T stop, Hynes Center.*

Museum of Afro-American History (Tour 1: Boston Common and Beacon Hill) *T stop, Park St.*

Museum at the John F. Kennedy Library (The "Streetcar Suburbs") *T stop, JFK/UMASS.*

Museum of Fine Arts (Tour 8: The Fens) *T stop, Museum.*

Museum of Science (Tour 2: The Old West End) *T stop, Science Park.*

Museum of the Ancient and Honorable Artillery Company of Massachusetts (Tour 5: Downtown Boston) *T stop, Haymarket.*

Museum of the National Center of Afro-American Artists represents Black artists in all media with regularly changing exhibits. *300 Walnut Ave., Roxbury, tel. 617/442–8614. Admission: $1.25 adults, 50¢ children under 16 and senior citizens. Open Sept.–May, Tues.–Sun. 1–5; June–Aug., Wed.–Sun. 1–6. T stop, Ruggles, then take bus #64, get off at Combden St., and walk 1 block.*

Old State House (Tour 5: Downtown Boston) *T stop, State.*

Parks and Gardens

Arnold Arboretum contains more than 7,000 kinds of trees and shrubs. (The "Streetcar Suburbs") *T stop, Forest Hills or Arborway.*

The Back Bay Fens, designed by Frederick Law Olmsted, consists of irregular reed-bound pools surrounded by broad meadows, trees, and flower gardens. (Tour 8: The Fens) *T stop, Museum.*

Belle Isle Park is the last local vestige of the living salt-marsh environment that was once predominant in the lands around Boston Harbor. Parts of the developed park are high and dry; for a more interesting experience, bring watertight boots and explore the marsh itself. It's a prime area for birding. *T stop, Suffolk Downs.*

Boston Public Garden (Tour 6: The Back Bay) *T stop, Boylston.*

Boston Harbor Islands State Park (Tour 5: Downtown Boston).

Castle Island Park is home to Fort Independence. (The "Streetcar Suburbs") *T stop, Broadway; then the City Point bus.*

Christopher Columbus Waterfront Park (Tour 3: Government Center and the North End) *T stop, Haymarket.*

Esplanade, on the Charles River, is a great place for a stroll or jog, bicycle ride or picnic. (Tour 1: Boston Common and Beacon Hill) *T stop, Charles/MGH.*

Franklin Park, encompassing more than 500 acres of Olmsted-designed space, has a very good zoo and the oldest public golf course in the country. (The "Streetcar Suburbs") *T stop, Ruggles; then the Franklin Park bus.*

Olmsted Park. A link in Frederick Law Olmsted's Emerald Necklace, the park stretches alongside the Riverway and Jamaicaway to Jamaica Pond. There is sailing on the pond.

Stony Brook Reservation. More than 464 acres near Boston's southern boundaries, including a municipal golf course. Good for walking and cross-country skiing. *Best reached by car via Route 1 (Jamaicaway/VFW Parkway) and West Roxbury Parkway.*

Tenshin Garden is a formal Japanese garden at the Museum of Fine Arts. (Tour 8: The Fens) *T stop, Museum.*

Waterfront Park. A wonderful spot to look out at the harbor and enjoy a picnic of Quincy Market delicacies. *Atlantic Ave. between Mercantile St. and Long Wharf. T stop, Aquarium.*

Churches

African Meeting House is the oldest African-American church building still standing in America. (Tour 1: Boston Common and Beacon Hill) *T stop, Park St.*

Arlington Street Church (Tour 6: The Back Bay) *T stop, Arlington.*

Cathedral of the Holy Cross is the premier church of the Archdiocese of Boston. (Tour 7: The South End) *T stop, Chinatown; then Bus 49 to Cathedral.*

Charles Street Meetinghouse, built in 1804 as a Baptist church, was bought in 1876 by the African Methodist Episcopal Church, which remained until 1939. It was used for community activities until recently, when it was converted into commercial stores. *Mt. Vernon and Charles Sts. Not open to the public. T stop, Charles/MGH.*

Christian Science Church is known for its Maparium, a 30-foot stained-glass globe that visitors can walk through. (Tour 6: The Back Bay) *T stop, Hynes Center.*

Church of the Covenant has Tiffany windows. (Tour 6: The Back Bay) *T stop, Arlington.*

Emmanuel Church of Boston (Tour 6: The Back Bay) *T stop, Arlington.*

First Baptist Church was designed by Henry Hobson Richardson. (Tour 6: The Back Bay) *T stop, Copley.*

First and Second Church of Boston. Built in 1867 as a new home for the city's oldest Puritan congregation, the church was destroyed by fire in 1968. The spire and frame of a rose window, all that were left standing, were incorporated into the design of the new church. *64-66 Marlborough St. at Berkeley St. Open weekdays 9–5, Sun. service at 11. T stop, Copley or Arlington.*

King's Chapel holds Paul Revere's largest bell. (Tour 5: Downtown Boston) *T stop, Park St. or Government Center.*

"New" Old South Church (Tour 6: The Back Bay) *T stop, Copley.*

Old North Church (Christ Church) is best known for the tower from which the signal lanterns of Paul Revere flashed warning to Charlestown of British troop movements. (Tour 3: Government Center and the North End) *T stop, Haymarket or North Station.*

Old South Meeting House is Boston's second oldest church. (Tour 5: Downtown Boston) *T stop, State.*

Park Street Church is where the hymn "America" was first sung. (Tour 1: Boston Common and Beacon Hill) *T stop, Park St.*

St. Paul's Cathedral is a massive Greek Revival structure. (Tour 1: Boston Common and Beacon Hill) *T stop, Park St.*

St. Stephen's is the only Bulfinch church still standing in Boston. (Tour 3: Government Center and the North End) *T stop, Haymarket or North Station.*

Trinity Church is Henry Hobson Richardson's masterpiece of Romanesque revival architecture. (Tour 6: The Back Bay) *T stop, Copley.*

Union United Methodist Church. A country-style parish church designed by A. R. Estey, who also planned the Emmanuel Church. *485 Columbus Ave. Open weekdays 9:30–4:30, Sun. service at 10:45. T stop, Ruggles.*

Cemeteries

Central Burying Ground contains the remains of Gilbert Stuart and many British casualties of the Battle of Bunker Hill. (Tour 1: Boston Common and Beacon Hill) *T stop, Boylston.*

Copp's Hill Burying Ground incorporates four cemeteries established between 1660 and 1819. (Tour 3: Government Center and the North End) *T stop, North Station.*

King's Chapel Burying Ground is the oldest graveyard in Boston. (Tour 5: Downtown Boston) *T stop, Park St. or Government Center.*

Old Granary Burial Ground is the final resting place for such prominent individuals as Samuel Adams, John Hancock, Peter

Faneuil, and Paul Revere. (Tour 1: Boston Common and Beacon Hill) *T stop, Park St.*

Phipps Street Burying Ground was laid out in 1631 and has tombstones dating from 1642. The obelisk memorializes John Harvard, the location of whose remains is uncertain. *Phipps St., Charlestown. T stop, Community College.*

Other Places of Interest

Boston Architectural Center, a school of architecture, was built in 1967 by Ashley, Myer & Associates, whose design won the school's competition. Note the Richard Haas trompe l'oeil. Exhibits and drawings. *320 Newbury St., tel. 617/536–3170. Admission free. Open Mon.–Thurs. 9–8, Fri. 9–5, weekends noon–5. T stop, Hynes Center.*

Chinatown (Tour 5: Downtown Boston) *T stop, Chinatown.*

City Hall (Tour 3: Government Center and the North End) *T stop, Government Center.*

Copley Place comprises two hotels and dozens of upscale shops and restaurants. (Tour 6: The Back Bay) *T stop, Copley.*

Fenway Park is one of the smallest and oldest major league baseball parks. (Tour 8: The Fens) *T stop, Kenmore.*

John Hancock Tower, New England's tallest building, has an observation deck that offers one of the best vantage points in the city. (Tour 6: The Back Bay) *T stop, Boylston.*

John F. Kennedy Federal Office Building was designed by the Bauhaus founder Walter Gropius. (Tour 3: Government Center and the North End) *T stop, Government Center.*

Swan Boats (Public Garden) (Tour 6: The Back Bay) *T stop, Arlington.*

4 Exploring Cambridge

Cambridge is an independent city faced with the difficult task of living in the shadow of its larger neighbor, Boston, while being overshadowed as well by the giant educational institutions within its own borders. It provides the brains and the technical know-how that, combined with Boston's financial prowess, has created the vibrant high-tech economy of which Massachusetts is so proud. Cambridge also continues to function as the conscience of the greater Boston area; when a new social experiment or progressive legislation appears on the local scene, chances are it came out of the crucible of Cambridge political activism.

Cambridge dates from 1630, when the Puritan leader John Winthrop chose this meadowland as the site of a carefully planned, stockaded village he named New Towne. Eight years later the town was renamed Cambridge in honor of the university at which most Puritan leaders had been educated.

In 1636 the Great and General Court of the Massachusetts Bay Colony established the country's first college here. Named in 1638 for John Harvard, a young Charlestown clergyman who died that year, leaving the college his entire library and half his estate, Harvard remained the only college in the New World until 1693, by which time it was firmly established as a respected center of learning.

By the middle of the 17th century, Cambridge was the New World's publishing center, and through 350 years it has remained a place to which people come primarily to learn and to teach, to discuss, to lecture, to write, and to think. At the same time, Cambridge is a city of 95,000 people in which half the population has nothing whatsoever to do with its universities.

The old Cambridge that took shape around the 17th-century college was a considerable journey from the several villages that grew up within its 22-mile expanse. In time the other communities broke away to form Lexington, Watertown, Arlington, and other cities, and in 1846 the college town was itself incorporated as a city. It then became affiliated politically with the industrial communities of Cambridgeport and East Cambridge, which lie below it on the west bank of the Charles River. Settled primarily in the 19th century, they produced furniture, brushes, caskets, bricks, glass, and reversible collars. In the 1840s the population of the two communities, made up of Irish, Polish, Italians, and French Canadians, was eight times that of the Harvard end of town.

The academic and industrial sections were effectively joined when the Massachusetts Institute of Technology moved to Cambridge in 1916. The striking modern buildings that have since been designed by graduates of the MIT and Harvard schools of architecture are in themselves sufficient reason for a visit to Cambridge today.

Numbers in the margin correspond to points of interest on the Cambridge map.

❶ Cambridge, just minutes from Boston by MBTA, is easily reached on the Red Line train to **Harvard Square.** The area is notorious for limited parking, so do consider taking the "T." If you insist on driving into Cambridge, you may want to avoid the local circling ritual by pulling into a garage. The $3-per-hour–$12-per-day parking fees may be well worth your sanity.

Cambridge

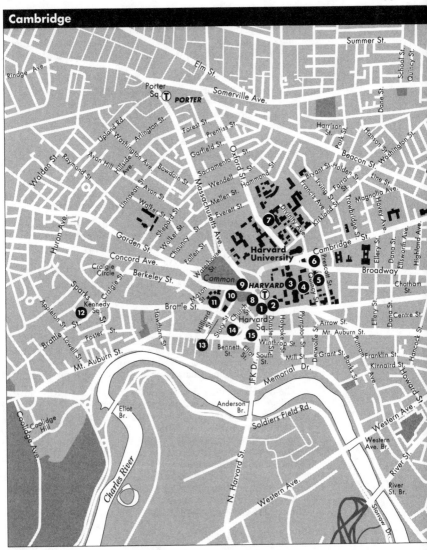

Arthur M. Sackler
Museum, **6**

Brattle House, **14**

Christ Church, **10**

Dawes Island, **9**

Dexter Pratt
House, **13**

First Parish Church, **8**

Fogg Art Museum, **5**

Hart Nautical
Gallery, **20**

Harvard Square, **1**

Harvard University
Museums of Cultural
and Natural History, **7**

Harvard Yard, **3**

Kresge
Auditorium, **17**

Longfellow National
Historic Site, **12**

Massachusetts
Institute of
Technology, **16**

MIT Chapel, **18**

MIT List Visual Art
Center, **21**

MIT Museum, **19**

Radcliffe College, **11**

The Square, **15**

Wadsworth House, **2**

Widener Library, **4**

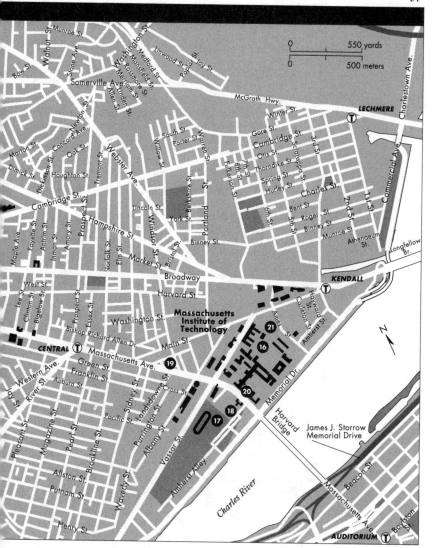

0 | 550 yards
0 | 500 meters

LECHMERE (T)

Charlestown Ave.

Commercial Ave.

Munroe St.
Walnut St.
Bow St.
Stone Ave.
Somerville Ave.
Marion St.
Dimick St.
Concord Ave.
Oak St.
Houghton St.
Dickinson St.
Cambridge St.
Maple Ave.
Fayette St.
Antrim St.
Inman St.
Prospect St.
Hampshire St.
Webster Ave.
Tremont St.
Windsor St.
Norfolk St.
Elm St.
Market St.
Broadway
Harvard St.
Washington St.
Bishop Richard Allen Dr.
Main St.

Medford St.
Mansfield St.
Rossmore St.
Merriam St.
Linden St.
Allen St.
Newton St.
Concord Ave.

Washington St.
Linwood St.
Poplar St.
Joy St.

McGrath Hwy.

Winter St.
Gore St.
South St.
Porter St.
Warren St.
Willow St.
Cambridge St.
Otis St.
Sciarappa St.
3rd St.
Thorndike St.
7th St.
8th St.
Fulkerson St.
Spring St.
Hurley St.
Charles St.
6th St.
Bent St.
5th St.
Roger St.
Binney St.
Munroe St.
Athenaeum St.

Lincoln St.
York St.
Berkshire St.
Portland St.
Bristol St.
Binney St.

KENDALL (T)

Longfellow Br.

1st St.
2nd St.

Howard St.
Carleton St.

West St.
Lee St.
Clinton St.
Bigelow St.
Prospect St.
Essex St.

CENTRAL (T) Massachusetts Ave.
Green St.
Franklin St.
Western Ave.
River St.
Auburn St.
Sidney St.
Pacific St.
Cross St.
Landsdown St.
Purrington St.
Albany St.
Vassar St.
Amherst Alley

Massachusetts Institute of Technology

Amherst St.
Memorial Dr.

(19)
(21)
(16)
(20)
(18)
(17)

Harvard Bridge

James J. Storrow Memorial Drive

Beacon St.
Boylston St.

Putney St.
Flagg St.
Pleasant St.
Magazine St.
Pearl St.
Brookline St.
Allston St.
Putnam St.
Waverly St.
Henry St.

Charles River

Massachusetts Ave.

AUDITORIUM (T)

N

Not a square at all, Harvard Square is where Massachusetts Avenue, coming from Boston, turns and widens into a triangle broad enough to accommodate a brick peninsula on which the MBTA station is located. Sharing the peninsula is a local institution, the out-of-town newsstand, which occupies the restored kiosk of 1928 that was the entrance to the MBTA station until its reconstruction when the Red Line was extended beyond Harvard Square.

The greater area of the square is a broad and busy one. The pedestrian flow is constant and varied, and wide sidewalks and miniparks encourage entertainers, promoters of causes, and those who want to share with you their religious convictions. Harvard Square is walled on two sides by banks, restaurants, and shops and on the third by Harvard University.

A good place to begin one's tour is the **Cambridge Discovery** information booth near the MBTA station entrance, where you will find maps, brochures, and information about the entire city. The walking tour brochures cover Old Cambridge, East Cambridge, and Revolutionary Cambridge. Cambridge Discovery also gives a rewarding tour of Old Cambridge conducted by a corps of well-trained high school students. *Cambridge Discovery, Inc., Box 1987, Harvard Sq., Cambridge 02238, tel. 617/497-1630. Open in winter, daily 9–5; in summer, daily 9–6.*

On the Harvard University side of Harvard Square stands ❷ **Wadsworth House,** a yellow clapboard structure built in 1726 as a home for Harvard presidents. It served as the first headquarters for George Washington when he arrived to take command of the Continental Army on July 2, 1775.

Step past Wadsworth House and through a gateway into ❸ **Harvard Yard.** While the college dates from 1636, the oldest buildings in Harvard Yard are of the 18th century; together the buildings chronicle American architecture from Colonial time to the present: **Holden Chapel,** built in 1744, is a Georgian gem. The graceful **University Hall** was designed in 1815 by Charles Bulfinch. **Memorial Hall,** completed in 1878 as a memorial to Harvard men who died in the Union cause, is High Victorian both inside and out. **Sever Hall,** designed in 1880 by Henry Hobson Richardson, represents the Romanesque revival that was followed by the Classical (note the pillared facade of Widener Library) and the Neo-Georgian, represented by the sumptuous brick houses along the Charles River. Harvard's four oldest buildings, Massachusetts Hall, Holden Chapel, Hollis Hall, and Harvard Hall, were occupied by the patriot regiments during the Revolution.

The Harvard University information office on the ground floor of the Holyoke Center (1350 Massachusetts Ave., tel. 617/495–1573), which, run by students, offers a free hour-long walking tour of Harvard Yard (during the academic year, weekdays at 10 and 2 and Sat. at 2; mid-June–Aug., Mon.–Sat. at 10, 11:15, 2, and 3:15, and Sun. at 1:30 and 3:30) and maps of the university area. The tour does not include visits to museums, but it provides a fine orientation and will give you ideas for further sightseeing.

❹ **Widener Library,** which boasts the country's second-largest collection of books, has a Gutenberg bible, a Shakespeare folio, and dioramas of Cambridge as it appeared in 1667, 1775, and

1936. Imagine what it must have been like to be here at the outbreak of the Revolution, when 16,000 patriots milled around
this town of 1,600 people. *Harvard Yard, tel. 617/495–2413.
Open during the academic year, weekdays 9 AM–10 PM, Sat.
9–5, Sun. noon–5; May 22–June 29, weekdays 9–5, Sat. 9–1;
June 30–Aug. 20, Mon.–Thurs. 9 AM–10 PM, Fri.–Sat. 9–5, Sun.
noon–5; Aug. 21–Sept. 20, weekdays 9–5, Sat. 9–1. Tours by appointment.*

Harvard has two celebrated art museums, each a treasure in
⑤ itself. The most famous is the **Fogg Art Museum.** Founded in
1895, it now owns 80,000 works of art from every major period
and from every corner of the world. Its focus is primarily on
European, American, and Far Eastern works; it has notable
collections of 19th-century French Impressionist and medieval
Italian paintings. Special exhibits change monthly. *32 Quincy
St., tel. 617/495–9400. Admission: $4 adults, $2.50 senior citizens and students, children under 18 free. Free Sat. 10–noon.
Open Tues.–Sun. 10–5.*

When you purchase a ticket to the Fogg, you are entitled to tour
⑥ the **Arthur M. Sackler Museum** (485 Broadway, tel. 617/495–
9400) across the street as well. It exhibits Chinese, Japanese,
ancient Greek, Egyptian, Roman, Buddhist, and Islamic
works. The Sackler keeps the same hours as the Fogg.

A ticket to the Fogg also gains you admission to Harvard's
Busch-Reisinger Museum (tel. 617/495–2317), now located in
the new Werner Otto Hall entered through the Fogg. The collection specializes in Central and Northern European art.
Hours are the same as at the Fogg and the Sackler.

⑦ Harvard also maintains the **Harvard University Museums of
Cultural and Natural History.** This vast brick building fulfills
the plan of the Swiss naturalist Louis Agassiz. His idea was to
bring under one roof the study of all kinds of life, plants, animals, and humankind. It contains four distinct collections: comparative zoology, archaeology, botany, and minerals. The most
famous exhibit here is the display of glass flowers in the *Botanical Museum.* Renting the taped tour will help you to appreciate
fully these models of more than 700 plant species, meticulously
recreated in glass by a father and son who worked continuously in Dresden, Germany, from 1871 to 1936.

The *Peabody Museum of Archaeology and Ethnology* holds one
of the world's outstanding anthropological collections; exhibits
focus on American Indian and Central and South American cul-
tures. The *Museum of Comparative Zoology* traces the evolution of animals and man. The best known among its wealth of
exhibits are the whale skeletons; the largest known turtle
shell; the Harvard mastodon, Kronosaurus; the giant sea ser-
pent; George Washington's pheasants; and the world's oldest
reptile egg. The *Mineralogical and Geological Museum,*
founded in 1784, has an extensive collection of exotic crystals
and meteorites; scale models of volcanoes and well-known
mountains are also on display. *26 Oxford St., tel. 617/495–3045.
Admission: $4 adults, $2 children 3–13, $3 students with ID
and senior citizens. Open Mon.–Sat. 9–4:30, Sun. 1–4:30. Free
Sat. 9–11. Closed major holidays.*

⑧ At the **Old Burying Ground** and **First Parish Church** on the corner of Church Street and Massachusetts Avenue, you can make
out through the iron railing of the cemetery a number of 17th-

century and 18th-century tombstones of ministers, early Harvard presidents, and Revolutionary War soldiers. The wooden Gothic Revival church was built in 1833 by Isaiah Rogers. *3 Church St., tel. 617/876–7772. Old Burying Ground open during daylight hours (access to cemetery through Christ Church's gate on Garden St.); church open in winter, weekdays 9–5; in summer, weekdays 9–3. Sun. service at 10:30, church open until 1.*

❾ Cross to **Dawes Island** in the middle of Garden Street to read the history legends and to see the bronze horseshoes embedded in the sidewalk. The horseshoes were a Bicentennial gift from the descendants of William Dawes, a doctor who galloped through Cambridge spreading the alarm ("The British are coming") on the eve of the Battle of Lexington. Beyond the ornamental arch is **Cambridge Common,** a public park since 1631.

❿ Cross back to Garden Street and stroll along the Burying Ground to **Christ Church,** designed in 1761 by Peter Harrison, the country's first trained architect. During the Revolution the church was used as a soldier's barracks until Washington ordered it reopened for services on New Year's Eve 1775. Step into the vestibule to look for the bullet holes made by a British soldier marching to Concord. The interior is airy and elegant in its simplicity. *Zero Garden St., tel. 617/876–0200. Open daily 7:30–6. Sun. services at 8, 10, and 12:30 (also at 5 during the academic year).*

⓫ At the next corner turn down Appian Way and take the first right through a small garden and into the yard of **Radcliffe College.** This is the heart of the college founded in 1897 "to furnish instruction and the opportunities of collegiate life to women and to promote their higher education." Still an independent corporation within Harvard University—to which it was wedded in 1977—Radcliffe maintains its own physical plant, including the Agassiz Theater. Exit through the gate next to the theater and continue down Mason Street to Brattle, where you turn right. Walk past the stone buildings and chapel of the Episcopal Divinity School.

Brattle Street is one of the country's most elegant. Elaborate mansions line both sides from this corner all the way to Elmwood, the great, square, mid-18th-century house that is the home of the Harvard president. In the 1770s this street was known as **Tory Row** because its mansions (then numbering seven), with their lands that stretched to the river, were owned by staunch supporters of King George. These properties were appropriated by the patriots when they took over Cambridge in the summer of 1775.

⓬ Washington himself quickly moved from the humbler Wadsworth House to the stately home at 105 Brattle Street, now maintained as the **Longfellow National Historic Site.** The house was built in 1759 by the son of a wealthy West Indies plantation owner who fled town in 1774. George Washington lived here throughout the siege of Boston. The poet Henry Wadsworth Longfellow rented a room here in 1837 and later received the house as a gift from his new father-in-law on his marriage to Frances Appleton, who burned to death here in a fluke accident. Longfellow filled the house with the exuberant spirit of his own work and that of his literary circle, which included Emerson, Thoreau, Holmes, Dana, and Parkman. This was the period in which Harvard students began shedding traditional theology and rote learning. Harvard's Tyrell Channing was probably the first university professor in this country to teach that the most important discipline is thinking. *105 Brattle St., tel. 617/876–4491. Admission: $2 adults, under 16 and over 62 free. Open for guided tours only; call ahead for tour times. Last tour departs at 4. Open daily 10–4:30.*

The absorption with ideas that still pervades old Cambridge can be savored in the dozen cafes and the half-dozen outstanding bookstores to be found around Harvard Square. Walk back **⓭** along Brattle Street to reach the yellow **Dexter Pratt House,** immortalized in Longfellow's "The Village Blacksmith." It is now owned by the Cambridge Center for Adult Education. The Blacksmith House Bakery on the first floor, and the Cafe (tel. 617/876–2725), up the incredibly skinny staircase from the Bakery, are both perfect stops for a strong pick-me-up coffee and sweet before continuing your tour. *56 Brattle St., tel. 617/547–6789. Admission free. Open Mon.–Sat. 9–7. Bakery and Cafe open weekdays 8–7, Sat. 8–6, Sun. brunch 11–3 in winter; Mon. 8–5 (bakery open until 7), Tues.–Sat. 8–8, Sun. brunch 11–3 in summer.*

⓮ **Brattle House** is an 18th-century gambrel-roofed Colonial that once belonged to the Loyalist William Brattle, who left Boston in 1774. From 1840 to 1842 it was the residence of Margaret Fuller, the feminist editor of *The Dial;* today it is headquarters for the Cambridge Center for Adult Education, and it is listed on the National Register of Historic Places. *42 Brattle St., tel. 617/547–6789. Admission free. Open Mon.–Thurs. 9–9, Fri. 9–7, Sat. 9–2.*

You can easily take an hour to walk this short block crammed **⓯** with shops and restaurants that locals call **The Square,** which is formed by the juncture of Massachusetts Avenue and John F. Kennedy Drive. An extension of it, the commercial end of Brattle Street, includes the stretch of Kennedy Drive that runs on to the Charles River. Give or take a few sidestreets, you can count 150 shops and an equal number of eating spots within this extended space.

An exploration of Cambridge would not be complete without a **⓰** visit to the **Massachusetts Institute of Technology.** The 135-acre campus of MIT borders the Charles River, 1½ miles south of Harvard Square. On a beautiful spring day it's a fine walk along Massachusetts Avenue that takes you from the historic richness of Harvard Square, through the bustle and ethnic diversity of urban Central Square (where there are some wonderful Middle Eastern and Indian spots for lunch), and into the warehouse openness of the Kendall Square area. If the weather is not so fine, take the "T" Red Line heading "inbound" from Harvard Square two stops to Kendall Square.

No one could have guessed that the founding of a small technological school in 1861 in Boston's Copley Square would one day meld the academic and industrial communities of Cambridge into an entirely new entity. Despite the pleas of the Harvard president that the school relocate in Allston, just across the river from its own campus (and thereby conveniently in Harvard's shadow), MIT President Richard MacLaurin opted for the new landfill at the opposite end of the city, abutting the riverside factories of East Cambridge.

The Massachusetts Institute of Technology moved to Cambridge in 1916 with great panoply, and it has long since fulfilled the predictions of its founder, the geologist William Barton Rogers, that it would surpass "the universities of the land in the accuracy and the extent of its teachings in all branches of positive science." Yet it has always been "the factory," even to its students, lacking as it does Harvard's ivy and aura.

In the 1930s there was a shift in focus from practical, applied engineering and mechanics to the outer limits of scientific fields. With the outbreak of World War II, the significance of such research became apparent. An emergency office of scientific research and development was set up, free of red tape, and manned by scientists from both Harvard and MIT. Here many of the components of modern warfare were developed and refined. The laboratories founded in wartime have since produced instrumentation and guidance devices for NASA flights and for nuclear submarines.

It can be argued that MIT (9,500 graduate and undergraduate students) has as much impact on Cambridge and Boston today as does Harvard (16,900 graduate and undergraduate students). In fact, one in five MIT graduates goes to work in the immediate area, many of them in the high-tech companies founded by fellow alumni that now fill many former industrial complexes in Cambridge.

Obviously designed by and for scientists, the MIT campus is divided by Massachusetts Avenue into the West Campus, which is devoted to student leisure life, and the East Campus, where the heavy work is done. The West Campus has some extraordinary buildings. The **Kresge Auditorium,** designed by Eero Saarinen with a curving roof and unusual thrust, rests on three instead of four points. The **MIT Chapel,** another Saarinen design, is lit primarily by a roof oculus that focuses light on the altar, as well as by reflections from the water in a small moat surrounding it, and it is topped by an aluminum sculpture by Theodore Roszak. **Baker House** was designed in 1947 by the Finnish architect Alvar Aaltoa in such a way as to give every room a view of the Charles River.

The East Campus, which has grown around the university's original neoclassical buildings of 1916, also boasts outstanding modern architecture and sculpture, notably the high-rise Earth Science Building by I. M. Pei and the giant stabile that Alexander Calder designed as a baffle for the wind so that the revolving doors in Pei's building can function (when the building first opened, they could not).

The Institute maintains an Information Center and offers free tours of the campus weekdays at 10 and 2. *Building Seven, 77 Massachusetts Ave., tel. 617/253–4795. Open weekdays 9–5.*

19 MIT has several fine museums. The **MIT Museum** contains photos, paintings, scientific instruments, and memorabilia relating to the Institute. *265 Massachusetts Ave., tel. 617/253–4444. Admission free for MIT students, children under 12, and senior citizens; $2 non–students. Open Tues.–Fri. 9–5, weekends 1–5.*

20 The **Hart Nautical Gallery** harbors a small but outstanding collection of ships' models. *55 Massachusetts Ave., tel. 617/253–5942. Admission free. Open daily 9–8.*

American Express offers Travelers Cheques built for two.

American Express® Cheques *for Two*. The first Travelers Cheques that allow either of you to use them because both of you have signed them. And only one of you needs to be present to purchase them.

Cheques *for Two* are accepted anywhere regular American Express Travelers Cheques are, which is just about everywhere. So stop by your bank, AAA* or any American Express Travel Service Office and ask for Cheques *for Two*.

Travelers Cheques

㉑ The MIT List Visual Art Center shows selections from the university's collection of 800 works of art; there are also changing exhibits and gallery talks. *20 Ames St., tel. 617/253–4680. Admission free. Open weekdays noon–6, weekends 1–5. Closed in summer.*

Cambridge for Free

The **Arco Forum of Public Affairs** (Kennedy School of Government, 79 JFK St., tel. 617/495–1380) sponsors an impressive list of speakers, including heads of state. Forums, many of which are broadcast on National Public Radio and C-Span, are held several nights a week during the academic year.

The world-renowned **Bunting Institute Colloquium** (Radcliffe College, 34 Concord Ave., tel. 617/495–8212) features women writers, scholars, artists, and scientists every Wednesday during the academic year.

The **Fogg Art Museum,** the **Arthur M. Sackler Museum,** and the **Harvard University Museums of Cultural and Natural History** are free on Saturday morning.

Harvard College Observatory. Harvard University opens its observatory to the public on the third Thursday of every month; programs begin at 8 PM and include a lecture, video or film, and, weather permitting, a view of the stars. The auditorium is small, so it's wise to arrive by 7:30. *Phillips Auditorium, 60 Garden St. (walking distance from Harvard Sq. and Porter Sq. T stops), tel. 617/495–7461.*

Longfellow Garden Concerts (105 Brattle St., tel. 617/876–4491) feature the poet's favorite music in the garden of the Longfellow House every other Sunday, June to early August, 3–4:30.

What to See and Do with Children

Cambridge Multicultural Arts Center (41 2nd St., tel. 617/577–1400) offers cultural events for children (often in collaboration with other groups around Cambridge), including workshops, storytelling, concerts, theater events, and dance performances.

Off the Beaten Track

Mt. Auburn Cemetery was one of the country's first garden cemeteries, and it remains one of the loveliest. Since it opened in 1831, more than 80,000 persons have been buried here, among them Henry Wadsworth Longfellow, Mary Baker Eddy, Winslow Homer, and Edwin Booth. The warbler migrations in the fall and spring make this a popular spot with bird watchers. Two tour maps are available at the office: one for horticultural points of interest, the other for tombstones of note. *Mt. Auburn St., Cambridge, tel. 617/547–7105. Open daily 8–7 in summer, 8–5 in winter. T stop, Harvard; then Watertown or Waverly bus to cemetery.*

5 Shopping

Boston's shops and stores are generally open Monday through Saturday from 9 or 9:30 until 6 or 7; many stay open until 8 late in the week. Some stores, particularly those in malls or tourist areas, are open Sunday from noon until 5. Most stores accept major credit cards—even the large department stores, like Filene's and Jordan Marsh, who have their own charge cards. Neiman Marcus accepts only its own card, but with the proper identification it's fairly easy to get one while you're there. Traveler's checks are welcome throughout the city (though it may be difficult for a small store to cash a check of large denomination). The state sales tax of 5% does not apply to clothing or food, except in restaurants. Boston's two daily newspapers, the *Globe* and the *Herald*, are the best places to learn about sales; Sunday's *Globe* often announces sales for later in the week.

Major Shopping Districts

Most of Boston's stores and shops are located in an area bounded by Quincy Market, the Back Bay, downtown, and Copley Square. There are few outlet stores in the area, but there are plenty of bargains, particularly in the world-famous Filene's Basement and Chinatown's fabric district.

The majority of Cambridge's stores are clustered around Harvard Square. The late shopping night in Harvard Square is Thursday. A few of the city's most original shops avoid the high rents in Harvard Square, you will find them on Massachusetts Avenue south of Porter Square and on Huron Avenue.

Boylston Street, in the heart of the Back Bay and parallel to Newbury Street, is home to more than 100 stores, among them Bonwit Teller and F.A.O. Schwarz. At the east end of Boylston Street is a very elegant complex, **Heritage on the Garden** (300 Boylston St., tel. 617/426–9500), home to Hermès, Saint John's Knits, Sonia Rykiel, and Escada; at the west end of Boylston Street is the Prudential Center complex, where specialty shops and department stores cluster in and around the center plaza, among them Lord & Taylor and Saks Fifth Avenue.

Cambridgeside Galleria (100 Cambridgeside Place, tel. 617/621–8666). Located in East Cambridge, is this three-story mall accessible by the Green Line Lechmere stop. It has more than 60 shops including the anchor stores of Filenes, Lechmere, and Sears. Parking costs $1 per 30 minutes.

Charles Street in Beacon Hill is a mecca for antiques and boutique lovers. Some of the city's finest and prettiest shops are here. **River Street,** which runs parallel to Charles Street, is an excellent source for antiques.

Copley Place, (tel. 617/375–4400), an indoor shopping mall connecting the Westin and Marriott hotels, is a blend of the elegant, the unique, the glitzy, and the overpriced. The Neiman Marcus department store anchors 87 stores, restaurants, and cinemas. Prices in the shops on the second level tend to be a bit lower. Some nearby parking garages offer lower rates with a validation from a mall retailer; inquire before parking.

Downtown Crossing, Boston's downtown shopping area, has been livened up: It's now a pedestrian mall with outdoor merchandise kiosks, street performers, and benches for people watchers. Here are the city's two largest department stores, Jordan Marsh and Filene's (with its famous Basement).

Boston Shopping

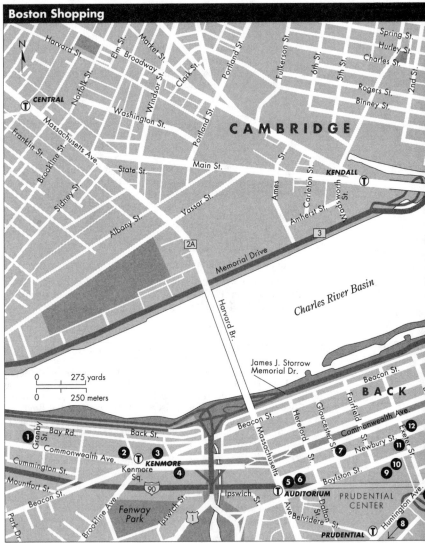

Alan Bilzerian, **25**

Ann Taylor, **32**

The Art Store
Gallery, **8**

Artsmart, **55**

Bally of
Switzerland, **17**

Bargain Box, **18**

Barnes and
Noble, **20, 50**

Beacon Hill Thrift
Shop, **36**

Bonwit Teller, **21**

Boston Antiques
Co-op, **39**

Boston University
Bookstore, **3**

Bova's Bakery, **41**

The Brattle
Bookstore, **53**

Brooks
Brothers, **24, 45**

Charles Street
Supply, **37**

Dairy Fresh
Candies, **43**

David P. Ehrlich and
Sons, **47**

Dorfman Jewels, **30**

Eastern Mountain
Sports, **1**

Emack & Bolio's, **7**

Emporio Armani, **11**

Eric Fuch's, **46**

F. A. O. Schwarz, **23**

Filene's, **51**

Giorgio Armani, **31**

Globe Corner
Bookstore, **48**

Helen's Leather
Shop, **38**

Hilton's Tent City, **40**

J. Pace & Son, **42**

James Billings
Antiques, **34**

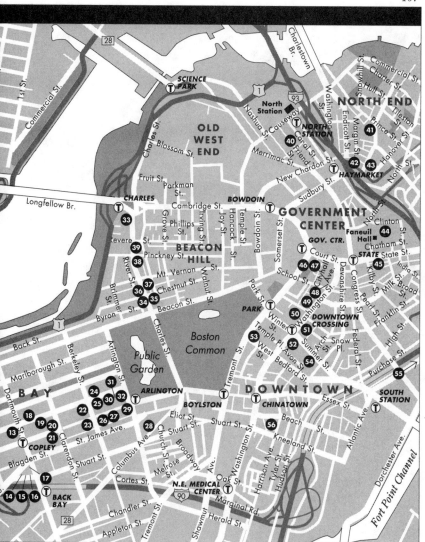

Jordan Marsh, **52**

Jos. A. Bank
Clothiers, **19**

Kennedy Studios, **35**

L. J. Peretti
Company, **28**

Lord & Taylor, **10**

Louis, **22**

Neiman Marcus, **14**

Newbury Comics, **6**

North End Fabrics, **56**

Nuggets, **4**

Planet Records, **2**

Roots, **26**

Saks Fifth Avenue, **9**

Savenor's, **33**

Shreve, Crump &
Low, **29**

The Society of Arts
and Crafts, **13**

Sweet Stuff, **44**

Tiffany & Co., **15**

Tower Records, **5**

Victoria's Secret, **16**

Warburton's, **49**

Waterstone's
Booksellers, **12**

Windsor Button
Shop, **54**

Women's
Educational and
Industrial Union, **27**

Cambridge Shopping

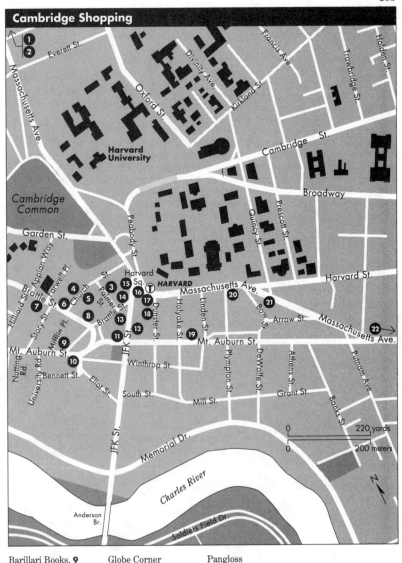

Barillari Books, **9**
Blacksmith House Bakery, **7**
The Bookcase, **5**
Cambridge Artists' Cooperative, **4**
Cambridge Discovery Booth, **17**
Cardullo's, **14**
Cheapo Records, **22**

Globe Corner Bookstore, **3**
Grolier Bookshop, **20**
Harvard Coop Society, **15**
Herrell's, **18**
Jasmin, **8**
The Music Emporium, **1**
Newbury Comics, **12**
Out-of-Town News, **16**

Pangloss Bookshop, **19**
Pepperweed, **2**
Reading International, **6**
Serendipity, **21**
Taang! Records, **10**
Tower Records, **11**
Wordsworth, **13**

Faneuil Hall Marketplace (tel. 617/523–3886), has small specialty shops, kiosks of every description, street performers, and
one of the great food experiences, Quincy Market. The intrepid
shopper must cope with crowds of people, particularly on
weekends. Saturday is the best day to walk through Haymarket Square, a jumble of outdoor fruit and vegetable vendors,
meat markets, and fish mongers. **Marketplace Center,** one of
the city's newest attractions, is adjacent to Faneuil Hall Marketplace and smack in the middle of the "Walkway to the Sea"
from Government Center to Boston's waterfront. Thirty-three
stores on two levels ring a central plaza; they include Banana
Republic, The Sharper Image, Doubleday Books, Brookstone,
The Gap, Williams-Sonoma, The Body Shop, an outdoor gelato
café, and a gourmet Japanese restaurant.

Harvard Square in Cambridge comprises just a few blocks but
boasts more than 150 stores selling clothes, books and records,
furnishings, and a surprising range of specialty items. Three
small weatherproofed shopping complexes are located just off
the square: The Garage (38 John F. Kennedy St.), The Galleria (57 John F. Kennedy St.), and Charles Square (Bennett and
Eliot Sts.). A new building has sprung up over the old bus terminal at One Brattle Square, housing HMV and The Limited.
And for better or worse, you can find a branch of just about any
popular chain within a few blocks: Urban Outfitters, The Body
Shop, Crate and Barrel.

Newbury Street is Boston's version of New York's Fifth Avenue. Near the Public Garden, Newbury Street is quite upscale
with the most stylish clothing boutiques, the most up-to-date
art galleries, and, in the Ritz-Carlton Hotel, the most delicious
blueberry muffins in town. Toward Massachusetts Avenue,
Newbury Street appeals more to the young and trendy—Urban Outfitters, Tower Records, several good bookstores, and
Johnson Paint Company, with an excellent art supply store upstairs, are just a sampling.

Department Stores

Filene's (426 Washington St., tel. 617/357–2100). This full-
service department store carries a complete line of men's and
women's formal, casual, and career clothing bearing the major
name brands and designer labels. Furs, jewelry, shoes, and
cosmetics are found in the eight floors of merchandise. Yet the
store's most outstanding feature is its two-level bargain basement, where items are automatically reduced in price according to the number of days they've been on the rack. The
competition can be stiff for the great values on discontinued,
overstocked, or slightly irregular items.
Harvard Coop Society (1400 Massachusetts Ave., Cambridge,
tel. 617/499–2000; at MIT, 3 Cambridge Center, tel. 617/499–
3200). Begun in 1882 as a nonprofit service for students and faculty, the Coop is now a full department store known for its extensive selection of records and books. It has a good assortment
of men's clothing, women's shoes, and stationery.
Jordan Marsh (450 Washington St., tel. 617/357–3000). For
more than 130 years Jordan's has been New England's largest
department store. It carries men's and women's clothing, including top designers, as well as housewares, furniture, and
cosmetics. There is a bargain basement.
Lord & Taylor (760 Boylston St., tel. 617/262–6000). Classic

clothing, from casual to elegant, by such designers as Anne Klein and Ralph Lauren; accessories, home furnishings, housewares, and a beauty salon.

Neiman Marcus (5 Copley Pl., 100 Huntington Avenue, tel. 617/536–3660). The flashy Texas retailer's home in New England has three levels of high fashion, Steuben glass, and gadgetry.

Saks Fifth Avenue (Prudential Center, tel. 617/262–8500). From the more traditional styles to today's avant-garde apparel, Saks offers clothing to satisfy everyone's needs.

Specialty Stores

Antiques   **Boston Antiques Co-op** (119 Charles St., tel. 617/227–9810). A collection of 14 dealers occupies two floors, carrying everything from vintage photos and paintings to porcelain, silver, bronzes, and furniture.

James Billings Antiques (34 Charles St., tel. 617/367–9533). An excellent selection of English antiques, mostly from before 1850. The store also offers interior design services.

The Music Emporium (2018 Massachusetts Ave., Cambridge, tel. 617/661–2099). This shop offers one of New England's best selections of new, old, and antique acoustic stringed instruments, including some from the 19th century. Contemporary acoustic and folk music and instruments are also available.

Shreve, Crump & Low (330 Boylston St., tel. 617/267–9100). The second floor has 18th- and 19th-century English and American furniture, silver, porcelain, and maps and prints. It has a good selection of Oriental porcelain as well.

Art Galleries   Art galleries display and sell works of art and antiques. Admission to galleries is normally free; call for hours.

Alpha Gallery (14 Newbury St., tel. 617/536–4465). Contemporary American and European painting, sculpture, and master prints.

The Art Store Gallery (621 Huntington Ave., tel. 617/232–1555). Affordable art and crafts—from jewelry and sculpture to prints and paintings—are created by students and alumni of the Massachusetts College of Art. Half of the profits go to the artists, the other half to the college's programs.

The Artful Hand (36 Copley Pl., 100 Huntington Ave., tel. 617/262–9601). Jewelry, glass, glass sculpture, wood, pottery, baskets, lamps, and furniture by more than 800 American artisans.

Artsmart (272 Congress St., tel. 617/695–0151). High quality art by more than 160 New England artists includes furniture, sculpture, jewelry, and hand-crafted eggs. The emphasis here is on affordable, accessible art.

Childs Gallery (169 Newbury St., tel. 617/266–1108). American and European paintings, prints, drawings, watercolors, and sculpture from the 17th to the 20th centuries.

Copley Society of Boston (158 Newbury St., tel. 617/536–5049). The works of well-known and aspiring New England artists; a nonprofit membership organization founded in 1879.

Eugene Galleries (76 Charles St., tel. 617/227–3062). Prints, etchings, old maps, city views, and books.

Gallery NAGA (67 Newbury St., tel. 617/267–9060). Contemporary works of photography and sculpture; furniture by local artists.

Guild of Boston Artists (162 Newbury St., tel. 617/536–7660).

Representational watercolors, oils, graphics, and sculpture by guild members; a nonprofit gallery.

Haley and Steele (91 Newbury St., tel. 617/536–6339). Rare 18th- and 19th-century prints, including 19th-century sporting and bird prints.

Robert Klein Gallery (207 South St., tel. 617/482–8188). Contemporary and vintage photographs by international and national photographers.

Barbara Krakow Gallery (10 Newbury St., tel. 617/262–4490). Contemporary American and European paintings, sculpture, drawings, and prints.

Nielsen Gallery (179 Newbury St., tel. 617/266–4835). Paintings, sculpture, drawings, and prints; German expressionist and master prints from the 19th and 20th centuries.

Pucker-Safari Gallery (171 Newbury St., tel. 617/267–9416). Contemporary paintings, sculpture, ceramics, and prints.

Rolly-Michaux (290 Dartmouth St., tel. 617/536–9898). Contemporary paintings, graphics, silkscreens, and sculpture; works by Calder, Picasso, Chagall, Miró, and Matisse.

Judi Rotenburg Gallery (130 Newbury St., tel. 617/437–1518). Principal gallery artists are the painters Zygmund Jankowski, Joseph Solman, and Harold and Judi Rotenburg, and the sculptor Marianna Pineda.

Vose Galleries (238 Newbury St., tel. 617/536–6176). American paintings of the 18th, 19th, and early 20th centuries.

Baked Goods **Blacksmith House Bakery** (56 Brattle St., Cambridge, tel. 617/354–3036). Rich German tortes, Viennese-style pastries, and *bouche de Noël* at Christmastime are the major temptations. There's also a café, which serves a Continental breakfast as well as light lunches.

Bova's Bakery (76 Prince St., tel. 617/523–5601). This is the place for freshly baked rolls and bread and wonderful bakery-style pizza. It's open 24 hours a day.

Warburton's (367 Washington St., tel. 617/426–7853). This British-based chain bakes meat-filled savories, nine varieties of muffins, danish, and croissants daily in each store. (Also at Government Center, across from the State House on Beacon Street, and on Brattle Street in Harvard Square.)

Books **Barnes and Noble** (395 Washington St., tel. 617/426–5502, and 607 Boylston St., tel. 617/236–1308). Boston's biggest discount bookseller specializes in reduced prices on recent best sellers and tables heaped with remainders (publisher's overstock of books printed in previous seasons) at bargain prices. Another department has classical records, tapes, and compact discs.

The Bookcase (42 Church St., Cambridge, tel. 617/876–0832). The basement is filled with an enormous selection of second-hand books.

Boston University Bookstore (660 Beacon St., tel. 617/267–8484). You'll find three floors of best sellers, out-of-print collections, magazines, and maps here in Kenmore Square.

The Brattle Bookstore (9 West St., tel. 617/542–0210). The late George Gloss built this into Boston's best used and rare bookshop, and his son Kenneth is carrying on. If the book you want is out of print, the Brattle has it or can probably find it.

The **Cambridge Discovery** booth supplies a wonderful map of bookstores in the area. And if you're serious about books, the map is worth getting: In the immediate Harvard Square area alone there are about 20 bookstores, including general discount shops like **Wordsworth** (30 Brattle St.) and **Barillari Books** (1

Mifflin Pl.), and specialty shops like **Grolier Bookshop** (6 Plympton St.) for poetry.

Globe Corner Bookstore (1 School St., tel. 617/523–6658, and 49 Palmer St., Cambridge, tel. 617/497–6277). These are the best sources by far for domestic and international travel books and maps; they also carry a very good selection of books about New England and by New England authors.

Pangloss Bookshop (65 Mt. Auburn St., Cambridge, tel. 617/354–4003). Stocks scholarly monographs in the humanities and social sciences and literary magazines and journals, as well as out-of-print books.

Reading International (47 Brattle St., Cambridge, tel. 617/864–0705). Has academic and nonacademic books, foreign newspapers and magazines, and a diverse collection of scholarly journals.

Waterstone's Booksellers (181 Newbury St., tel. 617/859–8030). This newcomer from England vies with Boston University Bookstore in size and obviously believes in bookshopping as ritual. From the spacious lobby and up through the third floor, display tables highlight an excellent selection of literature, health books, children's books, art, literary, and news journals. They also host an extensive author and event series.

Clothing for Men and Women

Alan Bilzerian (34 Newbury St., tel. 617/536–1001). For the most avant-garde and au courant men's and women's clothing in Boston, this is the only place to go.

Ann Taylor (18 Newbury St., tel. 617/262–0763, and Faneuil Hall Marketplace, tel. 617/742–0031). High-quality fashions for both classic and trendy dressers. When you want to know what's in style, this store's window is a reliable indication.

Bonwit Teller (500 Boylston St., tel. 617/267–1200). Imported and American designer clothing and accessories, and an International Boutique and Designer Salon.

Brooks Brothers (46 Newbury St., tel. 617/267–2600, and 75 State St., tel. 617/261–9990). Traditional formal and casual clothing. The styling is somewhat more contemporary in the third-floor Brooksgate shop, but basically Brooks is Brooks: correct and durable through the ages.

Giorgio Armani (22 Newbury St., tel. 617/267–3200). This top-of-the-line couture boutique is in contrast to **Emporio Armani** (210 Newbury St., tel. 617/262–7300), which sells sportier versions of Mr. Armani's distinctive clothing, in addition to jeans, children's clothing and home furnishings.

Jasmin (37 Brattle St., Cambridge, tel. 617/354–6043). Current designers from New York and Los Angeles sell their funky collections here.

JoS. A. Bank Clothiers (122 Newbury St., tel. 617/536–5050). For reasonably priced classic men's and women's apparel, Bostonians head to Bank's.

Louis (234 Berkeley St., tel. 617/262–6100). Louis carries elegantly tailored designs and a wide selection of imported clothing and accessories, including many of the more daring Italian styles. They also have subtly updated classics in everything from linen to tweeds.

Pepperweed (1684 Massachusetts Ave., Cambridge, tel. 617/547–7561). Features contemporary and unusual fashions from American, European, and Japanese designers.

Roots (419 Boylston St., tel. 617/247–0700). A handsome men's shop specializing in tastefully updated traditional styles. A good place to find well-cut flannels and tweeds.

Serendipity (1312 Massachusetts Ave., Cambridge, tel. 617/661–7143). The moderately priced imports of women's clothing are from India, Mexico, and South America; the shop also has jewelry, shoes, and accessories.

Crafts   **Cambridge Artists' Cooperative** (59A Church St., Cambridge, tel. 617/868–4434). Innovative jewelry, ceramics, glass, weavings, quilts, leather, and woodwork in almost every price range are featured in this artist-managed crafts gallery.

The Society of Arts and Crafts (175 Newbury St., tel. 617/266–1810). An excellent assortment of quality work by some of the country's finest craftspeople. Ceramics, jewelry, leather, batik, weaving, furniture.

Fabrics   **North End Fabrics** (31 Harrison Ave., tel. 617/426–2116). Almost everything in fabrics, including bridal, imported laces, designer fabrics, fun furs, theatricals, and woolens.

Windsor Button Shop (35 Temple Pl., tel. 617/482–4969). A large specialty store jammed with buttons, sequins, braids, trims, novelties, notions, muslin, felt, and other trimmings.

Food   **Cardullo's** (6 Brattle St., Cambridge, tel. 617/491–8888). Head here for exotic imports, sandwiches to go, cheeses, wines, and more than 270 varieties of beer.

Dairy Fresh Candies (57 Salem St., tel. 617/742–2639). A speedy turnover of goods means very fresh items. European packaged assortments, truffles, hard candy, dried fruits, nuts, and all kinds of chocolates are sold.

J. Pace & Son (42 Cross St., tel. 617/227–9673). These friendly neighborhood Italian grocers carry 25 types of olive oil, cheeses, fresh bread, olives, salami, imported prosciutto di Parma, and they can whip up a great deli sandwich for you.

Savenor's (160 Charles St., tel. 617/723–6328). Savenor's had a store in Cambridge where Julia Child shopped for gourmet items until it burned in 1991. It has now relocated to Charles Street and continues to carry the same outstanding cheeses, breads, prime cuts of meat, exotic game, and fine produce.

Sweet Stuff (Faneuil Hall Marketplace, North Market Building, tel. 617/227–7560). Chocolate-covered pretzels; candy pizza made of chocolate, marshmallow, and nuts; and jelly beans are among the house specialties.

Gifts   **Kennedy Studios** (31 Charles St., tel. 617/523–9868). Head to Kennedy's for fine prints, posters, and watercolors (especially classic Boston scenes). There are locations on Milk and Tremont streets, too.

Women's Educational and Industrial Union (356 Boylston St., tel. 617/536–5651). Cards, gifts, decorative items, children's clothing, and accessories are sold in the shop of this social and educational organization founded in 1877. There is an excellent needlework and collector's shop.

Ice Cream   **Emack & Bolio's** (290 Newbury St., tel. 617/247–8772). One of the original gourmet ice cream makers in Boston, this store is still on the short list of favorites.

Herrell's (15 Dunster St., Cambridge, tel. 617/497–2179). The original creator of Steve's is Steve Herrell, who, after selling his name, decided to get back in the ice-cream business. Nondairy ice cream and frozen yogurt complement the extensive variety of flavors: chocolate pudding is one of the more intense.

Jewelry   **Dorfman Jewels** (24 Newbury St., tel. 617/536–2022). An elegant shop with the finest watches, pearls, silver, and glass.

Shreve, Crump & Low (330 Boylston St., tel. 617/267–9100). The finest jewelry, china, crystal, and silver. Also an extensive collection of clocks and watches. Shreve's, one of Boston's oldest and most respected stores, is where generations of Brahmin brides have registered their china selections.

Tiffany & Co. (Copley Pl., 100 Huntington Ave., tel. 617/353–0222). Fifth Avenue comes to Boston, with the finest in gems and precious metal jewelry as well as flatware, crystal, china, and fragrances.

Newspapers and Periodicals **Out-of-Town News** (Harvard Square, Cambridge, tel. 617/354–7777). A staggering cross section of the world's newspapers and magazines is on sale here daily 6 AM–midnight. Also serves as a ticket agency.

Records, Tapes, and Compact Discs **Cheapo Records** (645 Massachusetts Ave., Cambridge, tel. 617/354–4455). New and used R&B, rock, and jazz LPs and 45s are available.

Newbury Comics (332 Newbury St., tel. 617/236–4930; 36 JFK St., Cambridge, tel. 617/491–0337). A very friendly, very cool staff sells the best selection of new rock and roll, especially independent pressings.

Nuggets (486 Commonwealth Ave., tel. 617/536–0679; 1354-A Beacon St., Brookline, tel. 617/277–8917). Used and out-of-print jazz and rock records, and a tremendous selection of new releases on CD and tape. The prices are excellent.

Planet Records (536 Commonwealth Ave., Kenmore Sq., tel. 617/353–0693). This second-floor store has an interesting and extensive selection of new and used records, from jazz and rock to reggae and international.

Taang! Records (12 Eliot St., Cambridge, tel. 617/876–2411). Taang! supports local music and sells underground rock. A great Boston find.

Tower Records (360 Newbury St., tel. 617/247–5900; 95 Mt. Auburn St., Cambridge, tel. 617/876–3377). This chain has opened its largest store (so far) in the Back Bay. Three enormous floors stock every kind of music imaginable. The selection in its Cambridge branch is just as wide.

Shoes **Bally of Switzerland** (Copley Pl., 100 Huntington Ave., tel. 617/437–1910). Quality imported footwear and accessories for men and women.

Helen's Leather Shop (110 Charles St., tel. 617/742–2077). New England's biggest Western boot dealer for men and women carries a variety of exotic animal-skin boots. There are leather jackets, belts, luggage and accessories, briefcases, sandals, and leather backpacks. Boots from Lucchese, Larry Mahan, Dan Post, Tony Lama, Justin, and Frye.

Sporting Goods **Eastern Mountain Sports** (1041 Commonwealth Ave., Brighton, tel. 617/254–4250). New England's best selection of gear for the backpacker, camper, climber, skier, or all-round outdoors person. Everything from tents and sleeping bags to technical mountaineering equipment—and a wide selection of casual clothing. A good source for books and maps for those planning trips into the New England backcountry.

Hilton's Tent City (272 Friend St., tel. 617/227–9242). An excellent selection of hiking, backpacking, and camping equipment as well as boots and clothing, including hard-to-find items.

Thrift Shops **Bargain Box** (117 Newbury St., tel. 617/536–8580). Operated by a non–profit organization, they sell donated or consignment clothing of high quality, often designer labels.

Beacon Hill Thrift Shop (15 Charles St., tel. 617/742–2323). When Beacon Hill families do their spring cleaning, many of their cast-offs end up here. Proceeds benefit the New England Baptist Hospital School of Nursing. Because the store is run by volunteers, it keeps irregular hours.

Tobacconists **David P. Ehrlich and Sons** (32 Tremont St., tel. 617/227–1720). A wide selection of finely blended tobaccos; cigars and pipes; and masculine gift items of the Dunhill variety. Fine beers and ales.

L. J. Peretti Company (2½ Park Square, corner of Boylston and Charles Sts., tel. 617/482–0218). A Boston institution since 1870, this is one of the few places that still makes pipes. Peretti sells its own blends of tobacco, a large selection of others, and handmade imported cigars.

Toys **Eric Fuch's** (28 Tremont St., tel. 617/227–7935). Offers great deals in toy replicas and miniatures, as well as fine model trains.

F.A.O. Schwarz (440 Boylston St., tel. 617/266–5101). This branch of the famed New York toy emporium offers the highest quality (and the highest priced) toys. A wide selection of trains, dolls, stuffed animals, games, and other intriguing playthings.

6 Sports, Fitness, Beaches

Spectator Sports

Sports are as much a part of Boston as codfish and Democrats. Everything you have heard about the zeal of Boston fans is true, and out-of-towners wishing to avoid controversy would do well not to flaunt their partiality to the teams back home. (Visitors from New York, for example, should not bring their Yankees hats.) College teams are followed with enthusiasm, especially Boston College and Harvard football. College hockey fans look forward to the Beanpot Tournament in February.

Baseball **Boston Red Sox,** American League (Fenway Park, tel. 617/267-8661 or 617/267-1700 for tickets). Baseball season begins early in April and finishes the first weekend in October. The Sox won the American League pennant in 1967, 1975, and 1986, though they haven't won a World Series since 1918. The small ball park is the country's oldest (built in 1912), infamous for the 37-foot-high left-field cement wall called the "Green Monster."

Basketball **Boston Celtics,** NBA (Boston Garden, tel. 617/523-3030 or 617/931-2000 for tickets). Basketball season runs from October to May, and they're running out of room for hanging the Celtics' championship flags among the rafters of the Garden. The Celtics have won the NBA championships 16 times since 1960, the last time in 1986.

Football **New England Patriots,** NFL (Sullivan Stadium, Foxboro, tel. 800/543-1776). Sullivan Stadium is 45 minutes south of the city. The Patriots fumble more often than not, but they did make it to the Super Bowl in the 1985 season.
Boston College Eagles (Alumni Stadium and Shea Stadium, Chestnut Hill, tel. 617/552-3000).
Boston University Terriers (Nickerson Field, off Commonwealth Ave., tel. 617/353-3838).
Harvard University Crimson (Harvard Stadium, North Harvard St. and Soldiers Field Rd., Allston, tel. 617/495-2211).

Hockey **Boston Bruins,** NHL (Boston Garden, tel. 617/227-3223). The Bruins are on the ice, underneath the Celtics' parquet, from October until April, frequently on Thursday and Sunday evenings. The Bruins have won the Stanley Cup five times, the last one in 1972.

Rowing Rowing is big in Boston; its popularity spawned the country's first rowing club, the Union Boat Club (tel. 617/523-9717), which hosts the world's biggest rowing event, the annual **Head of the Charles Regatta.** In mid-October over 3,000 male and female collegiate rowers from all over the world compete, while thousands of spectators line the shores of the Charles River and use the race as a reason to lounge on blankets and drink beer. (Imbibe with caution, the police have been known to disapprove.)

Tennis The **Longwood Cricket Club** (564 Hammond St., Brookline, tel. 617/731-2900) hosts the week-long U.S. Pro Tennis Championships in mid-July. Order tickets by calling 617/731-4500.

Participant Sports and Fitness

The mania for physical fitness is big in Boston. Lots of people play racquet sports on their lunch hours, and runners and roller skaters can be seen constantly on the Storrow Embankment. Most public recreational facilities, including skating rinks and tennis courts, are operated by the Metropolitan District Commission (MDC) (20 Somerset St., tel. 617/727–5215).

Bicycling The **Dr. Paul Dudley White Bikeway,** approximately 18 miles long, runs along both sides of the Charles River from Watertown Square to the Museum of Science. For other path locations, call the MDC (tel. 617/727–5215).

Minuteman Bicycle Trail. The 11-mile trail runs from the Alewife Red Line Station in Cambridge through Arlington, Lexington, and Bedford along the bed of an old railroad track.

The Bicycle Workshop (259 Massachusetts Ave., Cambridge, tel. 617/876–6555) rents bicycles, fixes flat tires while you wait, and delivers bicycles to your hotel. In downtown Boston during the spring and summer, **Community Bicycle Supply** (490 Tremont St., tel. 617/542–8623) rents cycles.

For more detailed information on bicycling in the area and for scheduled group rides, contact the **New England Mountain Biking Association** (69 Spring St., Cambridge, 02141, tel. 617/776–4686). The **Boston Area Bicycle Coalition** (Box 1015, Kendall Sq. Branch, Cambridge 02142, tel. 617/491–7433) publishes the newsletter "Spoke 'N Word," has information on organized area rides, and sells an area bike map for $3.50.

Billards **Jillian's Billiards Club** (145 Ipswich St., tel. 617/437–0300) is a semi-posh joint with the atmosphere of an English gentleman's library. Professional lessons are available and the 53-table pool hall also has three bars, a cafe, darts, shuffleboard, backgammon, chess, and a batting cage.

Boating On the Charles River and Inner Harbor to North Washington Street, all types of pleasure boats (except inflatables) are allowed on the waters of Boston Harbor, Dorchester inner and outer bays, and the Neponset River from the Granite Avenue Bridge to Dorchester Bay.

Public landings and floats are located at **North End Waterfront Park,** Commercial Street, Boston Harbor; **Kelly's Landing,** Day Boulevard, South Boston; and at these locations along the Charles River:

Clarendon Street, Back Bay; **Hatch Shell,** Embankment Road, Back Bay; **Pinckney Street Landing,** Back Bay; **Brooks Street,** Nonantum Road, Brighton; **Richard T. Artesani Playground,** off Soldiers Field Road, Brighton

There is another launching area at the **Monsignor William J. Daly Recreation Center** (tel. 617/727–4708) on the Charles River, Brighton. Owners of trailerable boats planning to use this facility should make arrangements in advance.

Community Boating (21 Embankment Rd., tel. 617/523–1038). Near the Charles Street footbridge that crosses Storrow Drive, the boating program is America's oldest and largest public sailing program. From April through October they offer seven-day memberships with unlimited boat use for $70, and two days for $50, to those qualified to sail solo. Month-long memberships, during which you may learn to sail solo, are available for $80.

Rent your own canoe, kayak, or shell from May through October from **Charles River Canoe and Kayak Center** (2401 Commonwealth Ave., Auburndale, tel. 617/965–5110).

Camping Of Boston's **Harbor Islands,** Lovells, Great Brewster, Grape, Bumpkin, and Peddocks Calf have campsites. A camping permit is required. Contact MDC headquarters, 98 Taylor St., Dorchester, MA 02122, tel. 617/727–5290, for Lovells and Peddocks islands. For the others, contact Harbor Islands State Park, 349 Lincoln St., Bldg. 45, Hingham, MA 02043, tel. 617/740–4290.

Fishing There are just two locations for freshwater fishing in Greater Boston: along the shores of the Charles River; and at Turtle Pond, Stony Brook Reservation, Turtle Pond Parkway, Hyde Park. For fishing from shore, try the John J. McCorkle Fishing Pier, Castle Island, and the pier at City Point, both located off Day Boulevard in South Boston. The Harbor Islands also permit fishing.

Boston Park Rangers (Boston Parks and Recreation Dept., tel. 617/522–2639) offer fishing lessons for individuals and groups in parks throughout the city. Call for program information and reservations.

Golfing The **Massachusetts Golf Association** (190 Park Rd., Weston, tel. 617/891–4300) represents more than 270 clubs in the state and will provide information on courses that are open to the public and equipment rentals. The office is open weekdays 9–4:30.

Franklin Park William Devine Golf Course (Franklin Park, Dorchester, tel. 617/265–4084), after years of neglect, underwent a $1.3-million restoration in 1989. The 6,100-yard, par-70 course was created in the early 1900s by Donald Ross and is open year-round, weather permitting. Greens fees are $9.50 for 9 holes and $16 for 18 holes on weekdays, and $10.50 and $19 respectively on weekends.

Hiking There are excellent footpaths for hikers in the 450-acre Stony Brook Reservation in Boston's Hyde Park and West Roxbury sections. A 20-minute drive south of Boston, the **Blue Hills Reservation** (Exit 3, Houghton's Pond, off Rte. 128, Milton, tel. 617/698–1802) offers 6,500 undeveloped acres of woodland and about 150 miles of trails, some ideal for cross-country skiing, some designated for mountain biking. If the headquarters is not open, maps are always available on the front porch. The **Blue Hills Trailside Museum,** operated by the Massachusetts Audubon Society, features discussions on natural history, live animals, and special events such as organized hikes and walks. *Exit 2B off Rte. 128 to Rte. 138, Milton, tel. 617/333–0690. Admission: $3 adults, $2 senior citizens, $1.40 children. Open Wed.–Sun. 10–5; closed major holidays.*

Boston's **Harbor Islands** (*see* Tour 5 in Chapter 3) also provide a convenient and off-the-beaten-path venue for hiking.

Jogging Both sides of the Charles River are quite popular with joggers (*see* Bicycling). For the location of other paths in greater Boston, contact the MDC or the Department of Environmental Management, Division of Forests and Parks (tel. 617/727–3180). Another great source of information is the **Bill Rodgers Running Center** (Faneuil Hall Marketplace, tel. 617/723–5612); Bill Rodgers is a four-time marathon winner. Many hotels provide jogging maps for guests.

Physical Fitness The **Westin Hotel** (Copley Place, Back Bay, tel. 617/262–9600) has complete health club facilities. Nonguests are welcome to use the facilities for an $8 fee.

The extensive facilities of the **Greater Boston YMCA** (316 Huntington Ave., tel. 617/536–7800) are open for $5 per day to members of other YMCAs for up to two weeks, and to nonmembers for $10 per day or $150 for a three-month membership. Lap pools, squash, and racquetball courts available.

Numerous hotels offer health club facilities for guests only (*see* Lodging): Back Bay Hilton, Boston Harbor Hotel at Rowes Wharf, Boston Marriott Copley Place, Boston Park Plaza Hotel & Towers, Copley Square Hotel (use of The Westin's Club and Back Bay Racquet Club for a small fee), 57 Hotel/Howard Johnson's (access to Boston Harbor Tennis Club), Four Seasons, Guest Quarters Suite Hotel, Hilton at Logan Airport, Lafayette Hotel, Marriott Long Wharf, Hotel Meridien, Midtown, Omni Parker House (use of nearby Fitcorp Health and Fitness Center), Ramada Inn, Ritz-Carlton, Sheraton Boston Hotel & Towers, The Westin.

The **Boston Athletic Club** (653 Summer St., tel. 617/269–4300) offers use of its facilities, including a pool, to guests of downtown hotels for $20 per day. **Fitcorp** (1 Beacon St., tel. 617/248–9797; Prudential Center, tel. 617/262–2050; 133 Federal St., tel. 617/542–1010) offers a similar arrangement but does not have a pool. They charge $12 per day, or $100 for 10 days.

Roller Blading From May through October, Memorial Drive on the Cambridge side of the Charles River is closed to auto traffic on Sundays from 11 AM to 7 PM, and the area between the Western Avenue Bridge and Eliot Bridge is transformed into Riverbend Park. **Beacon Hill Skate Shop** (135 Charles St., tel. 617/482–7400) rents blades for $5 per hour or $15 per day year-round. Safety equipment is included.

Skating Listed here are a few of the 20 public ice-skating rinks operated by The Metropolitan District Commission. For a complete schedule of hours of operation contact the Department of Parks and Recreation (tel. 617/727–9547).

Charlestown Rink, Rutherford Avenue near Prison Point Bridge; **Jamaica Plain Rink,** Jamaicaway, Willow Pond; **Brighton Rink,** Nonatum Road, Brighton; **Cleveland Circle Rink,** Cleveland Circle, Brighton; **North End Rink,** Commercial Street; **South Boston Rink,** Day Boulevard; **Neponset Rink,** Garvey Playground, Morrissey Blvd., Dorchester; **Hyde Park Rink,** Turtle Pond Parkway.

In winter skaters flock to the frozen waters of the Boston Public Garden's lagoon and the Frog Pond at Boston Common. Ice on one side of the bridge is for figure skating, while the other side is for faster-paced ice hockey. **Beacon Hill Skate Shop** (135 Charles St., tel. 617/482–7400) rents skates for use in the Public Garden.

Skiing **Blue Hills Ski Area,** Blue Hills Reservation, Washington Street, Canton, exit 2B from Route 128, is an MDC-managed downhill facility with a 1,400-foot double chair lift, 2 j-bars, and a rope tow. Its facilities include seven slopes, snowmaking, a ski school, and a restaurant. *Just south of Boston city limits off Rte. 128, tel. 617/828–5090 for ticket and ski school information, 617/828–5070 for recorded report on snow conditions.*

For those who are interested in serious skiing, Loon Mountain (tel. 603/745–8111) and Waterville Valley (tel. 603/236–8311) are both about 2½ hours north of Boston.

Tennis The Metropolitan District Commission maintains tennis courts throughout Boston. No permit is required to use these courts, which operate on a first-come, first-served basis:

John J. Moynihan Playground, Truman Highway, Hyde Park; **Francis D. Martini Music Shell,** Truman Highway, Hyde Park; **Monsignor Francis A. Ryan Memorial Playground,** River Street, Mattapan; **Charles Weider Park** (lighted), Sharon and Dale streets, Hyde Park; **Marine Park** (lighted), South Boston.

Beaches

Yes, Boston is on the ocean, and no, it is not renowned for its beaches. The harbor is a working harbor, one that has several million people living nearby, and consequently the water is not Bahamas-pure. There are public beaches, however, and the Metropolitan District Commission (MDC) opens them only when certain standards of cleanliness are met. The only swimming off Harbor Islands is Lovells Island. The mainland beaches, concentrated in Dorchester and South Boston, are largely neighborhood affairs, where occasional incidents have occurred when one group's sense of territory was violated by another. (These areas have been calm in recent years.)

The main beaches are Malibu Beach, Savin Hill Beach, and Tenean Beach, off Morrissey Boulevard, in Dorchester; Carson Beach, Castle Island Beach, City Point Beach, M Street Beach, and Pleasure Bay, off Day Boulevard, in South Boston.

These beaches are open from the end of June to the beginning of September. Lifeguards are on duty daily from 10 to 6 during this season. High temperatures and high tide may cause schedule changes. For further information, call the MDC Harbor District Office (tel. 617/727–5215).

Several excellent beaches a short distance from the city make lovely day trips. Among the nicest are Nantasket Beach in Hull, Crane's Beach in Ipswich, Plum Island (*see* Chapter 10, Excursions) in Newburyport, and Wingaersheek Beach in Gloucester.

7 Dining

The restaurants were selected by Mary H. Frakes, who covers the Boston dining scene for a number of national publications.

Updated by Julia Lisella.

Not so long ago, Boston was considered the home of the bean and the cod and not much else where fine dining was concerned. Part of the reason was the legacy of the Puritans, for whom eating was a necessity rather than an entertainment. But a Yankee emphasis on value for dollar has in recent years given rise to restaurants that emphasize relatively reasonable prices and yet manage to turn out dishes that are innovative, rich in flavor, and carefully prepared. And there's still a lot of good seafood to be had.

The choice of dining experience in Boston is unusually wide. At one extreme, respected young chefs emphasize the freshest ingredients and the menu reflects what's local and seasonal; at the other, the tradition of decades mandates recipes older than the nation and the menu seems forever unchanged. Between the extremes lies an extensive range of American, French, Italian, and other national and ethnic cuisines.

Most bars offer meals—some even pride themselves on their food—but offerings are usually limited and lean toward whatever is microwavable. Outdoor vendors, chiefly around Boston Common, have pretzels, popcorn, and occasionally hot dogs. In the Quincy Market area it's a short stroll from the indoor food stands to a bench in the colorful outdoor marketplace.

Bostonians are not traditionally late diners. Many of the city's finest restaurants are busy by 7 PM, and those near the theater district begin filling up earlier. (Advise your server when you sit down if you plan to attend an after-dinner performance.) Some of the more popular restaurants will offer two seatings on weekends, generally at around 7 and 9; those who like to linger over coffee and cognac will find the second sitting more relaxing.

Many restaurants now offer "early bird" specials at greatly reduced prices. They are an excellent bargain, especially for those who like to eat early. The one drawback may be that some offer only a limited menu, and sampling a particular entrée may mean going off the special. Restaurants often have luncheon specials whose quality equals that of dinner selections—at significantly lower prices.

While a more casual style has become evident in Boston restaurants, the formality that has always been an important aspect of the city still lingers. T-shirts and walking shorts may be acceptable in many places, but they are not appropriate in others. In most of Boston's better restaurants a man would feel comfortable wearing coat and tie, and a woman wearing a dress. Some restaurants still require coats and ties for men.

As a general rule, you can expect to tip about 15% on a check of less than $60, about 20% on a check larger than $60.

The following price categories are based on the average cost of a three-course dinner for one person, food alone, not including beverages, tax, and tip.

Category	Cost*
Very Expensive	over $40
Expensive	$25–$40

Moderate	$15–$25
Inexpensive	under $15

per person; add 5% tax

The following credit card abbreviations are used: AE, American Express; D, Discover Card; DC, Diners Club; MC, Master-Card; V, Visa.

The most highly recommended restaurants are indicated by a star ★.

French

Back Bay
★ **L'Espalier.** In the spring of 1988 the chef's toque and the keys to the restored 19th-century town house passed from the acclaimed Moncef Meddeb, who had established this very special restaurant, to Frank McClelland, whom *Food and Wine* called one of America's top chefs. While the use of fresh native ingredients continues to be the starting point for the daily menu, the style of cooking has moved away from the nouvelle and esoteric toward the simpler, lighter preparations and larger portions that characterize contemporary French and American cuisine. The $56 fixed-price, three-course dinner might include roast native partridge with chanterelles, salmon steak with mint and wild onion butter and a salad of peas and radishes, and for dessert a luscious but low-calorie arrangement of figs and peaches with wild strawberry sauce and mascarpone cheese. A *menu dégustation* ($72), which provides a sampling of many items, is available on weekdays. Under McClelland, the waiting staff and general atmosphere have become more relaxed; unchanged are the excellent wine list of 150 choices and the decor of the three intimate but elegant dining rooms, each with a marble fireplace and striking arrangements of fresh flowers. All have well-spaced tables. Large windows give the Salon and Parlor rooms a light, airy feeling, while the upstairs Library, with its dark peach walls and mahogany paneling, is more masculine and clubby. *30 Gloucester St., tel. 617/262–3023. Reservations required. Jacket and tie advised. AE, D, MC, V. No lunch. Closed Sun. Very Expensive.*

★ **Plaza Dining Room.** The romantic, Edwardian dining room at the Copley Plaza Hotel has always been elegant, its extensive menu sophisticated. The high-back, tapestry-covered chairs, the crystal chandeliers, a lavishly molded ceiling, mahogany Palladian-arched mirrors, and the baby grand playing discreetly in the background create an atmosphere suitable for haute cuisine. The seasonal menu offers dishes that are classically French, with innovative touches and ingredients. For example, the steamed shrimp is served with an orange and curry dressing while medallions of Maine lobster are garnished with avocado and apple. The wine list is impressive and the library at the entrance is perfect for an after-dinner brandy. *138 St. James Ave., tel. 617/267–5300. Reservations advised. Jacket and tie required. AE, DC, MC, V. Very Expensive.*

Cambridge
The Peacock. This basement restaurant in a residential side street north of Harvard Square provides its loyal following with a romantic setting and a French provincial menu that changes every other week. The specialties are chicken liver pâté, sole suchet, and meringues. Beer and wine (including ports and sherries) only. *5 Craigie Circle, tel. 617/661–4073.*

Reservations advised. Jacket and tie optional. MC, V. No lunch. Closed Sun. Moderate.

Downtown **Julien.** Vaulted ceilings take on a new perspective in the formal
★ dining room of the Air France–affiliated hotel that occupies the
historic Federal Reserve Bank building in the heart of the
financial district. Limestone walls, massive chandeliers, and
wing chairs surrounding discreetly placed tables combine to
give diners a surpassing sense of privacy and well-being that is
equally conducive to business deals or marriage proposals. The
seasonal classical French menu emphasizes seafood and the devoted use of local fresh produce. Consulting chef Marc
Haeberlin and his apprentice, Andre Chouvin, offer up a light
salmon souffle; lobster ragout with Riesling; rack of lamb;
breast of squab with savoy cabbage and truffles; and for dessert, la pêche Haeberlin (fresh pear poached in vanilla syrup
and served with homemade pistachio ice cream and a champagne sauvignon). The wine industry has acclaimed the excellence of the extensive, balanced list. *Hotel Meridien, 250
Franklin St., tel. 617/451–1900. Reservations advised. Jacket
and tie required. AE, DC, MC, V. No lunch weekends. Very
Expensive.*

French/American

Back Bay **Ritz-Carlton Dining Room.** The hotel and its formal dining
room are traditional to such an extent that whenever the chef
has tried to introduce changes in the age-old menu, the loyal
patrons have stirred up an uncharacteristic fuss. Thus you
shall ever find such tried-and-true dishes as New England clam
chowder, lobster bisque, broiled scrod, chateaubriand béar-
naise, Boston cream pie, dessert soufflés, and of course caviar.
Each season a few extra dishes sneak onto the menu: Venison
and wild mushroom pâté and smoked pheasant breast with cabbage and Riesling sauce. The wine list offers rarities among its
200 labels. Impeccably trained and attentive waiters in tuxedos
provide royal service—and have served royalty, the Prince of
Wales for one. Doubtless royalty feels right at home in the regal
but understated elegance of the room, with its color scheme of
gold accented by cobalt blue. Ample windows provide a com-
manding view of the Public Garden, and an accomplished pian-
ist adds the grace note. *Ritz-Carlton Hotel, 15 Arlington St.,
tel. 617/536–5700. Reservations recommended. Jacket and tie
required. AE, D, DC, MC, V. Very Expensive.*

South End **Hamersley's Bistro.** Fiona and Gordon Hamersley opened their
★ bistro in 1987 and have received rave reviews. The black decor
in both dining rooms is accented by a fire-engine-red bar and
maître d' station; the walls have been painted goldenrod, giving
the place a warm look. Specialties that have a permanent place
on the daily menu include a garlic and mushroom sandwich
served as an appetizer (the mushrooms change seasonally), and
roast chicken with garlic, lemon, and parsley. The wine list,
which changes to match the menu, includes French, Italian,
Spanish, and Californian selections by the bottle and glass. *578
Tremont St., tel. 617/267–6068. Reservations recommended.
Dress: informal. D, MC, V. Expensive.*

Boston Dining

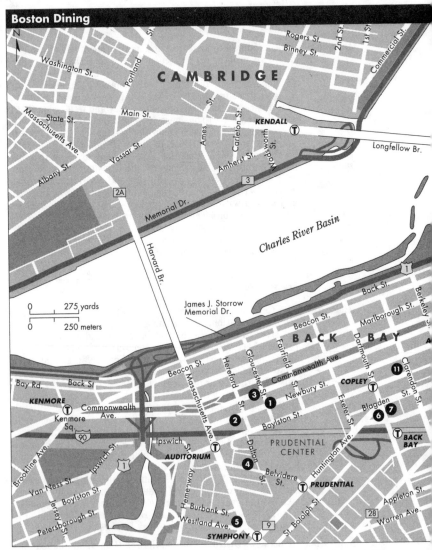

Another Season, **23**
Anthony's Pier 4, **39**
Aujourd'hui, **16**
Biba, **15**
Blue Diner, **47**
Boodle's, **4**
Carl's Pagoda, **45**
Charley's Eating and
Drinking Saloon, **2**

Cornucopia on the
Wharf, **29**
Cottonwood Cafe, **13**
The Daily Catch, **26**
Durgin-Park, **33**
Felicia's, **27**
Grill 23, **12**
Hamersley's Bistro, **9**
Ho Yuen Ting, **46**
Houlihan's Old
Place, **34**

Icarus, **8**
Imperial Teahouse
Restaurant, **43**
Jimmy's
Harborside, **40**
Joseph's Aquarium, **30**
Julien, **37**
Legal Sea Foods, **17**
L'Espalier, **3**

The Library Grill at
the Hampshire
House, **21**
Locke-Ober Café, **36**
Mr. Leung, **11**
Miyako, **1**
Montien, **42**
Morton's of
Chicago, **20**
No-Name
Restaurant, **41**

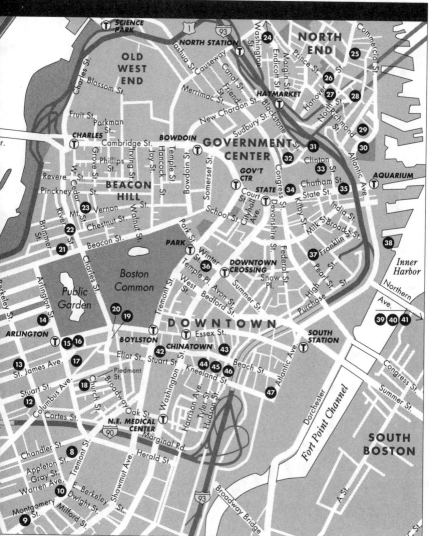

Olives, **24**

Plaza Dining Room, **7**

Restaurant Jasper, **28**

Ristorante Lucia, **25**

Ristorante
Toscano, **22**

Ritz-Carlton Dining
Room, **14**

Rocco's, **19**

Rowes Wharf
Restaurant, **38**

St. Cloud, **10**

Seasons, **31**

Siam Square, **44**

Star of Siam, **18**

Tatsukichi-Boston, **35**

Thai Cuisine, **5**

Turner Fisheries, **6**

Union Oyster
House, **32**

Cambridge Dining

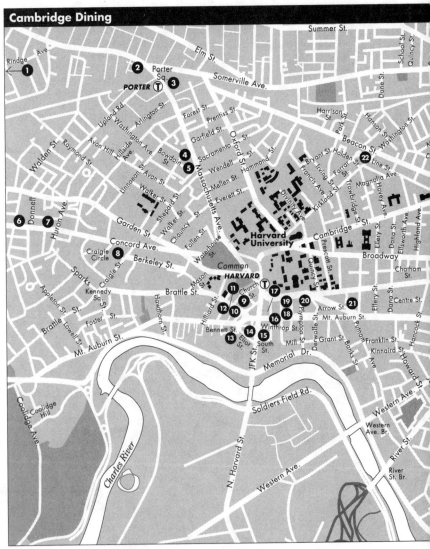

Acropolis, **5**
Anago Bistro, **33**
Averof, **2**
Bartley's Burger Cottage, **20**
Bertucci's, **10**
The Blue Room, **27**
The Border Cafe, **9**
Cafe Sushi, **21**
Cajun Yankee, **24**
Casablanca, **11**

Casa Mexico, **16**
Casa Portugal, **26**
Chez Nous, **7**
Cottonwood Cafe, **3**
Dali, **22**
East Coast Grill, **25**
The Elephant Walk, **23**
Elsie's Deli, **18**

Goemon Japanese Noodle Restaurant, **30**
Green Street Grill, **32**
Grendel's Den, **14**
Harvest, **12**
Iruna, **15**
John Harvard's Brew House, **17**
Joyce Chen Restaurant, **1**
La Groceria, **31**

Legal Sea Foods, **29**
Lucky Garden, **6**
Mexican Cuisine, **4**
Michela's, **28**
The Peacock, **8**
Rarities, **13**
Upstairs at the Pudding, **19**

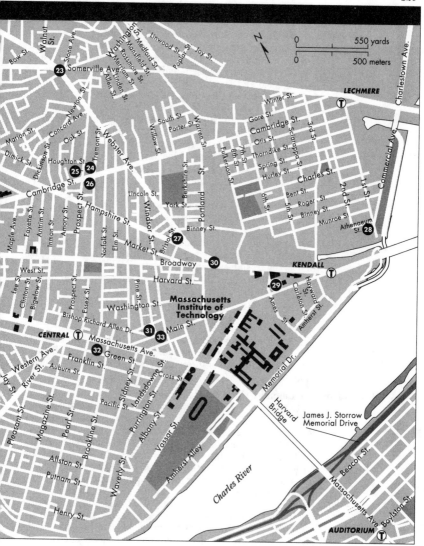

Classic American

Back Bay **Grill 23.** Gray business suits are prominent at this steak house. Dark paneling, gigantic marble columns, and waiters in white jackets give it a men's-club feel. The house salad, a mélange of vegetables, is justly praised, and the kitchen concentrates on grilling meat and seafood with skill. *161 Berkeley St., tel. 617/ 542-2255. Reservations suggested. Jacket and tie advised. AE, D, DC, MC, V. No lunch. Expensive–Very Expensive.*

Morton's of Chicago. The steaks are prime, the baked potatoes huge, the room packed and often noisy in one of Boston's classic steak houses. If you're particularly hungry, you might want to tackle the 24-ounce T-bone; if you haven't eaten for a week, try the 48-ounce super steak. The seafood selection includes swordfish. The Caesar and blue cheese dressings are homemade. Everything on the menu is à la carte. *1 Exeter Plaza, tel. 617/266-5858. Reservations advised (be prepared to wait up to 1½ hours Sat.). Jacket and tie advised. AE, DC, MC, V. No lunch weekends. Expensive.*

Boodle's. Under new management, this once London-style chophouse now features burgers, sandwiches, and salads, as well as the fresh local fish and variety of vegetables that have made Boodle's one of the Back Bay's best kept restaurant secrets. The split-level dining room is furnished like a 19th-century club. *40 Dalton St. in the Back Bay Hilton, tel. 617/266-3537. Reservations advised. Dress: casual. AE, D, DC, MC, V. Inexpensive–Moderate.*

Charley's Eating and Drinking Saloon. A 19th-century Victorian saloon serving American food: hamburgers, prime rib, sirloin steak, and London broil. *284 Newbury St., tel. 617/266-3000. Dress: casual. AE, D, MC, V. Inexpensive.*

Beacon Hill **The Library Grill at the Hampshire House.** The restored 19th-century Federal town house holds several drinking and dining establishments. Downstairs is the Bull and Finch Pub, model for the TV series *Cheers*. The second floor lounge, with its polished paneling and moose heads, has the feel of an elegant hunting lodge. Overlooking the Public Garden, it is a fine place to have a drink and watch the world go by. (Enjoy the New Orleans jazz brunch with their in-house quartet on Sundays.) The Gallery on the first floor is now a gift shop, and the restaurant has moved upstairs to the Library Grill, which looks out onto the Public Garden. The new chef has lightened the fare and offers such specials as swordfish with roasted red-pepper sauce and asparagus tips, grilled tenderloin, and duck over Oriental-style vegetables. *84 Beacon St., tel. 617/227-9600. Reservations advised. Dress: casual. Valet parking. AE, D, DC, MC, V. Expensive.*

Cambridge **Bartley's Burger Cottage.** Famed for its 42 varieties of burgers and fried onion rings, Bartley's is good for salads and sandwiches, too. Daily specials might include baked meatloaf with mashed potatoes and a vegetable. The small, crowded tables and bustling waitstaff qualify the place as a real burger joint. It's popular with students. *1246 Massachusetts Ave., tel. 617/ 354-6559. No reservations. Dress: casual. No credit cards. Closed Sun. Inexpensive.*

Elsie's Deli. Elsie has retired, but the quality of her revered sandwiches persists. We recommend the hot pastrami, the roast beef, and the super salads. *71A Mount Auburn St., tel.*

617/354–8362. No reservations. Dress: informal. No credit cards. Inexpensive.

Downtown   **Locke-Ober Café.** This Boston landmark has changed little since it opened in 1875. It did, at last, admit women to the Men's Café in 1972, and several years ago it added a new bar, albeit with the authentic Victorian stained glass and hand-carved Dominican mahogany used elsewhere in the building. A bastion of Boston's Brahmins, Locke's has probably seen the consummation of more business deals and political agreements than any other place in Boston. Its mix of traditional Continental and New England food is immune to innovation: lobster Savannah, oysters Winter Place, hash, Dover sole, steak tartare, Indian pudding, and John F. Kennedy's favorite, lobster bisque, have been house specialties for decades. Some of the staff (who wear black ties and long white aprons) have been there almost as long. The Men's Café, with its square dark mahogany bar and huge silver tureens, is a rare reminder of an era long past. Upstairs are the pleasant but less interesting Ober Room and the private dining rooms. Virtually everything on the menu is à la carte. *3 Winter Pl., tel. 617/542–1340. Reservations advised. Jacket and tie required. Valet parking after 6 PM. AE, D, DC, MC, V. No lunch weekends. Very Expensive.*

Blue Diner. This original 1945 diner has genuine diner food as well as more sophisticated offerings to please the mixture of blue-collar workers, architects, and artists that make up its regular clientele. It gets rave reviews for such original creations as grilled swordfish with melon chutney and down-home favorites like fresh roasted turkey with old-fashioned gravy, cranberry sauce, and mashed potatoes. Save room for a slice of the homemade coconut pie. It's one of the few places in Boston open 24 hours, Tuesday through Saturday. (It closes at midnight Sunday and Monday.) *178 Kneeland St., tel. 617/338–4639. No reservations. Dress: casual. AE, D, DC, MC, V. Moderate.*

Faneuil Hall   **Durgin-Park.** Diners here should be hungry enough to cope with enormous portions and to tolerate a long wait. This bustling Quincy Market restaurant was serving hearty fare when the building was a working market instead of a tourist attraction, and it requires only a little imagination to picture burly workingmen chowing down at the long communal tables where diners sit elbow to elbow with strangers. Durgin-Park still serves such homey New England fare as Indian pudding and haunches of prime rib that would keep your dog busy for hours. The atmosphere is uniquely Old Boston. *340 Faneuil Hall Marketplace, North Market Bldg., tel. 617/227–2038. Reservations for 15 or more. Dress: casual. AE, MC, V. Inexpensive–Moderate.*

Houlihan's Old Place. Steaks, burgers, fajitas, and pasta dishes are served amid art, antiques, and greenery. Half-price hors d'oeuvres are available in the lounge during weekday Happy Hour, 4–7. *60 State St., State St. Bldg., tel. 617/367–6377. Dress: casual but neat. Cover charge Thurs.–Sat. after 8 PM in the lounge. AE, D, DC, MC, V. Moderate.*

New American

Back Bay   **Aujourd'hui.** This formal dining room of the Four Seasons Hotel
     ★   has become one of the power rooms of the city. Its chairs are upholstered in tapestry, the china is antique, and the food re-

flects an inventive approach to regional ingredients and new American cuisine. Some entrées, such as rack of Colorado meadow lamb with layered potato and lasagna can be extremely rich, but the seasonal menu also offers low-calorie, low-cholesterol, "alternative cuisine" choices. Try for a window table overlooking the Public Garden. *200 Boylston St., tel. 617/451–1392. Reservations required. Jacket and tie advised. AE, DC, MC, V. Very Expensive.*

★ **Biba.** The wildly inventive Biba was a place to see and be seen from the day it opened in 1989. Its relaxed, eclectic decor combines bright colors and a cryptic mural of well-fed diners. The menu, which groups dishes as *meats, legumina,* and *offal,* encourages inventive and inexpensive combinations, and the gutsy fare mixes flavors from five continents. Dishes can be as simple as spaghetti with breadcrumbs or as elaborate as grilled duck over cherry chips and black olive butter. The wine list emphasizes adventurous selections from lesser-known areas. The downstairs bar, where street-level windows permit people-watching, is good for an afternoon snack or late-night grazing. Allow plenty of time for dining; service can be slow. *272 Boylston St., tel. 617/426–7878. Reservations advised. Dress: casual but neat. D, MC, V. Moderate–Expensive.*

Beacon Hill **Another Season.** Here the Continental menu changes every month, with nightly specials; the offerings are creative variations on classical European themes. Trout stuffed with hazelnuts, shallots, and fresh herbs with a beurre blanc; chicken Amsterdam, and homemade sorbets are representative selections. Only beer and wine are served, but the excellent wine list is well suited to the menu. A $22 prix-fixe menu is served Monday–Thursday. *97 Mount Vernon St., tel. 617/367–0880. Reservations advised. Dress: casual but neat. AE, MC, V. Closed Sat. and Mon. lunch, Sunday. Expensive.*

Cambridge **The Blue Room.** This hip and funky spot tucked below street level in an office complex blends together a global assortment of ethnic cuisines and manages to pull off the mix admirably, with lots of grilled or smoked fare and an eclectic hand with spices and ingredients. The emphasis in such favorite dishes as tacos al carbon and the pork-and-hominy posole is on flavor rather than formality. Brightly colored furnishings, counters where you can meet others while you eat, and a friendly waitstaff add up to a good-time place that is serious about food. *One Kendall Sq., tel. 617/494–9034. Reservations suggested. Dress: casual. MC, V. No lunch. Moderate–Expensive.*

John Harvard's Brew House. The person for whom Harvard College was named is said to have been interested in the brewing of beer, and this microbrewery/restaurant has capitalized on that reputation. Behind the long bar are the giant tanks that produce the restaurant's own lagers and ales. The menu mixes standard fun food—burgers, sandwiches, barbecue—with such New England favorites as smoked scallops and chicken pot pie. The dark-wood decor is enlivened by plaques illustrating high points of John Harvard's career. It's fun to identify the '60s celebrities depicted in stained glass along one wall. *33 Dunster St., tel. 617/868–3585. Dress: casual. AE, D, MC, V. Moderate.*

Rarities. The subdued contemporary decor complements a New American cuisine based on regional cooking and seasonal ingredients. The à la carte menu includes porterhouse of veal with vegetable strudel and a Rhode Island wine-based sauce.

Charles Hotel, 1 Bennett St., tel. 617/864–1200. Reservations advised. Dress: casual. AE, DC, MC, V. No lunch. Closed Sun. Expensive.

Faneuil Hall **Seasons.** Popular with businesspeople and politicians (City Hall
★ is just a block away), this solarium-like restaurant on the fourth floor of the Bostonian Hotel overlooks the bustling Faneuil Hall Marketplace and is a good place to entertain when you want to impress. The cuisine of chef Anthony Ambrose is American with international influences and changes seasonally. Selections from a summer menu included steamed halibut with oriental spices and apple paper, rack of lamb with lemon thyme sauvignon, and for dessert, macadamia nut and coconut flan with mango sorbet. The wine list is exclusively American. It is a private club at lunchtime. *Bostonian Hotel, North and Blackstone Sts., tel. 617/523–3600. Reservations advised. Dress: casual but neat. AE, DC, MC, V. Expensive.*

North End **Restaurant Jasper.** Jasper White, who trained a number of
★ Boston's best chefs, has a national reputation as a creator of contemporary New England cuisine. The menu leans heavily on local seafood and seasonal produce. Dishes might be as nouvelle as a salad of grilled duck with cranberries and spiced nuts—or as traditional as a New England boiled dinner cooked to perfection. The exposed brick walls and red lacquer furniture create a contemporary atmosphere, and the luscious desserts are anything but Puritan. *240 Commercial St., tel. 617/523–1126. Reservations advised. Dress: casual but neat. D, MC, V. No lunch. Closed Sun. and Mon. Very Expensive.*

South End **Icarus.** This elegant two-tier dining room offers a sophisticated menu and excellent service within walking distance of the theater district. The dark wood, well-spaced tables, flower arrangements, and subdued lighting make a pleasing atmosphere for highly inventive fare. The menu changes frequently; chef Chris Douglass prepares such specialties as polenta with braised exotic mushrooms and grilled eggplant with lemon tahini dressing as appetizers; entrées such as grilled tuna on a fennel and white bean salad, Wellfleet clams with tomato, zucchini, garlic, and basil over toasted noodles, and roast rack of lamb with roasted red peppers and ratatouille are served with color and flair. The freshly baked *focaccia* served in the bread basket is a treat. An extensive wine list complements the fare. Portions are ample; save room for the chocolate mousse torte dessert. A different menu is served at Sunday brunch. *3 Appleton St., tel. 617/426–1790. Reservations accepted. Dress: informal. AE, DC, MC, V. Closed Mon.–Sat. lunch. Expensive.*
St. Cloud. The setting is sleek, the clientele chic at this trendy bistro in a historic South End brownstone. The menu has lately consisted of contemporary American fare with a slight French influence: pappardelle noodles with smoked rabbit in a molasses cider vinegar sauce; potato-crusted salmon with mustard horseradish sauce and warm cabbage slaw; as well as good old American bluefish. The entrées lean to simply grilled meats and fish with interesting condiments. When available, the date pear tart is the dessert to have. *557 Tremont St., tel. 617/353–0202. Reservations advised. Dress: informal. AE, D, DC, MC, V. Expensive–Very Expensive.*

Waterfront **Cornucopia on the Wharf.** This highly regarded restaurant has
★ traded the historic background and intimacy of its old location downtown for a terrific waterfront view and a greatly ex-

panded space. The innovative cuisine that made Cornucopia's reputation is still featured, but a greater proximity to waterfront-strolling tourists has led to the inclusion of more traditional New England dishes on the menu. The late autumn menu, for example, includes Lobster Wiggle (a traditional lobster stew) as an appetizer, as well as roasted lamb pizza–a startling combination of lamb, prosciutto, fresh figs, poached apricots, and goat cheese atop a polenta crust. It's wise to leave room for dessert, especially if the white chocolate bread pudding is on the menu. A firm believer in the appropriate pairing of wine and food, the restaurant suggests a specific wine to accompany each dish. Moreover, the wine list is reasonably priced and innovative, and there's a large selection of wines by the glass. *100 Atlantic Ave., tel. 617/338-4600. Reservations advised. Dress: casual but neat. AE, MC, V. Closed Sun. Expensive.*

Rowes Wharf Restaurant. The dining room of the Boston Harbor Hotel offers a waterfront view without the noise and mediocre food of the megarestaurants. Built in 1987, the restaurant nonetheless has such traditional touches as upholstered armchairs, gathered swag curtains, mahogany paneling, and shaded wall sconces. The food is a subdued new American cuisine, with entrées such as fresh tagliatelli with mushrooms and poached Maine lobster over chorizo paella. The prix fixe menu is offered at $48. The outdoor waterside café is a winner in summer. *70 Rowes Wharf, tel. 617/439-3995. Reservations advised. Jacket required. AE, D, DC, MC, V. Expensive.*

Cajun

Cambridge **Cajun Yankee.** After eating the crawfish étouffée, the spicy jambalaya, or the duck with orange chipotel here, you'll begin to understand why Paul Prudhomme weighs as much as he does. Whitewashed walls, ceiling fans, and mahogany chairs foster a down-home atmosphere for the most authentic Louisiana cooking in Boston. *1193 Cambridge St., tel. 617/576-1971. Reservations strongly advised. Dress: casual. DC, D, MC, V. No lunch. Closed Sun. and Mon. Moderate.*

Chinese

Back Bay **Mr. Leung.** The black lacquered walls, exquisite flower arrangements, waiters in tuxedos, and a ceiling studded with tiny spotlights make this an unusual setting for a Chinese restaurant. But one taste of the Peking duck (for two) or lobster sautéed with ginger and scallops and you'll know you're in the Chinese equivalent of nirvana. *545 Boylston St., tel. 617/236-4040. Reservations required. Jacket advised. AE, D, DC, MC, V. Expensive.*

Cambridge **Joyce Chen Restaurant.** Joyce Chen offers a gracious setting and an extensive menu of Mandarin, Shanghai, and Szechuan food. Specialties include hot and cold soups, Szechuan scallops, and moo shu dishes. *390 Rindge Ave., tel. 617/492-7373. Reservations advised for large parties. Dress: informal. AE, D, DC, MC, V. Inexpensive-Moderate.*

Lucky Garden. Cambridge's first Szechuan restaurant offers hot-and-sour soup, scallops, Peking duck, and fried dumplings in a pleasant, comfortable atmosphere. No liquor. *282 Concord*

Ave., tel. 617/354–9514. Reservations accepted, but there's often a wait anyway. Dress: informal. MC, V. Inexpensive.

Downtown **Carl's Pagoda.** No one would come to this small upstairs restaurant looking for atmosphere, but its devoted clientele raves about the outstanding Cantonese cuisine, particularly the tomato soup, clams in black bean sauce, ginger shrimp, and Chinese sausages with vegetables. The knowing or adventuresome diner will simply ask Carl to prepare a meal and expect to be surprised, for some of his special dishes are not on the menu. *23 Tyler St., tel. 617/357–9837. Reservations advised for large parties. Dress: informal. No credit cards. No lunch. No liquor. Moderate.*

Weylu's Wharf. On the waterfront, with a view of the Boston skyline, Weylu's specializes in Mandarin and Szechuan cuisine. To such traditional dishes as hot and sour soup and moo shu pork, the chef has added new specialties, among them *fu young three-treasure* (shrimp, chicken, scallops, and vegetables in white wine sauce) and General Tso's Chicken, a deep-fried chicken dish in a tangy, orange sauce. Try also the scallion pancakes and crispy aromatic beef. The decor is contemporary Chinese, set in peach and green. *254 Summer St., tel. 617/423–0243. Reservations accepted. Dress: informal. AE, D, MC, V. Moderate.*

★ **Ho Yuen Ting.** Every night a waiting line forms outside this Chinatown hole-in-the-wall. The reason is simple: Ho Yuen Ting serves some of the best seafood in town. The house specialty is a sole and vegetable stir-fry served in a spectacular whole, crisply fried fish. Come with friends so you can also enjoy the clams with black bean sauce, lobster with ginger and scallion, and whole steamed bass. *13A Hudson St., tel. 617/426–2316. Reservations accepted for 7 or more. Dress: informal. No credit cards. Inexpensive–Moderate.*

Imperial Teahouse Restaurant. On the first floor is a traditional Cantonese restaurant with a representative menu. The livelier second floor is a large, airy dining room with the most extensive dim sum selection in Chinatown. *Dim sum* denotes both the meal (a veritable Chinese brunch, served daily 8:30–3:30) and the variety of dumplings and buns, tiny spareribs, morsels of pork, chicken, clams, shrimp, and other foods that you select from roving carts and pay for by the item. *70 Beach St., tel. 617/426–8543. Reservations accepted; the line moves fast, but expect a 15-min. wait for dim sum. Dress: informal. AE, DC, MC, V. Inexpensive–Moderate.*

Contemporary (Mixed Menu)

Cambridge **Chez Nous.** The menu changes daily in this simply decorated storefront dining room. Dinner might begin with smoked salmon, followed by roast free-range chicken and oven-poached halibut, then chocolate almond torte and raspberries for dessert. *147 Huron Ave., tel. 617/864–6670. Reservations advised. Dress: casual but neat. MC, V. No lunch. Closed Sun. Moderate.*

★ **East Coast Grill.** The chef calls his food "equatorial cuisine" to acknowledge the hot pepper and spices common in fare served near the equator. A number of ethnic dishes such as grilled tuna with West Indies sofrito, grilled sweetbreads, jerk chicken, and "pasta from Hell"—a pasta livened with inner beauty hot sauce—share the menu with southern regional specialties

such as North Carolina barbecue. The dining room is small,
bright, and very busy. *1271 Cambridge St., tel. 617/491–6568.
Reservations accepted for 5 or more. Dress: informal. MC, V.
No lunch. Moderate–Expensive.*

★ **Green Street Grill.** The tables are small, the room very plain,
the service casual, yet the chef is turning out some of the city's
most imaginative dishes. Reflecting his West Indian background, the food tends to be hot and spicy. Among the specialties are West Indian conch stewed with hot chili in a tomato and
thyme lemon butter sauce, and grilled swordfish with a spicy
white rum passion fruit lime and thyme dressing. The dishes
use lots of sauces, many of which show a decidedly French influence. *280 Green St., tel. 617/876–1655. No reservations. Dress:
informal. AE, MC, V. No lunch. Moderate–Expensive.*

Harvest. This is the sort of place where junior Harvard faculty
might come to celebrate getting a fellowship. It adopted nouvelle American cuisine early on, hosting a game festival in January or February every year that features the likes of elk and
antelope. The menu changes nightly, but always includes game
and fresh fish. The leafy patio is a good choice for an outdoor
meal in summer, and the bar attracts young, brainy singles.
The less expensive café section doesn't take reservations. *44
Brattle St., tel. 617/492–1115. Reservations strongly advised.
Jacket and tie advised. AE, D, DC, MC, V. Expensive.*

Cottonwood Cafe. This Southwestern eatery is to Tex-Mex
what Ralph Lauren is to Wrangler jeans. Sweet beet tamales, a
terrific smoked tomato sauce, and seafood paella draw a trendy
crowd. There is outdoor seating during warm weather. This
cafe is close to the Porter Square stop on the T's Red Line, and a
new branch opened recently in Boston. *1815 Massachusetts
Ave., tel. 617/661–7440. Boston: 222 Berkeley St., tel. 617/247–
2225. Reservations advised. Dress: casual but neat. AE, D,
MC, V. Moderate–Expensive.*

Casablanca. Interest in this downstairs spot has been renewed
since the restaurant switched places with Cafe Algiers and re-
vamped its menu. The back room still exudes that cool Casablanca atmosphere—with its wicker chairs, ceiling fans, and
murals. The front room is not quite as atmospheric—
banquettes are zebra striped which unfortunately gives it a
startlingly disco look—but the menu makes up for it. For lunch
try the penne pasta, with wild mushrooms, tomatoes, and a
fontina cream sauce, or grilled tuna with cous cous and squash
on the side. For dinner you can count on fresh, seasonal ingredients, attractive presentation, and interesting combinations,
such as Maine crab cakes served with chili sauce and shaved
fennel; grilled salmon; seafood cous cous; skewers of marinated
pork; and saffron fettucine. Desserts are fresh, and there is always a variety of fruit tortes. *40 Brattle St., tel. 617/876–0999.
Reservations advised. Dress: casual. AE, MC, V. Moderate.*

Grendel's Den. Housed in a former Harvard College fraternity
building, Grendel's has an unusually warm (three fireplaces),
clubby atmosphere, a downstairs bar, and an eclectic assortment of cuisines, including Middle Eastern, Greek, Indian,
Italian, and French. Diners are welcome to mix and match
small-portion dishes, which generally include such diverse
items as shish kebab, fettucine, moussaka, hummus, and
broiled fish. And there's a large salad bar. *89 Winthrop St., tel.
617/491–1160. Reservations accepted, advised on weekends.
Dress: informal. AE, DC, D, MC, V. Moderate.*

The Border Cafe. Excellent, reasonably priced Sunbelt fare—

Tex-Mex with Cajun and Caribbean touches—brightly painted murals advertising Tabasco and Dixie beer, and a small but lively bar scene has the Harvard Square crowds packed in on weekends. *32 Church St., tel. 617/864-6100. No reservations. Dress: casual. AE, MC, V. Inexpensive.*

French/Cambodian

Somerville ★
The Elephant Walk. This restaurant in Union Square (just outside Cambridge) has a loyal following. You can expect a wait on weekend evenings, but there's a pleasant area up front with wicker chairs and a small bar. This is a good place to come for well-prepared food and attentive service, without the hefty bill. Images of elephants come in all shapes and sizes, from the salt and pepper shakers on the white linen–covered tables to drawings of these mild beasts all along the walls. Large palm trees and black-and-white photographs of Cambodia also set the mood. The menu is divided into French on one side and Cambodian on the other, making it possible to begin a meal with a French appetizer like *Moules* (mussels) swimming in garlic butter, alongside delicately fried Cambodian spring rolls, which are served on a *tuk trey* with mint, basil, and beansprouts and can then be wrapped in a crispy piece of lettuce and dipped in a sweet fish sauce. Entrées include *Amok* (a spicy dish of sliced catfish with coconut milk and other seasonings, served in a banana leaf cup) and *Mee Siem* (rice noodles sautéed with pork, red pepper, garlic, shallots, Chinese chives, and beansprouts, and topped with shredded omelet). On the French side, there are such traditional choices as Canard à l'Orange and Steak au Poivre, as well as some fresh fish choices: salmon filet sautéed with a sorrel cream sauce or monkfish in an aioli sauce. The desserts are not particularly spectacular, but the custard caramel is creamy enough if you're in the mood for something sweet. *70 Union Square, Somerville, tel. 617/623-9939. Dress: casual. No reservations on weekends; reservations advised Sun.–Thurs. MC, V. Moderate.*

Greek

Cambridge
Acropolis. At the Acropolis you'll find a basic blue-and-white Aegean decor with predictable lamb dishes and Greek wines. The daily specials are a good value. *1680 Massachusetts Ave., tel. 617/354-8335. Reservations accepted weekends. Dress: casual. AE, DC, MC, V. Moderate.*

Iberian

Cambridge
Casa Portugal. Here is an intimate, genuinely Portuguese restaurant near Inman Square whose specialties include pork with clams, squid stew, seafood dishes, and native wines. *1200 Cambridge St., tel. 617/491-8880. Reservations advised for weekends. Dress: informal. AE, D, MC, V. No lunch. Moderate.*

Iruna. This Spanish restaurant, popular with students for years, specializes in paellas and seafoods and has great salads. Outdoor dining is possible in warm weather. Wine, beer, and sangria only. *56 John F. Kennedy St., tel. 617/868-5633. Reservations accepted. Dress: informal. AE, D, MC, V. Closed Sun. lunch. Moderate.*

★ **Dali.** Situated just outside Harvard Square, this gem offers a wide selection of Spanish tapas and entrées and the best list of

Spanish wines and sherries in the area. *415 Washington St., tel. 617/661–3254. Dress: casual but neat. AE, MC, V. No lunch. Inexpensive–Moderate.*

Italian

Back Bay **Rocco's.** The emphasis at Rocco's is on a colorful dining experience. The atmosphere is lavish: Two enormous brass chandeliers hang from a 20-foot ceiling decorated with murals of cherubs, maidens, and satyrs. Carved wooden fish and tropical birds adorn the tabletops. Once an "international" restaurant with a menu as eclectic as the room, Rocco's now serves Italian cuisine from all of its regions. The "experience" begins with a basket of warm crusty rolls, with soft garlic for a spread and olive oil for a dip. Sicilian baked tuna; vermicelli puttanesca; and roasted chicken cacciatora are some of the treats offered. For dessert there's tiramisù and hazelnut torte. *5 Charles St. S, Transportation Bldg., tel. 617/723–6800. Reservations advised. Dress: informal. AE, D, DC, MC, V. Moderate–Expensive.*

Beacon Hill **Ristorante Toscano.** Here is the food mama would make—if
★ mama were an expert cook in a tiny village in Tuscany. Homemade pasta and *focaccia* (pizzalike bread), fork-tender veal, succulent game birds, and a rich tiramisù are among the dishes that attract a blue-blooded Beacon Hill clientele. The exposed brick walls of the dining room are tastefully decorated with Italian scenes and antique cooking utensils. *41 Charles St., tel. 617/723–4090. Reservations advised. Dress: casual chic. AE. Closed Sun. lunch. Expensive–Very Expensive.*

Cambridge **Michela's.** One of the city's most popular restaurants, Michela's
★ boasts a menu that changes every eight weeks or so. It promises imaginative dishes such as pizza *margherita* (with five cheeses, carmelized onion, and truffle oil), roast duck with balsamic vinegar, grain olives, and duck liver crostini, and lobster and Taylor bay scallops in a broth with fennel, black pasta, and hot red peppers. All sauces, breads, and pastas are made fresh daily. The decor combines the building's industrial past (with exposed heating ducts) and soft, Tuscany colors. An atrium café serves a lighter menu, with all dishes under $12 6–10 PM Mon.–Sat. *1 Atheneum St. (the former Carter Ink Bldg.), tel. 617/225–2121. Reservations advised. Jacket and tie optional. AE, DC, MC, V. Closed Sat. lunch and Sun. Expensive.*

★ **Upstairs at the Pudding.** The Harvard Club, famed for its theatrical presentations and other high jinks, is home to this elegant restaurant featuring Northern Italian cuisine. The walls are a deep ivy green, the tablecloths pink, the setting intimate. The four-course prix fixe dinner ($42) offers an opportunity to choose from among 10 items in each course—the best way to sample Chef Deborah Hughes' diverse talents. Some examples: for the first course, *tagliatelle* with sun-dried tomatoes, French goat cheese, artichoke hearts, and Moroccan lemons; for the main course, veal scallopini with a hazelnut Marsala sauce; and for the third course, salad or a dessert such as charlotte au chocolat. All main courses are served with an array of fresh vegetables. An à la carte menu is also available. Sunday brunch menu includes Belgian waffles, Welsh rarebit, and sweet red pepper corned beef hash. *10 Holyoke St., tel. 617/864–1933. Reservations advised. Jacket and tie optional. AE, D, MC, V. Closed Sat. lunch. Expensive.*

La Groceria. The atmosphere here is informal, that of a real Italian trattoria; the restaurant is composed of several small rooms. Specialties include homemade pasta, antipasto, veal dishes, and homemade cheesecake and cannoli. *853 Main St., tel. 617/547–9258 or 617/876–4162. Reservations accepted for 6 or more. Dress: informal. AE, DC, MC, V. Moderate.*

Bertucci's. Part of a small local chain, Bertucci's turns out some of the best pizza in Boston. The ingredients are fresh and interesting, and the pies are baked over a wood flame in brick ovens, which gives them a unique flavor. Also available are salads, pastas, and calzones. There are several branches throughout the Boston area. *21 Brattle St., tel. 617/864–4748. No reservations. Dress: casual. MC, V. Inexpensive.*

North End **Felicia's.** Since the 1950s Felicia Solimine has been providing the solid Italian home cooking that has earned her the devotion not only of Bostonians but of out-of-town luminaries as well. (Luciano Pavarotti is said to go off his diet here when he's in town.) There is now a lounge on the third floor, complete with a 60-foot mural of Venice. In recent years Felicia's has been riding on its reputation, and the quality of its fare has slipped. Favorite specialties are the chicken *verdicchio*, angel-hair pasta, and cannelloni. Only beer and wine are served. *145A Richmond St., tel. 617/523–9885. Reservations accepted before 7 PM weekends. Dress: casual. AE, DC, MC, V. Moderate.*

Ristorante Lucia. Some aficionados consider Lucia's the best Italian restaurant in the North End. Its specialties from the Abruzzi region include batter-fried artichoke hearts or mozzarella in carrozza as appetizers and the chicken alla Lucia or *pollo arrabiatta* (chicken breast sautéed with a spicy tomato sauce) for entrées. Check out the upstairs bar, with its takeoff on the Sistine Chapel ceiling. *415 Hanover St., tel. 617/523–9148. Reservations accepted. Dress: informal. AE, D, MC, V. No lunch Mon.–Thurs. Moderate.*

Japanese

Back Bay ★ **Miyako.** This ambitious little restaurant in a new bilevel space on Newbury Street serves some of the most exotic sushi in town. Among its estimable hot dishes are *age-shumai* (shrimp fritters), *hamachi teriyaki* (yellowtail teriyaki), and *agedashi* (fried bean curd). The waitresses are uncommonly personable. Tatami seating is available. *279A Newbury St., tel. 617/236–0222. Reservations advised. Dress: informal. AE, DC, MC, V. Moderate.*

Cambridge ★ **Cafe Sushi.** Here is an exceptional sushi bar that will please devotees. Try the *kaki* (oyster sushi) or *anago* (broiled eel). An introductory platter is available for novices. *1105 Massachusetts Ave., tel. 617/492–0434. No reservations. Dress: informal. MC, V. Moderate.*

★ **Goemon Japanese Noodle Restaurant.** Large bowls of Japanese noodles in broth, with a mix-and-match selection of meats and vegetables, are filling fare and a considerable bargain. The contemporary decor features sleek black lacquer, yet the atmosphere is relaxed, not cold, and the service attentive. Dining at the counter lets you study the chefs at work. *1 Kendall Sq., tel. 617/577–9595. Reservations required for parties of 6 or more. Dress: casual. AE, D, MC, V. Inexpensive.*

Faneuil Hall **Tatsukichi-Boston.** Sushi and sashimi are specialties, as are pot-cooked dinners and *kushiagi* (deep-fried kebobs). Meals are served in a modern Japanese setting with Western or Oriental seating. The downstairs Lounge has live entertainment. *189 State St., tel. 617/720–2468. Reservations advised. Dress: informal. AE, D, DC, MC, V. No lunch. Moderate.*

Mediterranean

Cambridge **Anago Bistro.** The owner of the former 798 Main restaurant has passed on the reins of this intimate Kendall Square bistro to chef Bob Calderone and a 798 Main veteran, Susan Finegold. Contemporary New England fare has given way to an inventive Mediterranean menu. Pale yellow and rust glazed walls complete the transformation. This is a perfect spot for both romance and an excellent meal. Choose your dishes à la carte, or place yourself in the hands of the chef. The $30 sampling menu offers four courses that often begin with a Calderone favorite: baked vegetable casserole topped with a creamy square of peppered goat cheese and served with grilled flatbread. Other appetizers include grilled portabella mushrooms and asparagus in a sweet red-pepper sauce and grilled marinated squid served with delicate slivers of purple potatoes and light greens. For entrées, the seafood stew features a light sweet broth and the salmon is cooked to perfection and presented atop a bed of savoy cabbage, surrounded by a colorful array of snap and canellini beans. There's a generous wine list. *798 Main St., tel. 617/876–8444. Reservations suggested. Dress: casual but neat. AE, DC, MC, V. No lunch. Closed Sun. and Mon. Expensive.*

Charlestown **Olives.** This sunny version of a contemporary trattoria is well
★ worth the short trip over the Charles. Occupying an intimate, relaxed storefront space, Olives provides imaginative cooking at a reasonable price. The bistro is named for Olivia English, who runs the front of the house while her husband, Todd English, tends the wood-fired brick oven and the spit-roasting in the kitchen. The name also connotes the Mediterranean-style cuisine, which is based on the foods of countries where olives are grown. The open-face roast lamb sandwich has become a signature dish. Come early or late—or be prepared for an extended wait at the bar; this is one of the area's most popular restaurants. *10 City Sq., Charlestown, tel. 617/242–1999. Reservations accepted for 6 or more. Dress: casual but neat. MC, V. No lunch. Closed Sun. and Mon. Moderate–Expensive.*

Mexican

Cambridge **Casa Mexico.** The attractive basement dining room has Mexican tiles set in the brick walls. Among the specialties are *mole poblano*, enchiladas, and tostadas. *75 Winthrop St., tel. 617/491–4552. Reservations accepted Mon.–Thurs. only. Dress: informal. AE, DC, MC, V. No lunch Sun. Moderate.*

Mexican Cuisine. The Mexican Cuisine restaurant features authentic regional seafood specialties such as *camarones borrachos* (shrimp in a "drunken" tequila sauce), Tampico-style scallops, and tuna *en pipian* (sauce made with pumpkin seeds). There's little ambience, a high noise level, and lots of customers. *1682 Massachusetts Ave., tel. 617/661–1634. No reservations (to avoid waiting, arrive before 6). Dress: informal. AE. No lunch Sun. Moderate.*

Middle Eastern

Cambridge **Averof.** A large restaurant specializing in Lebanese and Greek cuisine, Averof caters to groups. The house features a charcoal-grilled shish kebab with onions, tomatoes, and Greek peppers; fried *calamari* (squid); and *moussaka*—layers of eggplant, chopped beef, and a cream sauce. For dessert, try the baklava. Belly dancers try to draw you into their act from 8:30 nightly. *1924 Massachusetts Ave., tel. 617/354–4500. Reservations accepted. Dress: casual. AE, D, DC, MC, V. Inexpensive–Moderate.*

Seafood

Back Bay **Turner Fisheries.** The restrained Puritan gray, blue, and white decor, subdued contemporary jazz, green-shaded accountants' lamps, and mahogany sideboards all hint that this is a tasteful fish house. A wide selection of seafood may be ordered broiled, grilled, fried, baked, or blackened, but any meal should begin with the chowder—which has been inducted into the Chowderfest Hall of Fame, having won the yearly Chowderfest competition too many times to contend. Be judicious in ordering; that chowder packs a mighty rich punch. *10 Huntington Ave., tel. 617/424–7425. Dress: casual. Reservations strongly advised. AE, D, DC, MC, V. Moderate–Expensive.*

Legal Sea Foods. What began as a tiny adjunct to a fish market has grown to important status, with additional locations in Chestnut Hill, the Copley Place Mall, and Kendall Square in Cambridge. Always busy, Legal still does things its own way. Dishes are not allowed to stand until the orders for a table are completed but are brought when ready to insure freshness. The style of food preparation is, as always, simple: Seafood is raw, broiled, fried, steamed, or baked; fancy sauces and elaborate presentations are eschewed. You can have a baked stuffed lobster or mussels au gratin, but otherwise your choice lies among the range of sea creatures available that day, cooked in their simplest forms. The smoked bluefish pâté is among the finest appetizers anywhere, and don't miss the chowder. Homemade ice creams are welcome desserts. The wine list is carefully selected, the house wine equally so. Legal also has a shop in Terminal C at Logan Airport (tel. 617/569–4622). Stop in before your flight departs, and they will package their famous chowder, pâté, shellfish and lobster for you to take home on the plane. *35 Columbus Ave., next to the Boston Park Plaza Hotel, tel. 617/426–4444. Cambridge: 5 Cambridge Ctr., tel. 617/864–3400. No reservations; expect to wait. Dress: informal. AE, D, DC, MC, V. Moderate.*

Faneuil Hall **Union Oyster House.** Established in 1826, the Union Oyster House is Boston's oldest restaurant. For nearly two decades its best feature has been a first-floor shellfish bar where the oysters and clams are fresh and well chilled—a handy place to stop for a dozen oysters or cherrystone clams on the halfshell. The upstairs rooms at the top of the narrow staircase are dark with low ceilings—very Ye Olde New England. A recent bar addition has a lighter feel. *41 Union St., tel. 617/227–2750. Reservations accepted. Dress: casual. Valet parking. AE, D, DC, MC, V. Moderate.*

North End **Joseph's Aquarium.** Joseph's is a small restaurant with a small bar and, in good weather, a view past bobbing pleasure craft to the inner harbor. The fare is straightforward seafood in a simple setting, the clientele generally businessmen at lunch, a young crowd at dinner. *101 Atlantic Ave. (Mercantile Building), at the northern end of Waterfront Park, tel. 617/523–4000. Dress: casual. AE, D,DC, MC, V. Moderate–Expensive.*

The Daily Catch. Shoulder-crowding small, this storefront restaurant in the North End specializes in calamari dishes, lobster *fra diavolo*, linguini with clam sauce—at extremely reasonable prices that compensate admirably for the lack of atmosphere. Because it's almost always crowded, a second restaurant has opened at 261 Northern Avenue, across from Jimmy's Harborside. Hours of operation vary greatly; call for times. *323 Hanover St., tel. 617/523–8567. No reservations. Dress: casual. No credit cards. Inexpensive–Moderate.*

Waterfront **Anthony's Pier 4.** This is perhaps the most famous of Boston restaurants, and diners pay a price for its popularity in waiting time, assembly-line service, and often mediocre food. If you can bear the tourist trap atmosphere, you will find a terrific view of the harbor and a menu that offers a wide variety of seafood (as well as dishes for carnivores). New England specialties include finnan haddie, clam chowder, and Indian pudding for dessert. Excellent lobsters are ordered by size. The wine list is of award-winning stature, and the house wine is first rate. In good weather the outdoor patio is a great place to wait, and there's an indoor lounge. *140 Northern Ave., tel. 617/423–6363. Reservations advised. Jacket required, tie preferred. AE, DC, MC, V. Moderate–Expensive.*

Jimmy's Harborside. Rivaling Anthony's—and preferred by many—Jimmy's is an exceedingly popular seafood establishment with a solid reputation. The bright, three-tiered main dining room was designed to ensure that every table has an unobstructed view of the harbor, and the Early American decor is enhanced by magnificent tapestries made in Appalachia. Upstairs, the Merchants Club dining room, with its China trade theme, is reserved for private functions. In addition to the many fresh seafood preparations that have long been standard fare, the menu now offers such specials as pasta primavera with a medley of sautéed shrimp, veal, and pork tenderloin. As a change from chowder or traditional bouillabaisse, try the scampi Luciana, a bouillabaisse made with white wine, cream, and a variety of fresh fish and shrimp. The wine list has been expanded and revised to showcase American wines. The Boat Bar, the scene of high-spirited camaraderie, is a favorite watering hole of politicians. *242 Northern Ave., tel. 617/423–1000. Reservations accepted. Jacket preferred after 6 PM. AE, DC, MC, V. No lunch Sun. Moderate.*

No-Name Restaurant. From its humble beginning as a nameless hole-in-the-wall for Fish Pier workers, the No-Name has grown into one of Boston's favorite seafood restaurants. It still attracts the workers, but now they share the usually crowded quarters with businesspeople, tourists, and families in town from the suburbs. An added dining room upstairs has reduced the waiting time, yet diners still sit elbow to elbow, feasting on the No-Name staples: fried seafood, boiled lobster, broiled scallops, and the fish of the day—always in generous servings. *15½ Fish Pier, off Northern Ave., tel. 617/338–7539. Reservations accepted for large groups only. Dress: informal. No credit cards. Inexpensive–Moderate.*

Thai

Back Bay **Star of Siam.** Here you'll find the cooking of Thailand, with many highly seasoned dishes. Among the selections are sautéed beef in curry sauce, sautéed shrimp with cashews, dancing squid, and *pad Thai* (pan-fried noodles). *93 Church St., behind Boston Park Plaza Hotel, tel. 617/451–5236. Reservations accepted. Dress: informal. AE, MC, V. Inexpensive.*

Thai Cuisine. Those who have business at Northeastern University, tickets for a Symphony Hall event, or simply an adventurous palate will welcome Thai Cuisine. Dishes can be very highly spiced, but the kitchen will make adjustments. The food is not merely exotica; it is well cooked, and the kitchen uses first-rate ingredients. A main course of half a duck is the only single-size entrée on the menu; the rest are the kind you order and share, Oriental fashion, with two or three. *14A Westland Ave., tel. 617/262–1485. No reservations. Dress: informal. AE, DC, MC, V. No lunch Sun. Inexpensive.*

Downtown **Montien.** A favorite with theatergoers, the Montien restaurant features dishes seldom seen on Thai menus, like *kat thuong-tong* (chicken tartlets with corn and coriander) and stuffed boneless chicken wings, called cupid wings, in addition to such Southeast Asian classics as *pla sarm ros* (spicy whole fish) and *pad Thai* (pan-fried noodles). Decorated with canopied booths, chandeliers, and a large centerpiece of silk flowers, the dining room has a romantic atmosphere. *63 Stuart St., tel. 617/338–5600. Reservations advised for large parties. Dress: casual. AE, D, DC, MC, V. No lunch weekends. Moderate.*

Chinatown **Siam Square.** Black-and-white photographs of Thailand hanging on peach-colored walls are the only ornament in this bright, clean restaurant with formica tables, but you won't notice the ambience once the food arrives. In addition to the ubiquitous *satay* (grilled chicken or beef strips served with a sweet and tangy peanut sauce) and *pad Thai* (pan-fried rice noodles with shrimp, egg, and vegetables), Siam Square offers a wonderful assortment of fish, steamed with ginger or deep fried and served with Tamarind sauce. Begin with the *tod mun* (minced shrimp and codfish cakes served with a cucumber sauce) or the grilled pork salad. Vegetarians will also be happy with the selection, which includes tofu pad Thai and Siam string beans. *86 Harrison Ave., tel. 617/338–7706. Reservations accepted. Dress: informal. AE, MC, V. Inexpensive.*

8 Lodging

Boston can be an expensive city in which to stay. A significant number of hotels have been built in recent years, and most of them fall in the *Expensive* to *Very Expensive* price range. Even some of the old, moderately priced standbys, such as the Lenox Hotel, have remodeled and raised their tariffs.

The good news is that many of the city's most costly lodging places offer very attractively priced weekend packages. These weekend rates (and their availability) will vary; for a free copy of the *Boston Travel Planner*, contact the Greater Boston Convention and Visitors Bureau (Box 490, Prudential Tower, Boston, MA 02199, tel. 617/536–4100).

Hotel facilities in Cambridge are severely limited and tend to be fully booked well in advance of such periods as student registration, football weekends, university commencements, and the autumn turning of the leaves. Three major hotels are located near the river, an awkward distance from public transport but easily accessible by car (and the views are fine).

Travelers who seek alternatives to hotel accommodations will find a variety of options in bed-and-breakfast establishments, hostels, YMCA and YWCA facilities, and rental apartments.

Hotels

The hotel reviews here are grouped first according to the price categories described below. While each category is defined only by specific dollar amounts, the hotels we have selected within a given category tend to share certain characteristics.

Very Expensive hotels tend to be either Boston traditions that deserve their continued reputations or new hotels that have set their sights high and are living up to their ambitions. Impeccable service is a hallmark; nearly all provide 24-hour room service and knowledgeable concierges, and fine dining is to be expected.

Expensive hotels offer much the same quality in room appointments, but they are often larger and their service less personal. Here are the better hotels catering to business travelers, usually of good value, with less of the grand manner.

Moderate hotels generally cost less because they emphasize comfortable accommodations rather than exceptional service, because their location is peripheral, or perhaps because they have been eclipsed by pretentious neighbors and have settled into a more modest niche.

Inexpensive hotels and motels are those that provide the clean basics without concern for replacing every cracked tile.

Within each price category, the hotel reviews are grouped by location. Visitors have an extensive choice of hotel location. There are hotels throughout the Back Bay, the Fens, Downtown Boston, in the Old West End, at Logan Airport, and in Cambridge.

The major hotel chains represented in Boston and Cambridge are Hilton, Holiday Inn, Howard Johnson, Hyatt, Marriott, Omni, Sheraton, Sonesta, and Westin.

With the area's many colleges, conventions, and tourist attractions, hotels generally maintain a very high rate of occupancy, particularly in spring, summer, and fall. To avoid inconvenience and frustration, do not arrive without a confirmed reservation.

Keep in mind that the prices of hotel rooms do not generally include parking, an expense that can run $10–$15 or more a night. A Massachusetts occupancy tax of 9.7% is added to all hotel bills.

The following rate categories apply to regular weekday rates for a double room for two, excluding tax and service charges. They do not reflect special weekend or package rates or seasonal promotions.

Category	Cost*
Very Expensive	over $195
Expensive	$150–$195
Moderate	$95–$150
Inexpensive	under $95

double room; add 9.7% state tax

The following credit card abbreviations are used: AE, American Express; D, Discover Card; DC, Diners Club; MC, MasterCard; V, Visa.

The most highly recommended properties are indicated by a star ★.

Very Expensive
Back Bay
★

Copley Plaza. The stately, bow-fronted classic among Boston hotels, built in 1912, acquired a new owner at the start of 1989, and has since been elegantly renovated. Guest rooms have carpeting from England, customized furniture from Italy, and new bathroom fixtures surrounded by marble tile. The Plaza Bar, rich in mahogany, has seating to accommodate a smoky piano bar; Copley's Bar has been redone. A separate concierge area has been created. The hotel staff is multilingual, children under 18 stay free in their parents' room, and pets are welcome. *138 St. James Ave., 02116, tel. 617/267–5300 or 800/826–7539. 319 rooms, 51 suites. Facilities: 2 restaurants, 2 bars, beauty and barber salons. AE, DC, MC, V.*

★ **Four Seasons.** The only hotel (other than the Ritz) to overlook the Public Garden, the newer 15-story Four Seasons specializes in luxurious personal service, old-world elegance, and comfort. The rooms have king-size beds, individual climate control, minibars, HBO, and 24-hour room service. A room overlooking the Garden is worth the extra money. The antique-filled public rooms include a relaxed piano lounge, and Aujourd'hui, a fine restaurant serving American cuisine. Small pets are welcome. *200 Boylston St., 02116, tel. 617/338–4400 or 800/332–3442. 288 rooms and suites. Facilities: lounge, concierge, heated indoor pool, sauna, exercise machines, whirlpool, valet parking. AE, DC, MC, V.*

Lenox Hotel. Constructed in 1900, the Lenox has long been a comfortable—if unexciting—hotel popular with those on a budget, but extensive renovations have transformed it into an elegant selection. Originally the Waldorf-Astoria, the Lenox has wide corridors that are now freshly carpeted and papered. The soundproofed guest rooms have spacious walk-in closets, color TV, AM/FM radio, and air-conditioning. Bathrooms come equipped with hair dryers, shaving mirrors, and amenities.

The decor is Early American or Chinese on the lower floors, French Provincial on the top floor. Structural renovations have uncovered a number of handsome archways and elaborate moldings, particularly in the airy and spacious corner rooms, where there are even some working fireplaces. The lobby is ornate and handsome, trimmed in blues and golds and set off by a large, welcoming fireplace that evokes the ambience of a country inn. Diamond Jim's Piano Bar, with its loyal local clientele, was recently remodeled, and an added wheelchair lift has improved accessibility to both Diamond Jim's and the main lobby. Children under 18 stay free in their parents' room. *710 Boylston St., 02116, tel. 617/536–5300 or 800/225–7676. 222 rooms. Facilities: 2 restaurants, valet service, valet pay parking, baby-sitting service, shuttle service to airport. AE, DC, MC, V.*

★ **Ritz-Carlton.** Since 1927 this hotel overlooking the Public Garden has been one of the most luxurious and elegant places to stay in Boston, and many people consider it the only place to stay in town. Its reputation for quality and service (there are two staff members for every guest) continues. All the rooms are traditionally furnished and equipped with bathroom phones and refrigerators. The most coveted rooms remain the suites in the older section, which have working fireplaces and the best views of the Public Garden. For an extra charge, guests can enjoy accommodations on the top three floors, with their own private club. Public rooms include the elegant café, with a window on chic Newbury Street; the sumptuous main dining room; the sedate Street Bar; and The Lounge. Small pets are welcome. *Arlington and Newbury Sts., tel. 617/536–5700 or 800/241–3333. 280 rooms, including 48 suites. Facilities: exercise room, affiliation with an excellent spa one block away, valet parking, concierge, 24-hr room service, laundry service, barber salon, multilingual staff, baby-sitting. AE, DC, MC, V.*

The Westin. The second of the two anchor hotels of Copley Place, with a skybridge connecting it to the shopping galleries, the 36-story Westin is one of Boston's tallest hotels. The rooms are big and handsomely furnished in an updated Queen Anne style; those on the Charles River side offer wonderful views. The restaurants include the Brasserie, the Ten Huntington Bar and Grill, and Turner Fisheries Bar and Restaurant, with an oyster bar. Small pets are welcome. *Copley Pl., tel. 617/262–9600 or 800/228–3000. 804 rooms, including 48 suites. Facilities: 3 restaurants, shops, excellent health club with indoor pool, Jacuzzi, sauna, exercise room, valet parking (very expensive). AE, DC, MC, V.*

Cambridge **Cambridge Center Marriott Hotel.** The 26-story hotel is two miles from downtown Boston in Kendall Square. All rooms have either two double beds or one king-size bed, plus color TV with free HBO. Two floors are designated Concierge Level—more services at a higher price. Children under 18 stay free in their parents' room. *2 Cambridge Center, tel. 617/494–6600 or 800/228–9290. 431 rooms. Facilities: indoor pool with whirlpool; Universal gym with sauna, lockers, stationary bikes, sundeck in season; restaurant; nightclub. AE, DC, MC, V.*

★ **The Charles Hotel.** The 296-room Charles anchors one end of the Charles Square development, which is set around a brick plaza facing the Charles River. The architecture is sparse and modern, softened by New England antiques and paintings by local artists. Guest rooms have quilts, TV in the bathroom, and

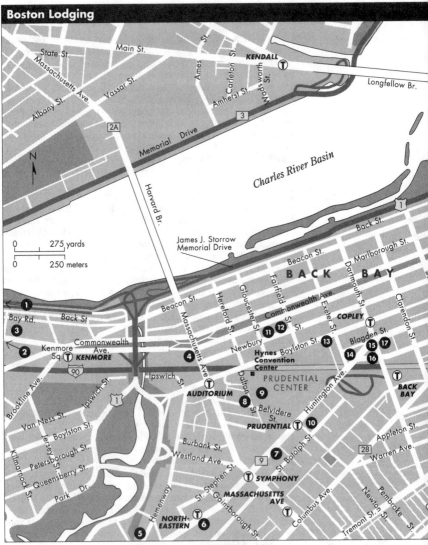

Boston Lodging

Back Bay Hilton, **8**

Beacon
Guesthouses, **12**

Berkeley Residence
Club (YWCA), **18**

Boston Harbor Hotel
at Rowes Wharf, **29**

Boston International
Hostel, **5**

Boston Marriott
Copley Place, **16**

Boston Park Plaza
Hotel & Towers, **20**

Bostonian, **27**

The Colonnade, **10**

Copley Plaza, **17**

Copley Square
Hotel, **14**

Eliot Hotel, **4**

57 Hotel/Howard
Johnson's, **21**

Four Seasons, **23**

Greater Boston
YMCA, **6**

Guest Quarters Suite
Hotel, **1**

Holiday Inn, **24**

Hotel Meridien, **31**

Howard Johnson's
Boston Southeast, **34**

Howard Johnson's
Kenmore Square, **3**

Lenox Hotel, **13**

Logan Airport
Hilton, **26**

Marriott Long
Wharf, **28**

Midtown Hotel, **7**

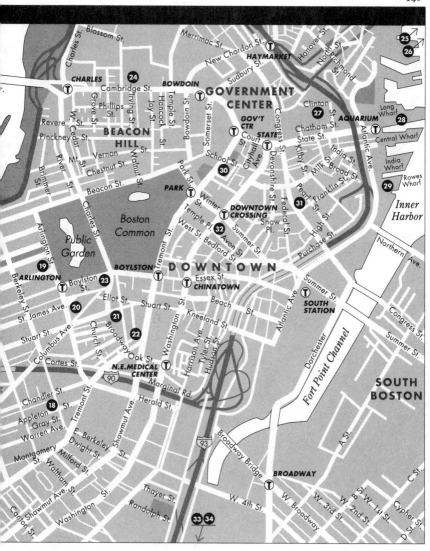

Newbury Guest House, **11**

Omni Parker House, **30**

Ramada Hotel, **25**

Ritz-Carlton, **19**

Sheraton Boston Hotel & Towers, **9**

Susse Chalet Motor Lodges, **33**

Swissôtel, **32**

Terrace Motor Lodge Best Western, **2**

Tremont House, **22**

The Westin, **15**

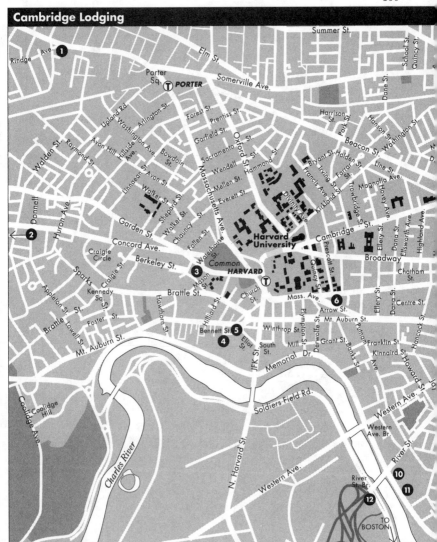

Cambridge Lodging

Cambridge Center
Marriott Hotel, **8**

Cambridge House Bed
and Breakfast, **1**

Cambridge YMCA, **7**

The Charles Hotel, **4**

Guest Quarters Suite
Hotel, **12**

Harvard Manor
House, **5**

Howard Johnson's
Cambridge, **10**

Hyatt Regency, **11**

The Inn at Harvard, **6**

Royal Sonesta Hotel, **9**

Sheraton
Commander, **3**

Susse Chalet Inn, **2**

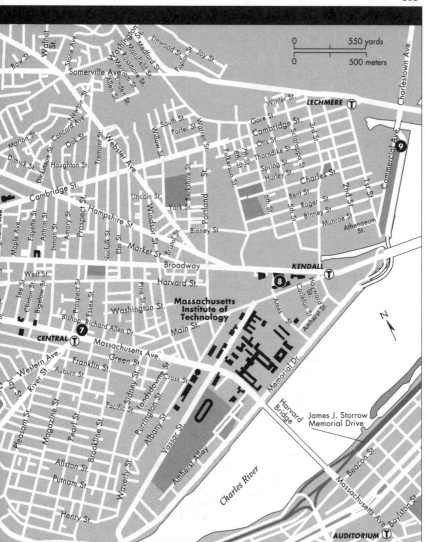

an honor bar. Though it is a new hotel, furniture and carpeting at the Charles were refurbished in 1991. The dining room, Rarities, serves New American cuisine. A Sunday buffet brunch is served in the Bennett Street Cafe. The Regattabar is one of the city's hottest spots for jazz. Children under 18 stay free in their parents' room. Small pets are allowed. *1 Bennett St., tel. 617/ 864–1200 or 800/882–1818. 296 rooms. Facilities: full spa services, swimming pool, 24 shops, 24-hr room service. AE, DC, MC, V.*

★ **Hyatt Regency.** Shaped like a ziggurat, the Hyatt Regency is a dramatic building on the Charles River. A glass-sided elevator hoists you through the 14-story atrium at its center. Some rooms have private balconies, all were renovated in 1992; most rooms have views of Boston across the river. There are two restaurants, a revolving rooftop lounge, sports bar, and two shops. Children under 18 stay free in their parents' room. *575 Memorial Dr., tel. 617/492–1234. 469 rooms. Facilities: indoor pool and Universal Health Club with whirlpool, steam bath, and sauna; bicycle rental, concierge, baby-sitting service, complimentary shuttle to points of interest. AE, DC, MC, V.*

Downtown **Boston Harbor Hotel at Rowes Wharf.** One of Boston's most ele-
★ gant luxury hotels is located right on the water, providing a dramatic entryway to the city for travelers arriving from Logan Airport via the water shuttle, which docks at the hotel. The Boston Harbor Hotel is part of an award-winning 15-story development recently completed at Rowes Wharf. With its dramatic 80-foot grand arch, it includes Foster's Rotunda, a copper-domed observatory that provides striking views of the harbor and city. The hotel is within walking distance of Faneuil Hall, downtown, the New England Aquarium, and the North End. The guest rooms have either a city view or a water view; the decor has hints of mauve or green and cream, and the traditional furnishings include a king-size bed, sitting area, minibar, and remote control TV. The bathrooms have phones, guest bathrobes, hair dryers, and amenity kits. Some rooms have balconies. The hotel is proud of its collection of more than 100 works of art celebrating the historical and artistic traditions of the city, all on display in the public spaces on the first and second floors. The hotel is also the home of the annual Boston Wine Festival each January through April. The elegant and comfortable Rowes Wharf Restaurant offers seafood and American regional cuisine as well as sweeping harbor views. The spectacular Sunday brunch is expensive at $35 per person but worthwhile for those with healthy appetites, or children under 12, who eat for free. There is also an outdoor café and a bar. Small pets are welcome. *70 Rowes Wharf, 02110, tel. 617/ 439–7000 or 800/752–7077. 230 rooms, including 26 suites. Facilities: health club and spa with 60-foot lap pool, whirlpool, sauna, steam and massage rooms; concierge, hair salons, gift shop, business center, marina, commuter boat to the South Shore, water shuttle, valet parking. AE, DC, MC, V.*

Bostonian. One of the city's smallest hotels and one of its most charming, the Bostonian epitomizes European-style elegance, with fresh flowers in its rooms, private balconies, and French doors. The Harkness Wing, constructed originally in 1824, has rooms with working fireplaces, exposed beam ceilings, and brick walls. The rooms tend to be small but are extremely comfortable, equipped with minibars and dual-line phone systems.

All bathrooms have telephones and oversize bathtubs. The service is attentive, and the highly regarded Seasons Restaurant has a glass-enclosed rooftop overlooking the marketplace. Children under 12 stay free in their parents' room. Some pets are allowed. *Faneuil Hall Marketplace, 02109, tel. 617/523–3600 or 800/343–0922. 152 rooms. Facilities: Jacuzzi in some suites, 24-hr room service, valet parking. AE, DC, MC, V.*

★ **Hotel Meridien.** The respected French chain refurbished the old downtown Federal Reserve Building, a landmark Renaissance-Revival building erected in 1922. The rooms, including some cleverly designed loft suites, are airy and naturally lighted, and all have been recently redecorated. Most rooms have queen-size or king-size beds; all rooms have a small sitting area with a writing desk, a minibar, modern furnishings, in-room movies, and two phone lines. Julien, one of the city's finest French restaurants, is here, as is the Café Fleuri, which serves a Saturday afternoon chocolate buffet and an elegant award-winning Sunday brunch. There are two lounges. Some pets are permitted. *250 Franklin St., 02110, tel. 617/451–1900 or 800/543–4300. 326 rooms, including several bilevel suites. Facilities: health club with whirlpool, dry sauna, and exercise equipment; indoor pool, concierge, 24-hr room service, nonsmoking floor, valet parking. AE, DC, MC, V.*

★ **Swissôtel.** Rising 22 stories above Washington Street and the new Lafayette Place, this Swissôtel borders Boston Common, the financial district, and the city's main shopping area. The designers have invested the hotel with an atmosphere of calm and elegant restraint, very much in the traditional European style. The mahogany lobby, with its Waterford crystal chandeliers and Chippendale reproduction room furnishings, enhance the genteel environment. All rooms offer complimentary Showtime and HBO, and bathroom phones. The ballroom may be Boston's most elegant. Café Suisse makes for a classy and leisurely lunch and there is also the Lobby Bar. Pets are welcome. *1 Ave. de Lafayette, 02111, tel. 617/451–2600, 800/992–0124, or (in MA) 800/325–2531. 500 rooms, including 43 suites. Facilities: health club, large indoor heated pool, concierge, 24-hr room service, multilingual staff. AE, DC, MC, V.*

Expensive
Back Bay

Back Bay Hilton. The 26-story Hilton occupies a corner pocket between the Prudential Center and the Christian Science complex and is close to the Hynes Convention Center. The Back Bay Hilton is a perfect spot for those who like quiet: all rooms are soundproofed, and there are only 16 on each floor. Tastefully decorated in warm contemporary colors, many of the standard-size rooms have balconies. Boodle's, a casual American restaurant, and Rendezvous Lounge are popular with locals as well as visitors. Children of all ages stay free in their parents' room. Pets are permitted. *40 Dalton St., 02115, tel. 617/236–1100 or 800/874–0663. 334 rooms. Facilities: fitness center, sauna, indoor swimming pool, sun deck, nonsmoking floors, lobby newsstand and gift shop, 24-hr garage. AE, DC, MC, V.*

Boston Marriott Copley Place. This is one of Boston's biggest and most ornate hotels, connected to the Copley Place shopping galleries and, by an enclosed footbridge, to the Prudential Center and Hynes Auditorium complex. The Marriott's 38 floors rise over an expansive four-story atrium that has lots of greenery and a waterfall. The rooms, tastefully decorated with Queen Anne furnishings, all have color cable TV with free HBO, AM/FM radio, and individual climate control. Four floors are designated nonsmoking. *110 Huntington Ave., 02116, tel. 617/236–5800 or 800/228–9290. 1,147 rooms including 70 Concierge Level. Facilities: 3 restaurants, 2 lounges, indoor pool, complete health club, business center, 24-hr room service, valet parking, game room, gift shop. AE, DC, MC, V.*

The Colonnade. Facing the Prudential Center from across Huntington Avenue, this small modern hotel has always seemed a little out of the way, not quite Back Bay, not quite the South End. Yet it is certainly convenient to Symphony Hall and the Christian Science Church complex, and it has a good restaurant and the Bar at Zachary's. Children under 12 stay free in their parents' room. *120 Huntington Ave., 02116, tel. 617/424–7000 or 800/962–3030. 288 rooms. Facilities: seasonal rooftop swimming pool, fitness room, valet and concierge service, multilingual staff, baby-sitting service. AE, DC, MC, V.*

Sheraton Boston Hotel & Towers. Boston's (and New England's) largest hotel and convention center is bustling and well equipped to provide all the amenities. Guest rooms are cozy, if not large, and comfortably furnished in traditional mahogany with mauve and gray accents. All rooms have color TV (with in-room movies) and wide windows. The higher floors facing the Charles River or the Christian Science Church complex provide the best views. Travelers wanting to escape the convention atmosphere should consider the Towers, which offers more luxurious and less hectic surroundings for approximately 20% more money. Small pets are allowed. Children under 17 stay free in their parents' room. Parking, with unlimited in and out, is $16 a day. *Prudential Center, 39 Dalton St., 02199, tel. 617/236–2000 or 800/325–3535. 1,250 rooms. Facilities: indoor/outdoor swimming pool with lifeguard and poolside service, fitness room, Jacuzzi, 2 restaurants, 2 lounges, business center, retail stores, concierge. AE, DC, MC, V.*

Cambridge   **Royal Sonesta Hotel.** A high-rise building near the Museum of Science and adjacent to the Cambridgeside Galleria, the Royal Sonesta has superb views of Boston's Beacon Hill across the Charles River. An impressive collection of modern art is scattered throughout the hotel and is heavily featured in the recently added West Wing. All newly decorated rooms have color TV, air-conditioning, and a mini-bar. Business-class rooms are equipped with IBM computers and printers, fax machines, and multiple phone lines. Children under 18 stay free in their parents' room. *5 Cambridge Pky., tel. 617/491–3600 or 800/766–3782. 400 rooms. Facilities: 2 restaurants, indoor heated swimming pool, courtesy van to points of interest, baby-sitting service. AE, DC, MC, V.*

★   **Sheraton Commander.** A nicely maintained older hotel on Cambridge Common, its rooms are furnished with four-poster beds. All rooms have color TV and air-conditioning, and some have kitchenettes. Children under 17 stay free in their parents' room. *16 Garden St., tel. 617/547–4800 or 800/325–3535. 176 rooms and suites. Facilities: fitness room, restaurant, lounge, business center, concierge, multilingual staff, valet service, free parking. AE, DC, MC, V.*

Downtown   **Marriott Long Wharf.** One of the newer hotels, the Long Wharf fits in nicely with the restored waterfront buildings in the vicinity of the New England Aquarium, Waterfront Park, and the North End. The rooms are not balconied, though they appear to be from the outside. Most rooms offer views of the harbor, and all rooms open onto the five-story atrium. The rooms have king-size or double beds, individual climate control and color TV with in-room movies. A small surcharge will put you in the concierge class on the top floor, with free Continental breakfast, cocktail hour, and the best views. A new business center has been installed. Children under 18 stay free in their parents' room. *296 State St., 02109, tel. 617/227–0800 or 800/ 228–9290. 400 rooms. Facilities: restaurant, lounge, indoor pool with poolside service, outdoor sun deck, health club, whirlpool, tanning salon, sauna, game room. AE, DC, MC, V.*

Omni Parker House. Said to be the oldest continuously operating hotel in America (though its present building dates only from 1927 and has had extensive renovations), the Parker House is centrally located one block from the Common and practically in the central business district. All rooms have color TV, air-conditioning, and in-room movies; some rooms have showers only. Parker House rolls, invented here, are still a feature in the main dining room, where Sunday brunch is an extravaganza. Children under 16 stay free in their parents' room. There are special rates for students. *60 School St., 02108, tel. 617/227–8600 or 800/843–6664. 535 rooms. Facilities: 2 restaurants, 2 bars, use of Fitcorp Health and Fitness Center, valet and room service, barber and beauty salons, concierge, gift shop, multilingual staff, baby-sitting service. AE, DC, MC, V.*

West of the Fens
★
Guest Quarters Suite Hotel. This 15-story hotel overlooking the Charles River is just off major highways, out of the city, and on the Boston–Cambridge line. Every unit is a suite containing a living room (with a sofa bed), a bedroom, and a bath. All suites have a refrigerator and entertainment bar, king-size bed, two TVs (with a movie channel) concealed in a custom-designed armoire, bedside desk, and armchair. One of the three telephones is in the bathroom, which is furnished with a large marble vanity and well-lit mirrors. The excellent Sculler's Jazz Club is frequented by guests and locals alike. Children under 18 stay free in their parents' room. *400 Soldiers Field Rd., 02134, tel. 617/ 783–0090 or 800/424–2900. 310 suites, including 5 bilevel penthouses. Facilities: indoor swimming pool, whirlpool and sauna, game room, exercise rooms, restaurant, lounge, downtown shuttle. AE, DC, MC, V.*

Moderate
Back Bay
★
Boston Park Plaza Hotel & Towers. Built in 1927 as the flagship for the Statler hotels, the Plaza has had extensive renovations and is an excellent choice for those who want to be at the heart of the action. The hotel is just a block from the Public Garden (of which some rooms on the top floor have a fine view), a stone's throw from the new Transportation Building, and a short walk from Newbury and Boylston streets, Copley Square, and downtown. The rooms vary in size, but all are equipped with direct-dial phones, air-conditioning, and in-room movies; some have two bathrooms. Unless you want to look out on a brick courtyard, ask for an outside room. Plaza Towers, at the top of the hotel, is an intimate 84-room hotel-within-a-hotel that offers larger and more luxuriously appointed rooms, express check-in and check-out, and more personalized service—at an increased rate. The lobby is spacious, elegant, and welcoming, with plants, crystal chandeliers, and comfortable couches. The popular Legal Sea Foods is one of four restaurants; there are two lounges, and the Terrace Room has live shows and entertainment. Children receive complimentary Swan Boat tickets and stay free in their parents' room. *64 Arlington St., 02116, tel. 617/426–2000 or 800/225–2008. 962*

rooms. Facilities: health club, 24-hr room service, overnight laundry and dry cleaning, concierge, foreign currency exchange, specialty shops, valet and garage parking, travel agency, hair salon, all major airline ticket offices. AE, DC, MC, V.

Copley Square Hotel. One of Boston's oldest hotels (1891), the Copley Square is still one of the best values in the city. It has recently undergone extensive renovations and a complete restoration of its facade, bringing it back to its turn-of-the-century look. The Original Sport Saloon has also been entirely renovated. The hotel is popular with Europeans and is European in flavor. The lobby is small, decorated in browns and subtle mauves, with oriental touches. The rooms, which are set off long, circuitous hallways, vary tremendously in size from very small to spacious. Some of the furnishings have been replaced; others will be refurbished. Yet all rooms have direct-dial phones, air conditioners, windows you can open, color TV, in-room safes, hair dryers, and automatic coffee makers with the necessary materials. If you want a quiet room, ask for one on the courtyard. The popular Cafe Budapest is downstairs. Children under 14 stay free in their parents' room. *47 Huntington Ave., 02116, tel. 617/536–9000 or 800/225–7062. 143 rooms. Facilities: use of a nearby health club for a small fee, family suites, airport limousine service, coffee shop, overnight parking across the street. AE, DC, MC, V.*

Eliot Hotel. An ambitious renovation has brought a new elegance and lots of marble to a formerly modest nine-floor, European-style hotel. The Eliot now offers marble baths, new period furnishings, and a marble-clad lobby. All rooms have air-conditioning and color cable TV. An extensive breakfast is offered for a small fee. The popular Eliot Lounge is next door to the hotel. Children under 12 stay free in their parents' room. *370 Commonwealth Ave., 02215, tel. 617/267–1607. 12 rooms, 82 suites. Facilities: valet parking. AE, DC, MC, V.*

57 Hotel/Howard Johnson's. The location is part Park Square, part theater district, which makes this centrally located hotel popular with business travelers. All rooms have color TV with free Showtime, air-conditioning, and private balconies. Children under 18 stay free in their parents' room. Pets are permitted. *200 Stuart St., 02116, tel. 617/482–1800 or 800/654–2000. 354 rooms. Facilities: 2 restaurants, heated indoor pool with lifeguard and poolside service, sun deck, sauna, free indoor parking. AE, DC, MC, V.*

Midtown Hotel. Side by side with several much more expensive hotels, the older, low-rise Midtown Hotel remains popular with tour groups and keeps a low profile. It's near Symphony Hall and the Christian Science Church complex and not far from the Museum of Fine Arts. All rooms have color TV and air-conditioning. Children under 18 stay free in their parents' room. *220 Huntington Ave., 02115, tel. 617/262–1000 or 800/343–1177. 159 rooms. Facilities: outdoor pool with lifeguard in season, restaurant, valet service, barber and beauty salons, free parking. AE, DC, MC, V.*

Cambridge
★ **Harvard Manor House.** This four-story motel in Brattle Square is the nearest lodging to Harvard Square shops and restaurants. All rooms have color TV and air-conditioning. Children under 16 stay free in their parents' room. *110 Mt. Auburn St., tel. 617/864–5200, 800/458–5886. 72 rooms. AE, DC, MC, V.*

Howard Johnson's Cambridge. This is a modern 16-story hotel overlooking the Charles River; some rooms have private balconies, and all rooms have views, some of them better than others. Children under 18 stay free in their parents' room. Pets allowed. *777 Memorial Dr., tel. 617/492–7777 or 800/654–2000. 205 rooms. Facilities: indoor pool, free parking, 2 restaurants, bar, baby-sitting service. AE, DC, MC, V.*

The Inn at Harvard. The newest hotel in the area, this understated four-story property sits on an island in the heart of Harvard Square. Owned by Harvard University and run by Doubletree Hotels, the Inn is intended to house university visitors, but it welcomes tourists and business travelers as well. Each room has cable TV and voice mail, and on the walls, original 17th- and 18th-century sketches on loan from the nearby Fogg Art Museum, as well as more contemporary watercolors. Although the guest rooms are modern, the sedate sand tones with light tapestries, the cherry-wood headboards and television cabinets, brass lamps, and well-crafted wood desks recall 18th-century America. Many rooms have tiny balconies and all rooms feature oversize windows with views out onto Harvard Square or Harvard Yard. Six of the rooms look out over the Inn's most spectacular feature, its Atrium lobby. Breakfast and dinner are served in the lobby to guests only. *1201 Massachusetts Ave., Cambridge 02138, tel. 617/491–2222 or 800/528–0444. 113 rooms. Facilities: underground valet parking, express check-in and check-out, laundry and dry cleaning services, 2 meeting rooms, business center. AE, DC, MC, V.*

Kenmore Square **Howard Johnson's Kenmore Square.** This is the best bet for those who want to be near the Boston University campus or Fenway Park. All of the recently refurbished rooms have modern furnishings, with color TV and air-conditioning. Small pets are allowed. Children under 18 stay free in their parents' room. *575 Commonwealth Ave., 02215, tel. 617/267–3100 or 800/654–2000. 179 rooms. Facilities: restaurant, lounge, indoor pool, free parking, multilingual staff, baby-sitting service, non-smoking rooms. AE, DC, MC, V.*

Logan Airport **Logan Airport Hilton.** The airport's proximity to downtown means that the Hilton is close to the action, too. The recently renovated rooms are modern, soundproofed, air-conditioned; each has color TV and pay-service HBO. There's a restaurant, sports bar, and lounge, and pets are allowed. Children stay free in their parents' room. *75 Service Rd., Logan International Airport, East Boston 02128, tel. 617/569–9300 or 800/445–8667. 542 rooms. Facilities: outdoor pool, fitness center, free parking, valet, baby-sitting service, free 24-hr shuttle service to airlines. AE, DC, MC, V.*

Ramada Hotel. The Ramada is in East Boston, 1½ miles from the airport and near the Suffolk Downs racetrack. All rooms have color TV and air-conditioning. Children under 18 stay free in their parents' room. *225 McClellan Hwy., East Boston, 02128, tel. 617/569–5250 or 800/228–2828. 350 rooms. Facilities: restaurant and bar, outdoor swimming pool, free 24-hr shuttle to airport, free "park-and-fly" up to seven days, room service until 10 PM. AE, DC, MC, V.*

Old West End **Holiday Inn.** This is the nearest hotel to Massachusetts General Hospital; it is also convenient to state and city offices and to Beacon Hill. The building's 14 floors include Foster's Bar and Grill and a grand ballroom on the top floor. All rooms have air-conditioning and TV. In 1993 all the rooms were renovated and Federalist period details added. Children under 18 stay free in their parents' room. *5 Blossom St., 02114, tel. 617/742–7630 or 800/465–4329. 303 rooms. Facilities: outdoor pool, laundry facilities, baby-sitting service. AE,DC, MC, V.*

Theater District **Tremont House.** The once-popular 12-story Bradford Hotel (closed for three years and completely renovated by Choice Hotels International) is again a welcome constituent of the Boston hotel scene. Because the Bradford was built as national headquarters for the Elks Club in 1925, when things were done on a grand scale, its spacious lobby has high ceilings, marble columns, a marble stairway, and lots of gold leaf. The 16-foot, four-tiered crystal chandelier is a replica of the original, which was made in West Germany (five similar chandeliers hang in the ballroom). The guest rooms tend to be small; they are furnished in 18th-century Thomasville reproductions and decorated with prints from the Museum of Fine Arts. (Note the authentic Elks Club brass doorknobs.) The double rooms have queen-size beds, but two double beds are available. The bathrooms also tend to be small; all have tub-and-shower combinations. All rooms have cable TV. Good news for deli lovers: One of New York's most popular spots for corned beef and blintzes, the Stage Delicatessen, has opened a deli here with a promise to truck in authentic Kosher pickles from the Big Apple. The Juke Box, a nightclub, is popular. *275 Tremont St., 02116, tel. 617/426–1400 or 800/331–9998. 281 rooms. Facilities: room and laundry service, concierge, 2 non-smoking floors, disabled accessible, valet parking. AE, DC, MC, V.*

Inexpensive **Beacon Guesthouses.** These furnished studio apartments in
Back Bay converted town houses, similar to European *pensions*, offer simple, basic accommodations. All have private baths and kitchenettes. Weekly rates are available. *248 Newbury St., 02116, tel. 617/266–7276. 20 rooms in summer, 10 rooms in winter. MC, V.*

Boston **Susse Chalet Motor Lodges.** Two practically identical motels sit side by side, just off the Southeast Expressway (I–93) in Dorchester, 5 miles from downtown Boston. Both are part of a national chain and, as such, their rooms are clean, serviceable, and dependable. Rooms have HBO and air-conditioning. Children under 18 stay free in their parents' room. *800 and 900 Morrissey Blvd., 02122, tel. 617/287–9100 or 287–9200 or 800/258–1980. 176 and 106 rooms, respectively. Facilities: coin-operated laundry, outdoor swimming pool, 2 restaurants, piano bar, 24-hr reception, free parking. AE, DC, MC, V.*

Howard Johnson's Boston Southeast. Standard motel rooms with air-conditioning are offered in this HoJo's, 4 miles south of downtown Boston, just off the Southeast Expressway (I–93). Children under 18 stay free in their parents' room. *5 Howard Johnson's Plaza, 02125, tel. 617/288–3030 or 800/654–2000. 100 rooms. Facilities: 24-hr restaurant, free parking. AE, DC, MC, V.*

Brighton **Terrace Motor Lodge Best Western.** Out beyond Boston University, almost in Brookline, the Terrace has a somewhat incongruous appearance as a motel on a city street. Yet it's economical, all rooms have color TV and air-conditioning, and downtown is just a trolley ride away. Kitchenettes are available. Children under 16 stay free in their parents' room. *1650 Commonwealth Ave., 02135, tel. 617/566–6260. 73 rooms. Facilities: free parking, free Continental breakfast. AE, DC, MC, V.*

62·70

Cambridge **Susse Chalet Inn.** This is a typical Susse Chalet, clean, economical, and sparse. It's isolated from most shopping or sites, a 10-minute drive from Harvard Square, but it is within walking distance of the Red Line terminus, offering T access to Boston and Harvard Square. All rooms have color TV and air-conditioning. *211 Concord Turnpike, 02140, tel. 617/661–7800 or 800/258–1980. 78 rooms. Facilities: free parking. AE, DC, MC, V.*

Bed-and-Breakfasts

A bed-and-breakfast is overnight lodging and breakfast in a once-private residence. While Boston does not have a large number of bed-and-breakfasts, there are several, and they are usually reasonably priced. Bed-and-breakfasts are becoming increasingly popular in Cambridge, and the homes listed by the reservation services named here are inspected regularly and must meet specific standards. They offer daily rates of $55–$170 per room. Reservations may be made through these central information and booking organizations, or through the inns themselves.

Bed & Breakfast Agency of Boston (47 Commercial Wharf, Boston 02110, tel. 617/720–3540 or 800/248–9262) lists 120 homes in the most visited areas of the city.

Bed & Breakfast Associates Bay Colony Ltd. (Box 57166, Babson Park Branch, Boston 02157, tel. 617/449–5302 or 800/347–5088). This service has 150 Boston and Cambridge listings.

Bed and Breakfast Cambridge and Greater Boston (Box 665, Cambridge 02140, tel. 617/576–1492 or 800/888–0178) lists rooms in 30 Cambridge homes.

Cambridge Discovery (tel. 617/497–1631). The kiosk in Harvard Square lists a dozen B&Bs in the Cambridge area.

Cambridge House Bed and Breakfast (2218 Massachusetts Ave., Cambridge 02140, tel. 617/491–6300 or 800/232–9989). A gracious 1892 Greek Revival home listed on the National Register of Historic Places, Cambridge House has 16 antique-filled guest rooms, some with private baths. All are convenient to the T and buses. A full breakfast is included. There is also a reservations center here for host homes in the metropolitan Boston area.

Host Homes of Boston (Box 117, Waban Branch, Boston 02168, tel. 617/244–1308) has listings for about 35 rooms.

New England Bed and Breakfast, Inc. (1045 Center St., Newton 02159, tel. 617/244–2112) lists 20 homes in Boston and Cambridge.

Newbury Guest House (261 Newbury St., Boston 02116, tel. 617/437–7666). This elegant red-brick and brownstone row house built in 1882 offers 15 double rooms with baths, reproduction Victorian furnishings, Continental breakfast, and a central location on Boston's most fashionable street.

Hostels

Greater Boston Council of American Youth Hostels (1020B Commonwealth Ave., Boston 02215, tel. 617/731–5430) will provide information on low-cost hostels throughout the Boston area.

Boston International Hostel is an inexpensive, youth-oriented hostel near the Museum of Fine Arts and Symphony Hall.

Guests sleep in dormitories for three to five persons and must provide their own linens or sleep sacks (sleeping bags are not permitted). There are five family rooms available with reservations. The maximum stay is three nights in summer, seven nights off-season. Reservations (only members may make them) are strongly recommended. Doors close at 2 AM. *12 Hemenway St., 02115, tel. 617/536–9455. Capacity 190 in summer, 100 in winter. MC, V. Preference given to members of the American Youth Hostel network during high season. To become a member write to The Greater Boston Council of American Youth Hostels, 1020 Commonwealth Ave., Boston 02215, tel. 617/731–5430. You may also become a member at this hostel.*

YMCAs and YWCAs

Berkeley Residence Club, run by the YWCA, provides single and some double rooms for women only. Meals are available at additional charge. There is no curfew, and the desk is staffed around the clock. Children over 6 permitted; no pets. *40 Berkeley St., 02116, tel. 617/482–8850. 200 rooms. Shared bath. TV, lounge, laundry facilities. MC, V.*

Cambridge YMCA. The accommodations are single rooms for men only, with a maximum stay of ten days. The second oldest Y in the country, the Cambridge Y will complete a multimillion-dollar renovation in early 1994. *820 Mass. Ave., tel. 617/661–9622. 140 rooms. Access to pool and sports facilities. Pay parking. Shared bath. No credit cards. No children. No pets.*

Greater Boston YMCA, near the Museum of Fine Arts and Symphony Hall, is a coed facility with single and double rooms. No children or pets. You can write in advance for accommodations. *316 Huntington Ave., 02115, tel. 617/536–7800. 60 rooms in winter, 200 in summer. Almost all rooms have shared baths; all rooms have TV. Access to pool and sports facilities, laundry, cafeteria. Free breakfast. MC, V.*

Apartment Rentals

American Accommodations (91 Charles St., Boston 02114, tel. 617/523–2757) provides short-term (weekly and monthly) luxury furnished apartments throughout the city.

9 The Arts and Nightlife

The Arts

Boston is a paradise for patrons of all the arts, from the symphony orchestra to experimental theater and dance to Orson Welles film festivals. In Cambridge, because many events are associated with local colleges, admission costs are often less than those in Boston. Good sources of information are Thursday's *Boston Globe* Calendar and the weekly *Boston Phoenix* (published on Thursday). *Boston* magazine's "On the Town" section gives a somewhat less detailed but useful monthly overview.

Boston's supporters of the arts are avid, and tickets often sell out well in advance of an event. If you want to attend a specific performance, it is wise to buy tickets when you make your hotel reservations. Some theaters will take telephone orders and charge them to a major credit card. Ticket brokers usually have tickets for a variety of events. Most of them take major credit cards, and all charge a service fee of $1.50–$5 per ticket. If you order far enough in advance, your tickets will be mailed to you; otherwise they will be held at the box office.

Bostix is Boston's official entertainment information center and the largest ticket agency in the city. Half-price tickets are sold here for the same day's performances; the "menu board" in front of the booth announces the available events. Only cash and traveler's checks are accepted. People often begin queuing well before the agency opens. *Faneuil Hall Marketplace, tel. 617/723–5181. Open Tues.–Sat. 11–6, Sun. 11–4. Closed major holidays.*
Concert Theater Sport Charge (tel. 617/497–1118) is open Monday–Friday 9–6, Saturday 9–5:30.
Ticketmaster (tel. 617/931–2000) allows phone charges to major credit cards, Monday–Friday 9 AM–10 PM, Saturday and Sunday 9–8. No refunds, exchanges, or cancellations.

Theater

Boston has long played the role of tryout town, a place where producers shape their productions before taking them on to Broadway. While many shows come to Boston in this way, there is an equally strong tradition of local theater that dates from the first cracks in the wall of the Puritan disapproval of play-acting. The Boston theater scene today is a lively one that embraces the traditional and the avant-garde, performed by a vigorous mix of student groups and professionals. Cambridge boasts a nationally respected resident theater company, stagings of off-Broadway plays, and a dependable stream of classic productions by the MIT and Harvard companies.

Commercial Theaters
Charles Playhouse (74 Warrenton St., tel. 617/426–5225). *Shear Madness*, on the playhouse's Stage II since 1980, has become a local institution; it's an "audience participation" whodunit set in a hair salon. Stage I features other popular productions.
Colonial Theatre (106 Boylston St., tel. 617/426–9366). The Colonial is one of Boston's most lavish proscenium theaters even though it is situated within an office building. Designed by Charlence H. Blackhall and opened in 1900, the Colonial remains the home of major productions, often on the way to or

from Broadway. The period decor has been richly restored and preserved.

Emerson Majestic Theatre (219 Tremont St., tel. 617/578–8727). Emerson College, the nation's only private institution devoted exclusively to communications and performing arts, has undertaken the extensive multimillion-dollar job of restoring this 1903 Beaux-Arts building. The Majestic hosts professional productions from all walks of Boston's cultural scene, from avant-garde dance to drama to classical concerts.

The Huntington Theatre Company (264 Huntington Ave., tel. 617/266–3913). Occupying a theater opened in 1925 by Henry Jewett's repertory company, the Huntington is Boston's largest professional resident theater company. Under the auspices of Boston University, with Peter Altman as producing director, the company performs five plays annually, a mix of established 20th-century plays and classics.

The Loeb Drama Center (64 Brattle St., tel. 617/495–2668). The Loeb has two theaters, the main one an experimental stage. This is the home of the American Repertory Theater, the long-established resident professional repertory company founded by Robert Brustein, one of the artistic directors. The highly respected ART produces both classic and experimental works.

Shubert Theatre (265 Tremont St., tel. 617/426–4520). Owned and managed by the Shubert Organization since it opened in 1910, the theater primarily accommodates major productions en route to or voyaging from Broadway.

Wang Center for the Performing Arts (270 Tremont St., tel. 617/482–9393). Originally the Metropolitan, this huge theater designed by Blackhall opened in 1925 as a movie palace. Restructured today for opera, dance, and drama, the theater houses large-scale productions, notably the Boston Ballet seasons.

Wilbur Theatre (246 Tremont St., tel. 617/423–4008). Another of Blackhall's handsome theaters, the Wilbur ranks as the great Boston favorite. An intimate house that features quality productions, the theater has been impeccably restored to its 1914 elegance; its portals are modeled after the Thomas Bailey Aldrich home on Beacon Hill.

Small Theaters and Companies

Back Alley Theater (1253 Cambridge St., Inman Sq., Cambridge, tel. 617/576–1253). Led by artistic director Eileen Sullivan, the regular season of eight to ten newer and experimental plays have included premieres. ImprovBoston, the area's longest-running improvisational comedy troupe, is based here.

Harvard's Hasty Pudding Theatricals (12 Holyoke St., Cambridge, tel. 617/495–5205). The "oldest theatrical organization in the United States," produces one show annually; it usually runs from late-February to the end of March, then goes on tour.

Le Grand David and His Own Spectacular Magic Company (Cabot Street Cinema Theater) (286 Cabot St., Beverly, tel. 508/927–3677). The world-famous performance mixes magic, music, and comedy in the lavish style of the turn of the century.

Lyric Stage (140 Clarendon St., tel. 617/437–7172). Housed on the second floor of the YWCA building, the Lyric presents New England and American premieres as well as the classics.

Puppet Showplace Theatre (32 Station St., Brookline, tel. 617/731–6400). Since 1974, the Puppet Showplace, devoted entirely to puppetry, has drawn on puppeteers from far and near.

Theatre Lobby (216 Hanover St., tel. 617/227–9872). This intimate theater in the round seats 175; performances of the long-running *Nunsense* are given Wednesday–Sunday.

Wheelock Family Theatre (180 The Riverway (Rte. 1), tel. 617/734–5200, ext. 147). Associated with Wheelock College, the theater encourages plays and musicals with broad appeal. The producer is Susan Kosoff.

Music

Boston excels in the variety and caliber of its musical life. Whether the offerings are classical, contemporary, experimental, ethnic, traditional, or popular, whether locally produced or imported, Boston audiences expect and get first quality. Boston has been synonymous with culture for so long that the association is now a stereotype, but it is no less true. Of the many contributing factors, perhaps the most significant is the abundance of universities and other institutions of learning, which are a rich source of performers, music series, performing spaces, and audiences.

Concert Halls **Berklee Performance Center** (136 Massachusetts Ave., tel. 617/266–1400 or 617/266–7455 for recorded information). Associated with Berklee College of Music, the center is best known for its jazz programs.

Boston Conservatory of Music (31 Hemenway St., tel. 617/536–6340). Many of the musical events here are free.

Boston University Concert Hall (Tsai Performance Center, School for the Arts Bldg., 855 Commonwealth Ave., tel. 617/353–3831). Associated with Boston University, many of the concerts here are free.

Hatch Memorial Shell. The bank of the Charles River reverberates to the sounds of the Boston Pops at a series of free outdoor summer concerts.

Isabella Stewart Gardner Museum (280 The Fenway, tel. 617/566–1401 for schedule information). Concerts in the Tapestry Room at 1:30 PM Saturday and Sunday. Admission of $4 adults, $2 students and seniors is in addition to museum admission.

Jordan Hall at the New England Conservatory (30 Gainsborough St., tel. 617/536–2412). One of the world's acoustic treasures, ideal for chamber music yet large enough to accommodate a full orchestra, the hall is home to the Boston Philharmonic.

Kresge Auditorium (77 Massachusetts Ave., Cambridge, tel. 617/253–2826). Concerts hosted by the Massachusetts Institute of Technology are given here.

Longy School of Music Pickman Recital Hall (27 Garden St., Cambridge, tel. 617/876–0956). Pickman Hall is an excellent acoustical setting for smaller ensembles and recitals.

Museum of Fine Arts (465 Huntington Ave., tel. 617/267–9300, ext. 300). Jazz and folk concerts take place in the courtyard every Wednesday evening at 7:30 from late June through mid-August (bring a blanket and a picnic). The Boston Museum Trio and numerous guest artists appear on Sunday afternoons in **Remis Auditorium** from late September to mid-May.

New School of Music (25 Lowell St., Cambridge, tel. 617/492–8105). The school offers free classical music concerts one or two times monthly. The hall is a 15-minute walk from Harvard Square.

Orpheum Theatre (Hamilton Place, off Tremont St., tel. 617/482–0680). The Orpheum hosts major acts and local favorites primarily from the rock scene.

Sanders Theater (Cambridge and Quincy Sts., Cambridge, tel. 617/496–2222). This Harvard theater provides a fine stage for local and visiting classical and folk performers.

Symphony Hall (301 Massachusetts Ave., tel. 617/266–1492). One of the world's most perfect acoustical settings, Symphony Hall is home to conductor Seiji Ozawa, the Boston Symphony Orchestra and the Boston Pops and is used by visiting orchestras, chamber groups, and soloists and for presentations by many Boston performing groups. The Pops concerts take place in May and June. The Boston Symphony Chamber Players programs and the Youth Concert Series (led by Assistant Conductor Grant Llewellyn and Harry Ellis Dickson, conductor laureate) are also given here.

Wang Center for the Performing Arts (270 Tremont St., tel. 617/482–9393). The Wang Center is ideal for big productions where acoustical considerations are less critical.

Church Concerts Boston's churches offer outstanding music programs. The Saturday *Boston Globe* provides a current listing. Among the most impressive forums are:

Emmanuel Church (15 Newbury St., tel. 617/536–3355)
First Church in Cambridge Congregational (11 Garden St., Cambridge, tel. 617/547–2724)
King's Chapel (58 Tremont St., tel. 617/227–2155)

Concert Performers Boston's reputation as the Early Music Capital of America is unchallenged. Much of the credit goes to such organizations as the **Cambridge Society for Early Music** (Box 336, Cambridge 02238, tel. 617/484–5107), which since 1951 has prompted the performance and appreciation of early music and administers the annual Erwin Bodky competition for excellence in the performance of early music.

Alea III (855 Commonwealth Ave., tel. 617/353–3340). This group, associated with Boston University, presents a season of performances at Boston University.

Boston Camerata (140 Clarendon St., tel. 617/262–2092). Formed in 1954, the Camerata offers a series of medieval, Renaissance, and baroque vocal and instrumental concerts.

Boston Museum Trio (465 Huntington Ave., tel. 617/267–9300). This group, in residence at the Museum of Fine Arts, garners high praise for skilled performances of baroque chamber music.

Boston Musica Viva (Longy School of Music, 295 Huntington Ave., tel. 617/353–0556). Contemporary masterpieces and newly commissioned works are performed.

Choral Groups It is hard to imagine another city's having more active choral groups. Many outstanding choruses are associated with Boston schools and churches.

Boston Cecilia (1773 Beacon St., Brookline, tel. 617/232–4540). This chorus, led by Donald Teeters and dating back to 1875, holds regular concerts at Jordan Hall.

Cantata Singers (Box 375, Cambridge 02238, tel. 617/267–6502). The Cantata Singers, directed by David Hoose, perform music dating from the Renaissance to the present.

Chorus Pro Musica (645 Boylston St., tel. 617/267–7442). Under the direction of Jeffrey Rink, the chorus appears with various symphony orchestras.

Handel & Haydn Society (295 Huntington Ave., tel. 617/266–3605). America's oldest musical organization, with a history of

performances dating to 1815, the society presents instrumental and choral programs. Performances are at Symphony Hall.
Wintersauce Chorale (Box 8008, Boston 02114, tel. 617/523–4634). The brainchild of George Guilbault, this group delights audiences with a concert series of lighter fare at John Hancock Hall.

Chamber Music Boston is blessed with an impressive array of talented chamber groups, some of them the product of successful undergraduate alliances. Many colleges have their own resident string quartets and other chamber ensembles, and concerts, often free to the public, are given almost every night of the week.

Boston Chamber Music Society (286 Congress St., tel. 617/422–0086). Under the artistic direction of Ronald Thomas, the society gives a 12-concert series each year at Sanders Theater and Jordan Hall.
Boston Symphony Chamber Players (301 Massachusetts Ave., tel. 617/266–1492). Members of the Boston Symphony Orchestra are the personnel of this outstanding ensemble.
Longy School of Music (27 Garden St., Cambridge, tel. 617/876–0956). A continuing chamber music series presents free performances almost every week at the school.

Concert Series **Bank of Boston Celebrity Series** (Statler Bldg., Suite 832, 20 Park Plaza, Boston, tel. 617/482–2595). This series presents 50 events annually—renowned orchestras, chamber groups, recitalists, vocalists, dance companies.
Boston Early Music Festival (729 Boylston St., Suite 600, tel. 617/661–1812). This series focuses on medieval, renaissance, and baroque music, with eight events throughout the year at concert halls and churches in Boston and a week-long festival in early June that attracts both local and international participants.
Boston Globe **Jazz Festival** (tel. 617/929–2000 for Public Affairs). An annual event sponsored by the city's leading newspaper, the festival features prominent jazz musicians and attracts thousands of fans from across the country. Performances take place over a week in mid-June, at venues throughout the city.
Charles River Concerts (729 Boylston St., Boston, tel. 617/262–0650). The programs feature young and lesser known artists whose careers merit greater exposure; concerts are given at halls throughout the city.
Midday Performances (Federal Reserve Bank of Boston, 600 Atlantic Ave., tel. 617/973–3453). Forty minutes of music, dance, opera, and other cultural programs are given in the ground-floor auditorium at 12:30 on Thursdays. You may also wish to visit the bank's non-profit art gallery upstairs, where New England–based artists mount excellent exhibits.

Concert Cruises **Water Music, Inc.** (12 Arrow St., Cambridge, tel. 617/876–8742). Classical, jazz, reggae, blues—and other music—are performed on a boat that cruises Boston Harbor on Friday evenings, mid-June through September.

Opera

Boston Lyric Opera Company (114 State St., tel. 617/248–8660). The Lyric Opera, a professional company, presents three fully staged productions each season. They have performed operas of Massenet, Mozart, Strauss, and others, and they always include a 20th-century work in their repertoire. A composer-librettist workshop is held in February.

Opera Company of Boston (539 Washington St., tel. 617/426–5300). The celebrated Opera Company of Boston, under the brilliant direction of Sarah Caldwell, has established itself as a world force in opera. The company presents international and local artists in a season of four productions that are often innovative and include perennial favorites, infrequently performed standards, and world premieres of contemporary works.

Dance

Ballet **Boston Ballet** (19 Clarendon St., tel. 617/695–6950). The city's premier dance company performs at the Wang Center for the Performing Arts. In addition to a fine repertoire of classical and modern works, it presents annual performances of the popular *Nutcracker* around Christmas.

Copley Square Ballet (667 Boylston St., tel. 617/437–9401). A small, relatively new company based at the Ana Roje School of Ballet in Copley Square, the troupe has a style rooted in the Russian technique introduced by Nicholas Legat.

Contemporary **Dance Umbrella** (380 Green St., Cambridge, tel. 617/492–7578). This group is one of New England's largest presenters of contemporary dance performances. It provides services and advocacy for the area's dance companies and presents national and international touring companies. Performances are scheduled in theaters throughout Boston. The Umbrella also offers information on all dance performances in the Boston area.

Beth Soll and Company (tel. 617/547–8771). The choreographer Beth Soll, who teaches at MIT, draws on everyday life for dance themes; her style has been linked to European expressionism. The company performs at theaters all over Boston.

Dance Collective (33 Richdale Ave., Cambridge, tel. 617/576–2737). Themes from contemporary life are explored in the collaborative efforts of three local choreographers: Judith Chaffee, Martha Armstrong Gray, and Dawn Kramer.

Ethnic **Art of Black Dance and Music** (tel. 617/666–1859). The group performs the music and dance of Africa, Latin America, and the Caribbean.

Cambridge Multicultural Arts Center (41 Second St., Cambridge, tel. 617/577–1400). The Center hosts local performers in ethnic music and dance; two galleries showcase the visual arts.

Folk **Folk Arts Center of New England** (1950 Massachusetts Ave., Cambridge, tel. 617/491–6083). This group sponsors participatory international folk dancing at locations throughout the city.

Mandala (tel. 617/868–3641). A popular group of dancers and musicians, Mandala performs lively international folk dances in full costume.

Film

With its large population of academics and intellectuals, Boston has its share of discerning moviegoers. However, while there's no shortage of first-run cinemas, including the multiscreen theater at Copley Place, it has become difficult to find cinemas that specialize in revivals and foreign films. Many former art houses have closed or converted to first-run, and aficionados must content themselves with waiting for a library or college film festival or renting a film and watching it on a VCR. Cambridge, however, is the best place in New England for finding classic, foreign, and nostalgia films.

Boston   **Boston Film & Video Foundation** (1126 Boylston St., tel. 617/536–1540) features the work of local and national independent filmmakers.

Cine Club at The French Library (53 Marlborough St., tel. 617/266–4351) shows a different French film every weekend, with screenings Friday, Saturday, and Sunday at 8.

The Classic Film Series (270 Tremont St., tel. 617/482–9393) at the Wang Center for the Performing Arts takes place from January–April. Films are shown on Mondays at 7:30 PM, but from 6–7:30 PM the Jazz Pops Ensemble plays music from the era or the movie, sometimes both. Tickets are $6, and season subscriptions are available.

Coolidge Corner Theater (290 Harvard St., tel. 617/734–2500) programs first-run movies, retrospectives, foreign films, and documentaries. Since 1990 the art deco theater has experienced a renaissance, one of three remaining houses showing alternatives to "Big Mac movies."

Loews Nickelodeon Cinema (606 Commonwealth Ave., tel. 617/424–1500) is one of the few theaters in the city that shows first-run independent and foreign films as well as revivals.

Museum of Fine Arts (465 Huntington Ave., tel. 617/267–9300) screens international and avant-garde films, early cinema, and the work of local filmmakers in the Remis Auditorium.

New England Children's Film and Video Festival (tel. 617/666–0460) comprises almost three dozen film programs at seven different locations throughout Boston. Detailed schedule information is available at public libraries in the Greater Boston area and at most Videosmith video stores.

New England Film and Video Festival (Museum of Fine Arts, 465 Huntington Ave., and the Tsai Performance Center at Boston University, tel. 413/545–2360) honors award-winning videos in animation, documentary, experimental, and dramatic categories created by New England artists. The yearly festival takes place in late spring.

Cambridge   **The Brattle Theater** (40 Brattle St., Cambridge, tel. 617/876–6837) is a recently renovated landmark cinema for classic-movie buffs.

Harvard Film Archive (Carpenter Center for the Visual Arts, 24 Quincy St., Cambridge, tel. 617/495–4700) programs the works of directors not usually shown at commercial cinemas; two screenings daily.

Somerville   **Somerville Theater** (55 Davis Sq., Somerville, tel. 617/625–5700), just two stops from Harvard Square on the Red Line, shows classics, foreign films, and first-run movies in a classic theater.

Nightlife

Boston restaurants, clubs, and bars, often clustered in distinctive areas of the city, offer a broad spectrum of evening and late-night entertainment. Live music possibilities range from new wave efforts to punk rock to sophisticated jazz piano stylings, and there are comedy clubs and discos—and bars where socializing holds all one's attention.

The Quincy Market area may be the center of the city's nightlife; it has been thronged with visitors from the day the restoration opened in 1976. Here in the shadow of historic Faneuil Hall you'll find international cuisine and singles bars among the specialty shops and boutiques.

Copley Square is the hub of another major entertainment area, and Kenmore Square, near the Boston University campus, has clubs and discos devoted to rock and new wave groups.

For Boston and Cambridge, Thursday's *Boston Globe* Calendar, a schedule of events for the upcoming week, includes an extensive listing of live entertainment under *Nightlife*. The weekly *Boston Phoenix* has another excellent listing. The monthly *Boston* magazine, while a bit less current, is a good source of information.

Bars

Boston **Bay Tower Room.** By day a private club, by night this is an enchanted spot where you sip a drink, look out over the panorama of Boston Harbor, and enjoy the music of a fine jazz trio on weekend evenings. *60 State St., tel. 617/723–1666. Open Mon.–Sat. 4:30 PM–1 AM. Call 9–5 for reservations. No cover charge. Jacket required. AE, DC, MC, V.*

Boston Beer Works. All the working tanks, pipes, and gleaming stainless steel and copper kettles used in producing beer are exposed at this "naked brewery." A complement of brews that change with the season, in addition to a regular selection, is the other draw here. *61 Brookline Ave., tel. 617/536–2337. Open daily 11:30 AM–1 AM. AE, MC, V.*

Bull and Finch Pub. The original Bull and Finch was dismantled in England, shipped to Boston, and reassembled here, an obvious success. This was the inspiration for the TV series *Cheers;* you might not find Norm or Woody, but you'll be able to hoist a few with the Beacon Hill locals who congregate here. There is often a line out the door. *84 Beacon St., at the Hampshire House, tel. 617/227–9605. Open daily 11 AM–2 AM. No cover charge. Dancing Thurs., Fri., Sat. AE, DC, MC, V.*

The Cafe. This is a pleasant spot for late-night drinks or a light after-theater dinner. A jazz harpist provides the perfect background. *Ritz-Carlton Hotel, 15 Arlington St., tel. 617/536–5700. Open daily 5:30–midnight. AE, DC, MC, V.*

Chaps. This popular gay men's bar and dance club plays 70s oldies on Tuesday and pop and disco the rest of the week. *27 Huntington Ave., tel. 617/266–7778. Open daily 1 PM–2 AM. Cover charge. No credit cards.*

Claddagh. One of Boston's many Irish pubs, with all the Irish coat-of-arms hanging by the bar, the Claddagh has an informal atmosphere. *Dartmouth St. and Columbus Ave., tel. 617/262–9874. Open daily 11:30 AM–1 AM. Live entertainment Fri. and Sat. evenings. AE, MC, V.*

Copley's. With its old-world elegance, high ceiling, and spacious bar, Copley's is a place for the proper Bostonian. A recent face-lift has made it cozier. Located in the Copley Plaza Hotel. *Copley Sq., tel. 617/267–5300. Open daily 11 AM–2 AM. AE, DC, MC, V.*

Daisy Buchanan's. A favorite hangout of athletes; you might run into Larry Bird or Mike Greenwell at the bar. The jukebox is loud. *240a Newbury St., tel. 617/247–8516. Open daily 11 AM–2 AM. No credit cards. Free hot dogs Sat. and Sun.*

Frogg Lane Bar and Grille. This is a popular spot in the heart of the swinging Quincy Market. The jukebox is very loud. *Faneuil Hall Marketplace, tel. 617/720-0610. Open Mon.-Thurs. 11:30 AM-midnight, Fri.-Sat. 11:30 AM-12:30 AM, Sun. noon-11:30 PM. AE, MC, V.*

Jacob Wirth's. The founder's portrait hangs on the wall above the large, ornately carved back bar of the establishment he opened more than 115 years ago. It's a turn-of-the-century American tavern, the kind of place where your grandfather might have stopped for a cold one on his way home from work; but also the place that was recently named one of the best bars in Boston. Be sure to wash down your bratwurst or pigs knuckles with a mug of Wirth's own special dark beer. There is an excellent selection of other beers and liquors. *31-37 Stuart St., tel. 617/338-8586. Open Mon.-Sat. 11:30 AM-11 PM, Sun. noon-8 PM. AE, DC, MC, V.*

Library Grill at the Hampshire House. Located above The Bull and Finch Pub, the Hampshire House has the atmosphere of an old Back Bay drawing room with paneled walls, moose heads, and paintings. Entertainment includes nightly piano music, a dance combo on Friday and Saturday evenings, and a Sunday jazz brunch. *84 Beacon St., tel. 617/227-9600. Open daily 11:30 AM-10:30 PM. AE, DC, MC, V.*

Plough & Stars. This traditional Irish bar has Guinness and Bass on tap and Irish, country, and bluegrass music daily from 9 PM to 1 AM. It's a comfortable, friendly, noisy place, popular with students. *912 Massachusetts Ave., Cambridge, tel. 617/492-9653. Open Mon.-Fri. 11:30 AM-1 AM, Sat.-Sun. noon-1 AM. No cover charge. No credit cards.*

St. Cloud Restaurant and Bar. This cozy, friendly bar in the heart of the South End is pleasant for a late-evening rendezvous. *Tremont and Clarendon Sts., tel. 617/353-0202. Open daily 11:30 AM-midnight. No cover charge. AE, DC, MC, V.*

Top of the Hub. A wonderful view overlooking the entire city and sounds of hip jazz make the drinks pricey but worth it. *Prudential Center, tel. 617/536-1775. Open Mon.-Thurs. 11:30 AM-12:30 AM, Fri. 11:30 AM-1 AM, Sat. noon-1 AM, Sun. 10 AM-midnight. Entertainment Tues.-Sat. No cover. AE, DC, MC, V.*

Cambridge **Cambridge Brewing Company.** Beer lovers can order a hamburger here and wash it down with a beer sampler, a pint of Cambridge Amber, or one of the other standards—the dark Charles River Porter beer is one of which they're especially proud—at this microbrewery, a favorite among the college and early 20s crowd. *1 Kendall Sq., Building 100 (where Hampshire meets Broadway), Cambridge, tel. 617/494-1994. Open Tues.-Fri. 11:30 AM-1 AM, Sat. noon-1 AM, Sun. noon-midnight, Mon. 11:30 AM-midnight. AE, MC, V.*

Cantab Lounge. A local band plays rock, blues, and jazz Wednesday-Sunday from 9:30 until closing in this friendly and informal lounge. Downstairs there's comedy and dinner Friday-Sunday. *738 Massachusetts Ave., Cambridge, tel. 617/354-2685. Cover charge. No credit cards.*

Indigo. This predominately lesbian bar plays new wave and rock on a small dance floor lit in purple neon. Upstairs is a larger dance floor. *823 Main St., Cambridge, tel. 617/497-7200. Open Thurs.-Fri. 4 PM-2 AM, Sat. 9 PM-2 AM. No cover charge Thurs. and before 10:30 Fri. and Sat. AE, MC, V.*

John Harvard's Brew House. Behind the long bar a range of ales, lagers, pilsners, and stouts are dispensed. The most popular offering is the full-bodied Mass. Bay Brewing Company's pale ale. The Brew House, frequented by a 20's crowd, smells like a real English pub. *33 Dunster St., Cambridge, tel. 617/ 868-3585. Open Mon.-Wed. 11:30 AM-midnight, Thurs.-Sat. 11:30 AM-2 AM, Sun. 11:30 AM-10 PM. AE, MC, V.*

Man Ray. This art gallery and progressive rock bar is connected to **Campus,** a jukebox bar. Thursday night is gay men's night, Sunday gay women's night. Man Ray attracts listeners of industrial, urban, techno rock. *21 Brookline St., Cambridge, tel. 617/864-0400. Open Wed.-Sun. 9 PM-1 AM. Cover charge. No credit cards.*

The Middle East. Opened in late 1992 as a venue for music in addition to very good ethnic cuisine, the Middle East is one of Boston's best clubs for jazz, world music, and rock. Three beats under one roof and a coffeehouse make it the choice for discerning listeners. *472 Massachusetts Ave., Cambridge, tel. 617/ 354-8238. Open Sun.-Wed. 11 AM-1 AM, Thurs.-Sat. 11 AM-2 AM. Cover charge. AE, MC, V.*

Wursthaus. This German restaurant is a Harvard Square landmark, and the upstairs lounge serves 160 beers from all over the world. Frequented by academic types, the atmosphere is relaxing and friendly. *4 JFK St., tel. 617/491-7110. Open Sun.-Wed. 7:30 AM-10 PM, Thurs.-Sat. 7:30 AM-midnight. No cover charge. AE, DC, MC, V.*

Cafés and Coffeehouses

Cambridge boasts one of the best concentrations of cafés and coffeehouses in the New World and Boston is trying to catch up. Whether they serve wine or coffee, pastries or full meals, the atmosphere in these places is unhurried, geared to the single diner who may read while dining, and to the couple locked in discussion. Poetry readings and music are featured at a few locations, but basically they are low-key, genial lingering spots.

Boston **Other Side Cosmic Café.** Come on over to the Other Side for a college dorm ambience, good cup of java, fruit and vegetable juice bar, and no-frills soup and sandwiches. The first floor feels like a warehouse, while the second floor has low ceilings, red velvet curtains, and mismatched furniture. The art installations change occasionally, but Sunday afternoon jazz quartets and Monday night video and films are a constant. *407 Newbury St., tel. 617/536-9477. Open Sun.-Thurs. 10 AM-midnight, Fri. and Sat. 10 AM-2 AM. No credit cards.*

Trident Booksellers Café. This café on upper Newbury Street is bohemian cool with New Age overtones. It is here you'll find esoteric books, a great selection of magazines, creative haircuts, crowded tables, and a lot of journal-writing. *338 Newbury St., tel. 617/267-8688. Open daily 9 AM-11 PM AE, MC, V.*

Cambridge **The Blacksmith House.** This is the original 18th-century house where Longfellow's blacksmith lived (a nearby stone commemorates the long-gone chestnut tree). Now operated by the Cambridge Center for Adult Education (42 Brattle St.), it houses an outstanding German bakery with indoor tables and a warm-weather streetside café. Poetry readings, concerts, and plays are staged in the Spiegel Performance Center, a modern addition at the rear of the building. Pick up a schedule of events at the bakery or next door at CCAE. *56 Brattle St., Cambridge, tel. 617/354-3036 for the bakery, 617/547-6789 for CCAE. Open* *weekdays 8 AM–7 PM, Sat. 8 AM–6 PM, Sun. 11 AM–3 PM. Outdoor café open in summer until 9 PM. No credit cards.*

Cafe Algiers. This is a genuinely Middle Eastern café with a choice of strong coffees and tea and pita-bread lunches. It's a good place to meet for a serious conversation, especially since the service is rather relaxed. *40 Brattle St., tel. 617/492–1557. Open daily 8 AM–midnight. No credit cards.*

Coffee Connection. Where serious caffeine drinkers come to get a fix, the Connection has a wide selection of various beans and brews fully described in a menu. Caffeinated and herbal teas are available, too. Numerous branches have sprung up in Boston, including 2 on Newbury Street and one each in Copley Place, Charles Street, Federal Street, and Faneuil Hall. All keep similar long hours. *36 JFK St., tel. 617/492–4881. Open Mon.–Thurs. 6:30 AM–11 PM, Fri. 6:30 AM–midnight, Sat. 7:30 AM–midnight, Sun. 9 AM–11 PM. No credit cards.*

Passim's. One of the country's first and most famous venues for live folk music, Passim's by day is a gift shop and a quiet basement setting for a light lunch or a coffee break. By night it's a gathering place for folk and bluegrass music or poetry readings. *47 Palmer St., tel. 617/492–7679. Open Tues.–Sat. noon–5 and in the evenings for shows. Tickets may be purchased at the door 30 min. before the show. No credit cards.*

Jazz Clubs

Clubs often alternate jazz with other kinds of music; always call ahead for program information and times.

The Bar at Zachary's. Laid-back but swinging jazz sounds allow listening or dancing in an intimate, comfortable atmosphere. *Colonnade Hotel, 120 Huntington Ave., tel. 617/424–7000. Open Tues.–Sat. 5–1 AM. AE, DC, MC, V.*

Marriott Hotel Terrace Bar is an airy, comfortable bar with a jazz band performing weekend nights. *Marriott Copley Place, 110 Huntington Ave., tel. 617/236–5800. Open daily 3 PM–1 AM. Cover charge on weekends. AE, DC, MC, V.*

The Plaza Bar. Boston's answer to New York's Oak Room the elegant Plaza is one of Boston's very special places. *Copley Plaza Hotel, Copley Sq., tel. 617/267–6495. Open Mon.–Sat. 5 PM–1 AM. Live entertainment Mon.–Sat. nights. AE, MC, V.*

Regattabar. Some top names in jazz perform at this spacious and elegant club in the Charles Hotel. Even when there's no entertainment, it's a pleasant place for a drink (and drinks are expensive). *Bennett & Eliot Sts., Cambridge, tel. 617/864–1200 and 617/876–7777 for tickets. Shows Tues.–Thurs. at 9, Fri. at 8 and 10, Sat. at 9 and 11. Ticket prices vary. AE, MC, V.*

Ryles. Soft lights, mirrors, and greenery set the mood for first-rate jazz by local and national groups. This is one of Boston's best for new music and musicians, with a different group playing on each floor. *212 Hampshire St., Cambridge, tel. 617/876–9330. Open Sun.–Thurs. 5 PM–1 AM, Fri.–Sat. 5 PM–2 AM. No reservations. Cover charge. Sun. brunch. AE, MC, V.*

Scullers. This 100-seat place has made a very strong name for itself by hosting such well-knowns as Herb Pomeroy and the Victor Mendoza Quintet. On the second floor of the Guest Quarters Suite Hotel, this is a cozy place to relax; all but a few tables have a direct view of the performers. *400 Soldiers Field Rd., tel. 617/783–0811. Reservations strongly advised. Admission* *varies. Shows Tues.–Sat. 8:30 and 10:30 PM. Sun. acoustic brunch 11:30–2. AE, DC, MC, V.*

Westin Hotel. Jazz bands and soloists perform throughout the week in the warm and comfortable Turner Fisheries Bar in one of Boston's best hotels. *10 Huntington Ave., Copley Sq., tel. 617/262–9600, ext. 7425. Open Mon.–Sat. 3:30 PM–1 AM, Sun. 11 AM–1 AM. No cover charge. AE, DC, MC, V.*

The Willow. Even though it's not in Boston or Cambridge, the Willow cannot be overlooked. This small club seats only 100 people or so, and its devoted patrons come to hear excellent local jazz ensembles jam. *699 Broadway, Somerville, tel. 617/623–9874. No reservations. Shows nightly at 9 and 11. Admission varies. No credit cards.*

Rock Clubs

Axis. One of three dance places stacked on top of each other in this building outside Kenmore Square, Axis attracts a "funkier" mixed crowd with its selection of urban underground music. Sunday is gay night when Axis and Avalon, below it, combine forces and permit dancers to circulate between the two clubs. *15 Lansdowne St., tel. 617/262–2424. Open Thurs. 10:30 PM–2 AM, Fri. and Sat. 9:30 PM–2 AM, Sun. 9 PM–2 AM. Cover charge. AE, MC, V.*

Bunratty's. Here's a popular, often crowded spot to listen to local hard rock groups perform every day of the year. Large-screen TV and game room. *186 Harvard Ave., Allston, tel. 617/254–9820. Open Mon.–Sat. noon–2 AM, Sun. 2 PM–2 AM. Cover charge after 8 PM. No credit cards.*

The Paradise. This small club is known for big-name talent such as Sinéad O'Connor and Robin Trower. New wave, rock, jazz, folk, blues, alternative pop/rock, and country all take turns on stage here, and the audience mix varies with the entertainment. This is a good venue for live shows; artists play here for the intimate setting. Tickets may purchased in advance at Ticketmaster (tel. 617/931–2000) or at the box office. *967 Commonwealth Ave., tel. 617/254–2052 or 254–2053.*

The Rat (The Rathskeller). This popular Kenmore Square club showcases the best of the local rock scene. The Cars got their start here. Primarily frequented by students from nearby Boston University, it has cheap drinks, pinball, video, and an incredible noise level. *528 Commonwealth Ave., tel. 617/536–2750. Open Sun.–Tues. 4 PM–2 AM, Wed.–Sat. noon–2 AM. Cover charge. No credit cards.*

Blues/R&B Clubs

The House of Blues. Co-owners Dan Akroyd and the late John Belushi's wife, Judy, opened this venue in 1992. They consider it a headquarters for blues lovers, with a museum, store, restaurant, and recording facility. Live music begins at 10 PM; Sunday offers a Gospel brunch. *86 Winthrop St., Cambridge, tel. 617/491–2583. Open Sun.–Wed. 11:30 AM–1 AM, Thurs.–Sat. 11:30 AM–2 AM. Cover charge varies. MC, V.*

Johnny D's. A mix of styles permeates this 375-person capacity club, from world beat with a dancing beat to rhythm and blues to jazz and rockabilly shows. *17 Holland St., Somerville, tel. 617/776–2004. Open Mon.–Fri. 11 AM–1 AM, Sat. and Sun. 10:30 AM–1 AM. Shows nightly except Mon. Cover charge varies. AE, MC, V.*

Nightstage. The club's two levels present top names in blues, jazz, folk, Latin, pop, and bluegrass. National and local talent are featured. *823 Main St., Cambridge, tel. 617/497–8200. Admission varies; tickets recommended in advance. Open for shows only. AE, MC, V.*

Comedy Clubs

Catch a Rising Star. A New York club of the same name owns and operates this venue, where comedy is the fare seven nights a week. Nationally known acts appear Thursday–Saturday, new talents are showcased Sunday–Wednesday. *30B JFK St., Cambridge, tel. 617/661–9887 or 617/661–0167. Shows Mon.– Thurs. at 8:30, Fri.–Sat. at 8:30, 9:30, and midnight, Sun. at 8:30. Reggae show at 10:30 Thurs. and Sun. All ages admitted to comedy shows. Cover charge. AE, MC, V.*

Nick's Comedy Stop. Local comics perform every night at this club and bar in the theater district, and occasionally a well-known comedian pops in. *100 Warrenton St., tel. 617/482–0930. Shows Fri.–Sat. at 8:30 and 10:30, Sun.–Thurs. at 8:30. Tickets $6–$12. Reservations advised on weekends. AE, MC, V.*

Stand Up Comedy Cafe. Boston's top comedians perform in this popular cabaret-style club in the heart of the theater district. *Charles Playhouse, 76 Warrenton St., tel. 617/426–6339 or 617/ 426–3737. Shows Sun.–Thurs. at 8:30, Fri.–Sat. at 8:30 and 10:30.*

Stitches. "Where stars are born," according to *Boston* magazine, and a favorite for lovers of comedy, Stitches has shows nightly except Monday. Sunday is open mike night. *835 Beacon St., tel. 617/424–6995. Shows Tues.–Thurs. and Sun. at 8:30, Fri.–Sat. at 8:30 and 10:30. Tickets $6–$10. AE, MC, V.*

Dance Clubs

Avalon. This fast-paced club is also one of Boston's largest. Near Kenmore Square, it features high-energy disco and a giant dance floor that can accommodate more than 1000 people. *15 Lansdowne St., tel. 617/262–2424. Open Thurs. 10:30 PM–2 AM, Fri. and Sat. 9:30 PM–2 AM, Sun. 9 PM–2 AM. Cover charge. AE, MC, V.*

The Jukebox VHF. The decor includes old jukeboxes and a 1954 Ford plunging into the room over the bar. The music runs to 50s nostalgia in the larger room, but there is a contemporary disco in an adjoining space. *Tremont House Hotel, 275 Tremont St., tel. 617/542–1123. Open Fri. and Sat. 8 PM–2 AM. Cover charge. No credit cards.*

Quest. High energy and house music pervade the four-floor club; catering to a mixed gay/straight crowd Thursday, a gay male crowd on Friday and Saturday, and lesbians on Sunday. Quest is the only Boston club to boast a roof deck. *1270 Boylston St., tel. 617/424–7747. Open Thurs.–Sat. 5 PM–2 AM, Sun. 8 PM–2 AM. Cover varies. AE, MC, V.*

Rachel's. Dance nightly to the disco sound or enjoy wide-screen video in the Boston Marriott on the waterfront; Rachel's is popular for late-night revelry and for its $1.99 appetizers, weekdays 5–7. *Long Wharf, 296 State St., tel. 617/227–0800. Open Mon.–Thurs. 4 PM–1:30 AM, Fri.–Sun. 11:30 AM–1:30 AM. Cover charge on weekends after 9 PM. AE, DC, MC, V.*

Zanzibar. This tropical club caters to a youngish crowd who come to dance to 70s oldies on Wednesday, live reggae on

Thursday, and a DJ on weekends. *1 Boylston Pl., tel. 617/451–1955. Open Wed.–Sat. 8 PM–2 AM. Cover varies. AE, MC, V.*

Singles

Cityside Bar. A well-known singles haven, Cityside offers live entertainment nightly by local rock groups. It's a good spot, but it can be crowded and noisy. *262 Faneuil Hall Marketplace, tel. 617/742–7390. Open daily 11:30 AM–2 AM. Cover charge Fri.–Sun. AE, DC, MC, V.*

Houlihan's. This dance place and restaurant in the marketplace area is a favorite of professional singles. The DJ provides the music for dancing. *60 State St., tel. 617/367–6377. Dance nightly 9 PM–2 AM. Cover charge after 8 PM Fri. and Sat. AE, DC, MC, V.*

Napoleon Club. An attractive and popular gay club with piano music downstairs every night and a DJ Friday and Saturday. Draws an older crowd. *52 Piedmont St., tel. 617/338–7547. Open daily 5 PM–2 AM. Cover charge weekends for dancing. No credit cards.*

Tia's. The huge outdoor patio overlooking Boston Harbor is a favorite watering hole in the summer. *Long Wharf, 200 Atlantic Ave., tel. 617/227–0828. Open daily 11:30 AM–1 AM. No cover charge. AE, DC, MC, V.*

Other Attractions

The Golf Club boasts a 14,000-square-foot, 18-hole indoor mini-golf course with a restaurant, bar, 16-speaker sound system, and large-screen television. There are no windmills here. *3 Lansdowne St., tel. 617/262–0300. Open 5 PM–1 AM weeknights and noon–1 AM on weekends.*

Medieval Manor offers a 2½ hour, fixed-price, 12th-century dining orgy that features a six-course meal, serving wenches, strolling minstrels, court jesters dictating when you are permitted to use the bathroom, and a lot of good, messy fun (there's no silverware). The food is not gourmet cuisine, but it is plentiful, satisfying a primarily under 30 crowd. *246 E. Berkeley St., tel. 617/423–4900. Open for dinner only Mon.–Fri. 8, Sat. 5 and 9:30, Sun. 6. Reservations required. $22–$32 per person, depending on the day of the week and which show or meal you attend. MC, V.*

10 Excursions

West of Boston: Lexington and Concord

The events of April 19, 1775, the first military encounters of the American Revolution, are very much a part of present-day Lexington and Concord. In these two quintessential New England towns, rich in literary and political history, one finds the true beginning of America's freedom trail on the very sites where a colonial people began their fight for independence and a new nation.

Getting Around

By Car Cross the Charles River at the Massachusetts Avenue Bridge and proceed through Cambridge, bearing right for Arlington at Harvard Square. Continue through Arlington Center on Massachusetts Avenue to the first traffic light, turn left into Jason Street, and begin your tour. Travel time is 25 minutes one way.

By Train Boston and Maine trains run from North Station (150 Causeway St., tel. 617/722–3200 or 800/392–6099) to Concord and beyond. Travel time is one hour one way.

By Bus The **MBTA** (tel. 617/722–3200) operates buses to Lexington and Boston's western suburbs from Alewife Station in Cambridge. Travel time is about one hour one way.

Guided Tours

Brush Hill Charters and Bean-Town Trolley Tours (439 High St., Randolph 02368, tel. 617/986–6100) has daily motorcoach tours to Lexington's Battle Green and Concord's Old North Bridge area from mid-February to December 1.

The Gray Line (275 Tremont St., Boston 02116, tel. 617/426–8805) offers two tours west of Boston from mid-April to mid-October: "The Grand Combination" lasts seven hours and covers 75 miles, including Boston, Concord, and Lexington; the "Lexington, Concord, Cambridge" tour lasts about three hours.

Exploring Lexington

Numbers in the margin correspond to points of interest on the Lexington map.

As the Redcoats retreated from Concord on April 19, 1775, the Minutemen peppered the British with musket fire from behind low stone walls and tall pine trees before marching to the safety of Charlestown's hills. "The bloodiest half mile of Battle Road," now Massachusetts Avenue in Arlington, began in front of the **Jason Russell House,** a Colonial farmhouse. Russell, along with 10 other Minutemen, was killed here during the Battle of the Foot of the Rocks, which involved about 1,700 Minutemen and militia and a similar number of British soldiers, near the intersection of today's Lowell Street and Massachusetts Avenue. Another 10 Minutemen and more than 20 British soldiers were killed outside. Bullet holes are still visible in the house. Adjoining the Russell House, a much newer, barn-shape building (cir-

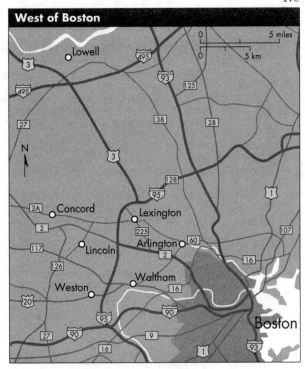

West of Boston

ca late 1970s) houses the **George Abbot Smith History Museum,** offering a contemporary look at American historical and cultural phenomena. Changing exhibits have included such varied topics as evolution of the Barbie Doll and early Jewish communities in the New World. *7 Jason St., Arlington, tel. 617/648–4300. Admission: $2 adults, 50¢ children under 13. Open Mon.–Fri. 1–5, weekends by appointment. 30-min. tours available.*

Head west on Massachusetts Avenue through Arlington Heights to the **Old Schwamb Mill** (turn off Massachusetts onto Lowell, then take the second right to Mill Lane). In 1650 this was the site of a gristmill; during the Revolution, the Battle of the Foot of the Rocks on Mill Brook took place here. Today private craftsmen produce and sell Shaker reproductions of furniture, rugs, baskets, and boxes. *17 Mill La., tel. 617/643–0554. Admission: free for drop-ins, $35 for a group of 6–10 with a full tour. Open weekdays 10–4 and on weekends for special tours (call ahead for information).*

Continue on Massachusetts Avenue through its intersection with Route 2A in East Lexington, and on your left will be the **Museum of Our National Heritage.** The contemporary brick and glass building, built and supported by the Scottish-Rite Masons, houses changing exhibits in a tasteful and subdued setting. The displays focus on America's heritage as seen through its artifacts, and there are events, lectures, and films. *33 Marrett Rd., tel. 617/861–6559 or 617/861–0729 for recorded information. Admission free ($1 donation suggested). Open Mon.–Sat. 10–5, Sun. noon–5. Closed major holidays.*

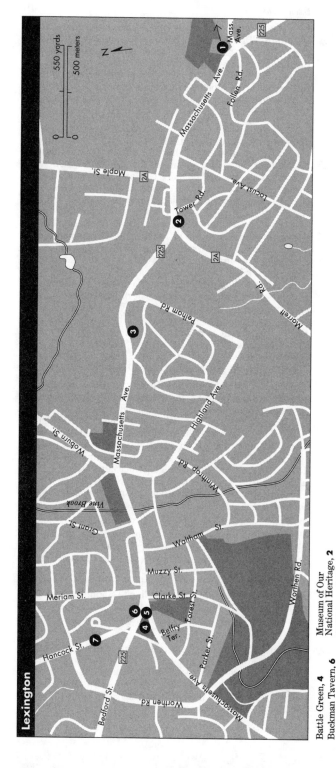

Lexington

550 yards
500 meters

N

Battle Green, **4**
Buckman Tavern, **6**
Hancock-Clarke
House, **7**
Minuteman Statue, **5**
Munroe Tavern, **3**

Museum of Our
National Heritage, **2**
Old Schwamb Mill, **1**

Less than a quarter of a mile west on Massachusetts Avenue, the **Munroe Tavern,** built in 1695 as a pub, is open to the public as a historic site. The Munroe family hid in nearby woods while the dazed and demoralized British rested and regrouped here on their retreat to Boston following their second encounter of the day with the rebels at Concord's Old North Bridge. *1332 Massachusetts Ave., tel. 617/861–0928. Admission: $2 adults, 50¢ children 6–16. Open weekend nearest Apr. 19–Oct. 31, Mon.–Sat. 10–5, Sun. 1–5.*

Massachusetts Avenue continues through the center of downtown Lexington, where it bustles with crafts and antiques stores, bookstores, and restaurants. **Battle Green,** a two-acre, triangular piece of land bounded by Harrington Road, Bedford Street, and Massachusetts Avenue is where the Minuteman Captain John Parker assembled his men to await the arrival of the British, who marched from Boston to Concord to "teach rebels a lesson" on the morning of April 19. Henry Hudson Kitson's renowned statue of Parker, the **Minuteman Statue,** stands at the tip of the Green, facing downtown Lexington. The **Revolutionary Monument** marks the site where seven of the Minutemen killed that day are buried. Captain Parker's command that morning to his 77 men, who formed two uneven lines of defense, is emblazoned on the **Line of Battle boulder,** to the right of the Minuteman Statue: "Stand your ground, don't fire unless fired upon; but if they mean to have war, let it begin here." *Visitors Center (Lexington Chamber of Commerce), 1875 Massachusetts Ave., Lexington 02173, tel. 617/862–1450. Open June 1–Oct. 31, daily 9–5; Nov. 1–Nov. 30 and Jan. 1– May 31, daily 10–4; Dec., weekdays 10–4, weekends 10–2.*

The British Major John Pitcairn was equally emphatic that morning, ordering his troops to surround the Minutemen and disarm them but not to shoot. A shot did ring out, and the rest is history. Word of the bloodshed in Lexington spread rapidly to surrounding towns. When the British marched into Concord later that day, more than 400 Minutemen were waiting on Punkatasset Hill, the high ground overlooking the Concord River and the Old North Bridge. A marker in the stone wall along Liberty Street, behind the Old North Bridge Visitors Center, announces: "On this field the minutemen and militia formed before marching down to the fight at the bridge."

Two questions remain unanswered. Who fired first? Why did Parker, a 45-year-old veteran of the French and Indian War, place his men behind the two-story, barnlike meetinghouse that stood where the Minuteman Statue stands today? (A memorial behind the statue marks the meetinghouse site.) The Minutemen couldn't see the advancing British, much less make a show of resistance. Indeed, why didn't Captain Parker tell his men to take to the hills overlooking the British route? It was an absurd situation, 77 men against 700, one of history's most celebrated accidents.

On the right side of the Green is **Buckman Tavern,** built in 1690, where the Minutemen gathered initially to wait for the British on April 19. A 30-minute tour visits the tavern's seven rooms. *1 Bedford St., tel. 617/862–5598. Admission: $2.50 adults, 50¢ children 6–16. Open weekend nearest Apr. 1–Oct. 31, Mon.– Sat. 10–5, Sun. 1–5.*

A quarter mile north of the Green stands the eight-room
❼ **Hancock-Clarke House,** a parsonage built in 1698. Here the patriots John Hancock and Sam Adams, who were attending the
Provincial Congress in session in Concord, were roused from
their sleep by Paul Revere, who had ridden out from Boston to
"spread the alarm through every Middlesex village and farm"
that the British were marching to Concord. Both Hancock and
Adams fled to avoid capture. A 20-minute tour is offered. *35
Hancock St., tel. 617/861–0928. Admission: $2.50 adults, 50¢
children 6–16. Open weekend nearest Apr. 19–Oct. 31, Mon.–
Sat. 10–5, Sun. 1–5.*

Note: The Lexington Historical Society offers a combination
ticket of $5 for admission to the Munroe Tavern, the Buckman
Tavern, and the Hancock-Clarke House.

The town of Lexington comes alive each *Patriot's Day* (the
Monday nearest April 19) to celebrate and re-create the events
of April 19, 1775, beginning at 6 AM, when "Paul Revere" rides
down Massachusetts Avenue shouting "The British are coming!
The British are coming!" "Minutemen" groups in costume partici-
pate in events throughout the day.

Exploring Concord

*Numbers in the margin correspond to points of interest on the
Concord map.*

To reach Concord from Lexington, take routes 4/225 through
Bedford and Route 62 west to Concord; or Route 2A west,
which splits from routes 4/225 at the Museum of Our National
Heritage. The latter route will take you through parts of **Minute Man National Historical Park,** whose more than 750 acres
commemorate the events of April 19; it includes Fiske Hill and
the **Battle Road Visitors Center,** approximately one mile from
the Battle Green on the right off Route 2A. *Tel. 617/862–7753.
Admission free. Open mid-Apr.–Dec., daily 8:30–5. Audiovisual programs; printed material; lectures in summer.*

❶ As you enter Concord, the Chamber of Commerce **tourist information kiosk** is a handy place to get your bearings; maps and
brochures are available here. *Heywood St., tel. 508/369–3120.
Open mid-Apr.–May, weekends 9:30–4:30; June–Oct., daily
9:30–4:30. Hours vary in winter.*

❷ Now a series of rotating art exhibits, the **Jonathan Ball House,**
built in 1753, was a station on the underground railroad for run-
away slaves during the Civil War. Ask to see the secret room.
The garden and waterfall are refreshing. *Concord Art Association, 37 Lexington Rd., tel. 508/369–2578. Admission free.
Open Feb.–mid-Dec., Tues.–Sat. 11–4:30, Sun. 2–4:30.*

Memorials to the Civil War dead will be found on Monument
Square, across from the Colonial Inn in downtown Concord.
❸ The **Wright Tavern** (2 Lexington Rd.), just off the square, was
headquarters first for the Minutemen, then the British, on April 19. The tavern was built in 1747; it's owned and maintained
by the First Parish (20 Lexington Rd., tel. 508/369–9602).

❹ At the **Old North Bridge,** a half-mile from Concord Center, the
tables were turned on the British later in the day on April 19.
Here Minutemen from Concord and surrounding towns fired
"the shot heard round the world," signaling the start of the

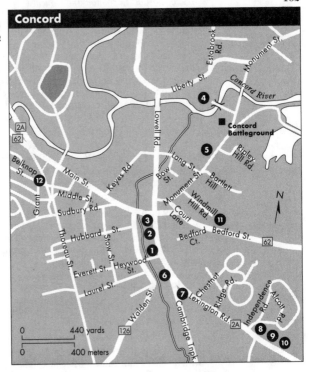

American Revolution, and here Daniel Chester French's Minuteman Statue (1875) honors the country's first freedom fighters. The Minute Man National Historical Park's North Bridge Visitors Center is a half-mile down Monument Street. *174 Liberty St., tel. 508/369–6993. Open daily 8:30–5. Audiovisual programs and printed material year-round; lectures Apr.–Oct.*

The Reverend William Emerson watched rebels and Redcoats ⑤ do battle from the back meadow of his home, the **Old Manse,** on Monument Street. The house, built in 1769–1770, was occupied by the family except for the 3½ years Nathaniel Hawthorne rented it. A 30-minute tour shows visitors Hawthorne's windowpane writings; furnishings and other details date to the late 18th century. *Monument St., tel. 508/369–3909. Admission: $4 adults, $3.50 senior citizens, $2.50 children 6–12. Open the weekend nearest Apr. 19–late Oct., Mon. and Wed.–Sat. 10–4:30; Sun. and holidays 1–4:30.*

The 19th-century essayist and poet Ralph Waldo Emerson, grandson of William Emerson, lived briefly in the Old Manse in ⑥ 1834–1835, then moved to what we know as the **Ralph Waldo Emerson House** at 28 Cambridge Turnpike. Here he wrote the famous *Essays* ("To be great is to be misunderstood"; "A foolish consistency is the hobgoblin of little minds, adored by little statesmen and philosophers and divines"). Emerson is even better remembered for the words from his "Concord Hymn" (1837): "Here once the embattled farmers stood And fired the shot heard round the world." (The lines are inscribed at the foot of the Minuteman Statue at the Old North Bridge.) The Emerson House furnishings are pretty much as Emerson left them, even down to his hat on the banister newel post. *28 Cambridge Turnpike, on Route 2A, tel. 508/369-2236. Admission: $3 adults, $1.50 children 6–17. Open the weekend nearest Apr. 19–mid-Oct., Thurs.–Sat. 10–4:30, Sun. 2–4:30. 30-min tours.*

7 The original contents of Emerson's study are in the **Concord Museum,** one-half mile southeast on Route 2A heading into Concord (with additional Emerson material at Harvard University's Houghton Library). The museum houses 15 period rooms, from Colonial to Empire; the bed in which Thoreau slept at Walden; powder horns; a diorama of the battle at the Old North Bridge; and one of the two lanterns hung at the Old North Church on the night of April 18, 1775. The museum, in an attractive country setting, occupies a 1930 Colonial Revival house. *200 Lexington Rd., tel. 508/369-9609. Admission: $5 adults, $4 senior citizens, $3 students, $2 children under 15, $12 families. Open Mon.–Sat. 10–5, Sun. 1–5.*

8 Louisa May Alcott's family home, **Orchard House,** is named for the apple orchard that once surrounded it. This was home for the Alcott family from 1857 to 1877. Here Louisa wrote *Little Women* and her father, Bronson, founded his school of philosophy. (Fourteen years earlier, Bronson, with the English reformer Charles Lane, Emerson, and Thoreau, tried to establish a Utopian community at an 18th-century farm, Fruitlands, in rural Harvard; today the Fruitlands Museum houses memorabilia associated with the venture, along with a Shaker House and an Indian artifact collection.) Nothing is roped off in Orchard House, allowing one a better sense of what life was like for the Alcotts. *399 Lexington Rd., tel. 508/369-4118. Admission: $4 adults, $3 students and senior citizens, $2 children 6–12, under 6 free. Open Apr. 1–Sept. 15, Mon.–Sat. 10–4:30, Sun. 1–4:30; Sept. 16–Oct. 31, daily 1–4:30; Nov. and Mar., weekends only 1–4:30.*

Nathaniel Hawthorne lived at the Old Manse in 1842–1845, working on stories and sketches, then moved to Salem (where he wrote *The Scarlet Letter*) and Lenox (*The House of the Seven Gables*). In 1852 he returned to Concord, bought a rambling
9 structure called **The Wayside,** and lived here until his death in 1864. The subsequent owner, Margaret Sidney (author of *Five Little Peppers and How They Grew*), kept Hawthorne's tower study intact. *455 Lexington Rd. (Rte. 2A), tel. 508/369-6975. Admission: $2 adults, under 16 and over 62 free. Open mid-Apr.–Oct. 31, Tues.–Sun. 10–5:30 (last tour leaves promptly at 5). A unit of Minute Man National Historical Park.*

10 Next door to The Wayside, the yard of **Grapevine Cottage** (491 Lexington Rd., not open to the public) has the original Concord grapevine, the grape the Welch's jams and jellies company made famous. Welch's moved its headquarters from New York to downtown Concord in 1983 to bring the company "back to its roots." A plaque on the fence tells how Ephraim Wales Bull began the Concord grape.

11 Each Memorial Day, Louisa Alcott's grave in the nearby **Sleepy Hollow Cemetery** (entrance on Route 62 West) is decorated. Along with Emerson, Thoreau, and Hawthorne, she is buried in a section of the cemetery known as Author's Ridge. A huge quartz stone marks Emerson's grave; its bronze tablet reads,

"The passive master lent his hand To the vast soul o'er which him planned." *Open weekdays 7–dusk.*

A short drive from Monument Square on Main Street to Thoreau Street, then left onto Belknap Street, takes you to the

⑫ **Thoreau Lyceum,** where the writer and naturalist's survey maps, letters, and other memorabilia are housed. A replica of his Walden Pond cabin is here. *156 Belknap St., tel 508/369–5912. Admission: $2 adults, $1.50 students, 50¢ children under 12. Open Feb., Sat. 10–5, Sun. 2–5; Mar.–Dec., Mon.–Sat. 10–5, Sun. 2–5. Closed holidays.*

Exploring Waltham, Weston, Lincoln

Other communities west of Boston, lacking Lexington and Concord's historical and literary significance, have different attractions for the visitor.

In downtown **Waltham,** a stone's throw from the Charles River and Route 20, approximately 12 miles west of Boston, the Boston Manufacturing Company experimented in 1813 with its own "industrial revolution": making a product from start to finish under one roof. The **Charles River Museum of Industry,** which opened in the fall of 1988, houses a history of American Industry from 1800 to the present that emphasizes steam power machinery. Exhibits include automaking and watchmaking, electronic equipment, and records on all the industries. *154 Moody St., tel. 617/893–5410. Admission: $4 adults, $2 children and senior citizens. Open Thurs. and Sat. 10–5, other weekdays by appointment. Closed major holidays.*

When it was obvious that the waters of the Charles were inadequate to supply enough energy to make cloth on the scale intended, the company moved its operations to Lowell, on the Merrimack River.

The other side of Waltham's industrial past can be found in two well-preserved pieces of architecture. One, the **Lyman Estate,** or The Vale, was built in 1793 by Theodore Lyman, a wealthy Boston merchant and entrepreneur. The Salem architect Samuel McIntire designed the elegant country house and laid out the surrounding grounds according to English design principles. An enthusiastic horticulturalist and gentleman farmer, Lyman erected greenhouses for the cultivation of exotic fruits and flowers. The camellias and grapevines that can be seen today are more than 100 years old. Today the property is under the supervision of the Society for the Preservation of New England Antiquities (SPNEA), which has a Conservation Center here. The house, substantially enlarged in 1882, is rented out for functions. *185 Lyman St., tel. 617/891–7095 (greenhouses) or 617/893–7232 (house). Admission to greenhouses: $2. Greenhouses open Mon.–Sat. 9:30–3:30; house open by appointment for groups of 10 or more.*

Gore Place, built nearby in 1805, is a 22-room Federal period mansion accented by a "flying staircase" that spirals three full flights upward. Built originally as the country house of Governor Christopher Gore, it now houses a museum of Early American, European, and Oriental antiques. The 40 acres of grounds includes cultivated fields, gardens, and woodlands. *52 Gore St., tel. 617/894–2798. Admission including a guided tour: $4 adults, $2 under 15, $3 senior citizens. Open Apr. 15–Nov. 15,*

Tues.–Sat. 10–5, Sun. 2–5 (last tour leaves at 4). Grounds and gift shop open daily, free of charge.

In **Weston,** further out on Route 20, the **Case Estates** (135 Wellesley St.) is a smaller version of Jamaica Plain's 265-acre Arnold Arboretum. Unusual perennials are sold here May through October.

The **Cardinal Spellman Philatelic Museum,** on the campus of Regis College, displays some 3,500,000 stamps. Director Joseph Muller's enthusiasm for the permanent collection and the special exhibits—everything from Walt Disney stamps to flower stamps—is contagious. *235 Wellesley St., tel. 617/894–6735. Admission free. Open Tues.–Thurs. 9–4, Sun. 1–5.*

Still farther out on Route 20 is **Longfellow's Wayside Inn,** restored by Henry Ford beginning in 1923. Known originally as John How's Black Horse Tavern in 1661, the tavern's name became linked forever with that of the poet Henry Wadsworth Longfellow in 1863, when his *Tales of a Wayside Inn* was published. The inn still offers "Food, Drink and Lodging for Man, Woman, and Beast."

A working 18th-century **gristmill** reproduction; the **schoolhouse** that "Mary" and her "little lamb" reportedly attended (moved here from Sterling by Henry Ford in 1926); and the **Mary Martha Chapel** are nearby.

To the north of Weston is **Lincoln,** located west of I–95 and south of Route 2, an elegant suburban hamlet that preserves more than 7,000 acres of land in conservation areas and is home to several interesting sites.

The Massachusetts Audubon Society's **Drumlin Farm** is a 180-acre working New England farm with domestic and wild animal exhibits, nature trails, hayrides, and a gift shop. *South Great Rd., Rte. 117, tel. 617/259–9807. Admission: $5 adults, $3.50 children 3–15 and senior citizens. Open Tues.–Sun. 9–5 in summer, 9–4 in winter.*

The **DeCordova & Dana Museum Park** is worth the good part of a morning or afternoon, especially on a sunny day when you can walk in and around the modern sculptures set on 30 acres of parkland overlooking Sandy Pond. Inside, the museum offers changing modern art exhibitions. Outdoor concerts are presented on Sunday afternoons in summer. *Sandy Pond Rd., tel. 617/259–8355. Admission to museum: $4 adults, $3 children and senior citizens. Open Tues.–Fri. 10–5, weekends noon–5. Grounds open daily 10–10, free of charge.*

The **Codman House,** originally a two-story, L-shaped Georgian building set amid agricultural land, was more than doubled in size in 1797–1798 by John Codman. (The design for the expansion is attributed to Charles Bulfinch.) The house is preserved with evidence of every period from the original Georgian paneled rooms to a Victorian dining room, and it is under the supervision of SPNEA. Codman also landscaped the grounds to resemble those of an English country estate. *Codman Rd., tel. 617/259–8843. Admission: $5 adults, $4.50 senior citizens, $4 students, $2.50 children 5–12. Open for hourly tours noon–5, June 1–Oct. 15, Wed.–Sun.*

The **Gropius House** was the family home of the architect Walter Gropius (1883–1969), director of the Bauhaus in Germany from

1919 to 1928. This was the first building he designed on his arrival in the United States in 1937; he used components available from catalogues and building supply stores in a manner that was revolutionary in appearance and expressed Bauhaus principles of function and simplicity. The house is under the supervision of SPNEA. *68 Baker Bridge Rd., tel. 617/259–8843. Admission: $5 adults, $4.50 senior citizens, $4 students, $2.50 children 5–12. Open June 1–Oct. 15, Fri.–Sun. noon–5; Nov. 1–May 30, the first full weekend of the month, noon–5. Tours are offered on the hour, noon–4.*

Route 2 from Lincoln will return you to Boston.

Dining

The restaurant price categories are based on the average cost of a three-course dinner (à la carte) for one person, food alone, not including beverages, tax, and tip.

The following credit card abbreviations are used: AE, American Express; D, Discover Card; DC, Diners Club; MC, MasterCard; V, Visa.

Category	Cost*
Very Expensive	over $20
Expensive	$12–$20
Moderate	$8–$12
Inexpensive	under $8

*per person; add 5% tax

Concord **Colonial Inn.** Traditional fare—from prime rib to scallops—is served in the gracious dining room of an inn of 1718. Lighter fare is offered in the lounge. Overnight accommodations are available in 54 rooms. *48 Monument Sq., tel. 508/369–9200. Reservations advised for dinner. Jacket advised at night. AE, DC, MC, V. Expensive.*
Walden Station. A casual restaurant in an old brick firehouse, Walden Station prepares American cuisine such as fresh seafood and beef filets. The fresh desserts are made on premises. *24 Walden St., tel. 508/371–2233. Reservations only for 5 or more. Dress: informal. AE, D, MC, V. Inexpensive–Moderate.*

Lexington **Versailles.** An intimate French restaurant, the Versailles serves such specialties as brie with caviar baked in puff pastry and quiche Lorraine for lunch, rack of lamb and veal Oscar for dinner. *1777 Massachusetts Ave., tel. 617/861–1711. Reservations advised. Jacket and tie optional. AE, DC, MC, V. No lunch Sun. Very Expensive.*
Yangtze River. The Yangtze is a big, contemporary-style Chinese restaurant with a good luncheon on weekdays and a dinnertime buffet Sunday through Thursday. However, if you're not particularly fond of fried foods, you may want to skip the buffet and try one of the steaming fish entrées instead. *25 Depot Sq. (right off Massachusetts Ave.), tel. 617/861–6030. Reservations only for 5 or more. Dress: informal. AE, MC, V. Moderate.*

Lowell

Everyone knows that the American Revolution began in Massachusetts. Until recently, however, little attention was paid to the fact that this state, and in particular the Merrimack Valley, was the nurturing ground of another great change in our national life: the Industrial Revolution that transformed a nation of farmers, merchants, and small tradesmen into a manufacturing colossus. The story of America's industrialization is vividly recalled in the quintessential mill town of Lowell, the site of state and national historic parks dedicated to the memory of the day when the power loom was queen along the Merrimack.

Getting Around

By Car Lowell lies at the intersection of Routes 459 and 3. Take the Mystic Bridge to I–93 and stay on I–93 to the junction of I–95. Go south on I–95 until you see the exit for Route 3–Lowell. Travel time is one hour.

By Train Trains operated by the Boston and Maine Railroad (tel. 617/722–3200 or 800/392–6099) leave daily from North Station. Travel time is one hour.

Exploring Lowell

On arrival in Lowell, head for the **National and State Parks Visitor Center** in the downtown Market Mills Complex for a thorough orientation and informative films. The center is located in what was the headquarters of the Lowell Manufacturing Company in the days when Lowell was "spindle city." You can follow a walking tour that highlights the city's history from "mill girls" to its 5.6 miles of canals. (The canals' gatehouses have their original equipment, and costumed gatekeepers play roles typical of the 1850s.) Guided tours, starting from the visitor center, are available October through April. Reservations are required. Barge rides on the canals and a trolley service, complete with replicas of turn-of-the-century cars (operates July through Columbus Day), are available. *246 Market St., tel. 508/459–1000. Admission: boat tours $2; trolley tours $2 adults, $1 senior citizens, under 16 free. Open daily 8:30–5.*

The new **Boott Cotton Mills Museum,** opened in the spring of 1992, is the first major National Park Service museum on industrial history. The Boott Mills Complex, originally constructed in 1836, underwent a multimillion-dollar restoration. The museum building, Mill #6, dates back to 1873. Visitors can watch ninety power looms at work in the weave room, or visit one of the exhibits on America's industrial history that explore such subjects as working conditions and union-building at the turn of the century. *169 Merrimack St., tel. 508/459–1000. Open daily 8:30–5. Admission: $3 adults, $2 senior citizens, $1 children 6–16, under 6 free.*

The **Brush Gallery and Artists' Studios,** located in **Market Mills,** offers visitors a chance to see local artists at work, with demonstrations on weaving, papermaking, painting, and sculpture, as well as other arts. Gallery exhibits specialize in contemporary art and change every six weeks. *Market St., tel. 508/459–7819. Open Jan.–Mar., Wed.–Sun. noon–4; Apr.–Dec., Tues.–Sun. 11–5.*

The **Lowell Heritage State Park** (25 Shattuck St.), now managed by the National Park in Lowell, boasts a major waterpower exhibit, visitors programs, walking tours, boating, fishing, and picnicking. You can pick up detailed information at the National and State Parks Visitor Center (*see* above).

The **New England Quilt Museum** displays historical and contemporary examples of the art of quilting. *At press time the museum was moving from Market Mills due to a flood. Call ahead for its new Lowell location and hours. Tel. 508/452–4207.*

Part of the fascination of Lowell is its amazing ethnic diversity, a legacy of the days when immigrants from throughout North America and Europe came here to work in the textile mills. (Today a major influx is from Cambodia, and it was a Chinese immigrant, Dr. An Wang, who made Lowell a center of computer manufacturing.) One major ethnic group to migrate to Lowell in the heyday of the mills was the French Canadians. The most famous son of French-Canadian Lowell was the poet and novelist Jack Kerouac, who was born here in 1922. Kerouac's memory is honored in the new **Eastern Canal Plaza,** where plaques bear quotes from his Lowell novels and from *On the Road.*

Two blocks from the Market Mills entrance to the Lowell National Historical Park is the birthplace and museum of another native son, James McNeill Whistler. Although the artist, who painted the classic *Arrangement In Grey and Black #1: Portrait of the Artist's Mother,* popularly known as *Whistler's Mother,* claimed to have been born in Baltimore, the Lowell Art Association purchased the gray clapboard house (built in 1823) to preserve Whistler's Lowell roots. The first floor of The Whistler House Museum of Art has a gallery; the upper floors house the collection of the society. *243 Worthen St., tel. 508/ 452–7641. Admission: $2 adults, $1 students, under 12 free. Open Tues.–Sat. 11–4, Sun. 1–4. Tours last about an hour. Closed Jan., Feb., and Tues. Mar.–May and Sept.–Dec.*

Dining

The restaurant price categories are based on the average cost of a three-course dinner (à la carte) for one person, food alone, not including beverages, tax, and tip.

Category	Cost*
Very Expensive	over $20
Expensive	$12–$20
Moderate	$8–$12
Inexpensive	under $8

*per person; add 5% tax

The following credit card abbreviations are used: AE, American Express; D, Discover Card; DC, Diners Club; MC, MasterCard; V, Visa.

The Olympia. One Greek-American presidential hopeful was born in Lowell, so it seems only patriotic that you eat Greek food when in this neighborhood. The specialty at this friendly, family-run restaurant—a favorite of workers at the nearby museums—is lamb, but the cook is also adept at preparing moussaka and a variety of fish dishes. Blue-and-white table-cloths brighten up the place; lunch specials are available. *457 Market St., tel. 508/452–8092. Reservations accepted for 4 or more on weekends. Dress: casual. No credit cards. Moderate.*

North of Boston: The North Shore

The slice of Atlantic Coast known as the North Shore extends from Boston's well-to-do northern suburbs, past grimy docklands, to the picturesque Cape Ann region, and beyond the Cape to Newburyport, just south of the New Hampshire border. It takes in historic Salem, which thrives on a history of witches, millionaires, and maritime trade; Gloucester, the oldest seaport in America; quaint little Rockport, crammed with crafts shops and artists' studios; and Newburyport with its red-brick center and rows of clapboard Federal mansions. Bright and busy during the short summer season, the North Shore is a tranquil area between November and June, when most holiday-making facilities have closed down.

Important Addresses and Numbers

Visitor Information The umbrella organization for the whole region is the **North of Boston Visitors and Convention Bureau** (Box 642, 248 Cabot St., Beverly 01915, tel. 508/745–2268). The following cover more specific areas:

Cape Ann Chamber of Commerce (33 Commercial St., Gloucester 01930, tel. 508/283–1601).

Essex North Chamber of Commerce (29 State St., Newburyport 01950, tel. 508/462–6680).

National Park Service Visitor Information (Museum Place, Essex St., Salem 02642, tel. 508/741–3648).

Rockport Chamber of Commerce Visitor's Booth (Box 67, Upper Main St., Rockport 01966, tel. 508/546–6575).

Salem Chamber of Commerce and Visitor Information (32 Derby Sq., Salem 01970, tel. 508/744–0004).

Salisbury Chamber of Commerce (Town Hall, Beach Rd., Salisbury 01952, tel. 508/465–2942).

Emergencies **Beverly Hospital** (Herrick St., Beverly, tel. 508/922–3000).

Getting Around

By Car The primary link between Boston and the North Shore is Route 128, which, just inland, follows the line of the coast as far north as Gloucester. To reach Newburyport directly from Boston, take I–95. The more scenic coastal road (it doesn't become scenic until you're north of Lynn) is Route 1A, which leaves Boston via the Callahan Tunnel. Beyond Beverly, Route 1A goes inland, and the new coastal route connecting Beverly, Gloucester, and Rockport is Route 127.

By Bus Buses between Boston and the North Shore are less frequent than the trains, but **The Coach Company** Bus Lines (tel. 800/

874–3377) offers service along Route 1 and an express commuter service between Boston and Newburyport.

On the Cape the **Cape Ann Transportation Authority** (CATA) (tel. 508/283–7916) covers the Gloucester/Rockport region and will pick up and drop off passengers anywhere on designated routes.

By Train Massachusetts Bay Transportation Authority (MBTA) trains leave North Station, Boston, for Salem, Beverly, Gloucester, Rockport, and Ipswich. Call 617/722–3200 for schedules.

By Boat A boat leaves Boston daily for Gloucester between May 30 and Labor Day, at 10 AM. The journey lasts three hours, and fares are $18 for adults, and $10 for children under 12. For information, call **A.C. Cruise Lines** (28 Northern Ave. Bridge, Pier 1, Boston, tel. 617/426–8419 or 800/422–8419).

Guided Tours

The Gray Line (275 Tremont St., Boston 02116, tel. 617/426–8805) offers a 4½-hour tour of Salem April through October, including Marblehead, and an eight-hour seacoast tour that takes in Newburyport; Portsmouth, New Hampshire; and York, Maine. All tours begin in Boston.

Special-Interest Tours The most popular special-interest tours on the North Shore are whale-watching excursions. Four breeds of whale feed in the *Whale-watching* area between May and October, and whales are so thick in the sea that you're practically guaranteed to see at least half a dozen—on "good" days you may see 40 or more. Some of the more reputable whale-watch operations include **Cape Ann Whale Watch** (415 Main St., Gloucester, tel. 508/283–5110), **Captain Bill's Whale Watch** (9 Travers St., Gloucester, tel. 508/283–6995), **New England Whale Watch** (54 Merrimac St., Newburyport, tel. 508/465–9885 or 800/848–1111), and **Yankee Fleet/Gloucester Whale Watch** (75 Essex Ave., Gloucester, tel. 508/283–0313).

Exploring the North Shore

Numbers in the margin correspond to points of interest on the North Shore map.

❶ Marblehead, with its ancient clapboard houses and narrow, winding streets, retains much of the character of the village founded in 1629 by fishermen from Cornwall and the Channel Islands. Yet today's fishing fleet is small compared to the armada of pleasure craft that anchors in the harbor. This is one of New England's premier sailing capitals, and Race Week (usually the last week of July) brings boats from all along the Eastern seaboard. But the men who made Marblehead prosper in the 18th century were merchant sailors, not weekend yachtsmen, and many of their impressive Georgian mansions still line the downtown streets.

While parking is difficult in Marblehead, you must walk through the narrow, winding streets to appreciate fully their charm. Your best bet is to park wherever you can and leave your car. There is a 30-car public lot at the end of Front Street. If you choose on-street parking, watch the time to avoid being ticketed.

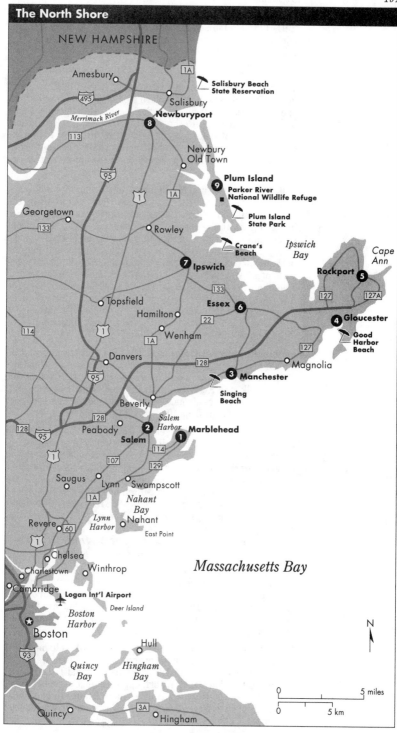

The North Shore

Time Out To experience the fisherman's Marblehead, visit the **Driftwood** (tel. 617/631–1145), a simple, red-clapboard restaurant by the harbor on Front Street. Fishnets hang from the ceiling and excellent, inexpensive breakfasts and lunches are served from 5:30 AM until 2 PM.

The town's Victorian municipal building, **Abbott Hall,** was built in 1876 and houses A. M. Willard's painting *The Spirit of '76,* one of America's treasured patriotic icons. Many people, familiar since childhood with the depiction of the three Revolutionary veterans with fife, drum, and flag, are surprised to find the original in an otherwise unassuming town hall. *Washington St., tel. 617/631–0528. Open weekday business hours and June–Oct., Sat. 9–6, Sun. 11–6.*

Follow Route 114 out of Marblehead, turn right onto Route 1A, ② and drive the short distance to **Salem.** Don't be put off by the industrial surroundings. The setting may be tarnished, but Salem is a gem, full of compelling museums, trendy waterfront stores and restaurants, a shopping area closed to traffic, and a wide open common with a children's playground and jogging path. Settled in 1630, the town is known for the witchcraft hysteria of 1692, a rich maritime tradition, and the architectural splendor of its Federal homes. The frigates of Salem opened the Far East trade routes and provided the wealth that produced America's first millionaires. Numbered among its native sons were Nathaniel Hawthorne, the navigator Nathaniel Bowditch, and the architect Samuel McIntire.

Park in the central parking lot at Riley Plaza by the information booth, and begin your exploration by following the Heritage Trail (painted on the sidewalk) around the town. If you prefer not to walk, the **Sightseeing Trolley and Shuttle Service** (tel. 508/744–5463) leaves from the same booth on narrated tours of the city, every hour from 10–4, April through November.

Salem unabashedly calls itself "Witch City." Witches astride broomsticks enhance the police cars; witchcraft shops, a local witch, and more recall the city's infamous connection with the witchcraft trials of 1692. Sites commemorating the witch hysteria, which resulted in the hangings of 19 innocent people, are numerous. The **Salem Witch Museum** offers a multisensory presentation re-creating the events with 13 stage sets and life-size models. *Washington Square N, Salem, tel. 508/744–1692. Admission: $4 adults, $2.50 children 6–14, $3.50 senior citizens. Open July–Aug., daily 10–7, Sept.–June, daily 10–5. Closed Thanksgiving, Christmas, New Year's Day.*

No witch ever lived at **Witch House,** but more than 200 accused witches were questioned there. The decor is authentic late-17th century, reflecting the era when the trials were held. *310½ Essex St., Salem, tel. 508/744–0180. Admission: $3 adults, $1.50 children. Open daily mid-Mar.–June and Labor Day–Dec. 1, 10–4:30; July–Aug. 10–6.*

Putting its macabre past behind it, Salem went on to become a major seaport, with a thriving overseas trade. **Salem Maritime,** a National Historic Site operated by the National Trust,, is situated right beside Derby Wharf, opposite the Customs House. Tours take in the Customs House, made famous in Nathaniel Hawthorne's *The Scarlet Letter;* the Government Warehouse; and historic shipowners' homes. *174 Derby St., tel. 508/744–*

4323. Admission free. Open daily 8:30–5. Closed Thanksgiving, Christmas, New Year's Day.

Many of the exotic items brought back by Salem's merchant ships are housed in the **Peabody and Essex Museum,** the oldest continuously operating museum in America. The museum also contains exhibits on New England's whaling and fishing past and documents from the witch trials and (for an additional fee) operates tours of several historic mansions that belonged to shipowners and other wealthy merchants. *East India Sq., Salem, tel. 508/745–1876. Admission: $6 adults, $3.50 children 6–16, $5 senior citizens and students. Open Mon.–Sat. 10–5, Sun. noon–5. Closed Thanksgiving, Christmas, New Year's Day.*

The **House of Seven Gables,** immortalized by Nathaniel Hawthorne in his book of the same name, should not be missed. Interesting points on the tour are period furnishings, a secret staircase discovered during 1886 renovations, and the garret with its model of the house. Hawthorne was born in Salem in 1804, and the house where he was born has been moved to this site. *54 Turner St., Salem, tel. 508/744–0991. Admission: $6.50 adults, $4 children 13–17, $3 children 6–12. Open daily July–Labor Day, 9:30–5:30; Labor Day–June, 10–4:30. Closed Thanksgiving, Christmas, New Year's Day, and last week in Jan.*

Just south of Salem on Route 1A, costumed "interpreters" at the **Pioneer Village and Forest River Park** re-create Salem of the 1630s, when it was the state capital. Replicas of thatched cottages, dugout homes, and wigwams have been constructed at the site. *Jct. Rte. 1A and Rte. 129, tel. 508/745–0525. Admission: $4 adults, $3.50 senior citizens and children 13–17, $2.50 children 6–12. Open mid-May–Oct., daily 10–5.*

❸ North of Salem, pass through Beverly on Route 127 and on to the small seaside town of **Manchester,** with its excellent Singing Beach, so-called because of the noise of the wind against the sand. Head down Hesperus Avenue in the village of Magnolia to see "Norman's Woe Rock," made famous by Longfellow in his poem *The Wreck of the Hesperus.*

The rock can also be viewed from **Hammond Castle Museum,** a stone building inspired by the castles of the Middle Ages and built in 1926 by the inventor John Hays Hammond Jr. It contains medieval furnishings and paintings, and the Great Hall houses an impressive organ with 8,600 pipes and 126 stops. *80 Hesperus Ave., Gloucester, tel. 508/283–2080. Admission: $5.50 adults, $3.50 children 6–12, $4.50 senior citizens and students. Open Wed.–Sun. 10–5. Open Mon. on national holidays. Closed Thanksgiving, Christmas, New Year's Day.*

❹ As the road continues along the coast, you enter **Gloucester** along a fine seaside promenade. The first sight you'll see is the famous statue of a man at a ship's wheel, eyes on the horizon, dedicated to those "who go down to the sea in ships." The statue was commissioned by Gloucester's citizens in 1923 in celebration of the seaport's 300th anniversary. Gloucester, the oldest seaport in the nation, is a workaday town and still a major fishing port. Another side to its personality is illustrated by **Rocky Neck,** the oldest working artists' colony in America.

❺ Route 127 continues to **Rockport,** at the very tip of Cape Ann. The town derives its name from the granite formations, and many Boston-area structures are made of stone from the town's long-gone quarries. Today, Rockport is a mecca for summer tourists who are attracted by its hilly rows of colorful clapboard houses, historic inns, dozens of artists' studios, and its beach (albeit rather small). While known primarily as a tourist's town, Rockport has not gone overboard on T-shirt emporia and the other accoutrements of a summer economy: shops sell crafts, clothing, and cameras, not trashy souvenirs, and restaurants serve quiche, seafood, or home-baked cookies rather than fast food. The best time to visit Rockport is during the off-season, when many of the shops remain open, the crowds are gone, and one can see the place for the lovely New England seacoast town it is. Walk out to the end of Bearskin Neck for an impressive view of the open Atlantic and the nearby lobster shack affectionately known as "Motif No. 1" because of its popularity as a subject for amateur artists.

❻ Head west out of Cape Ann on Route 128 and then turn north on Route 133 for the village of **Essex.** Surrounded by salt marshes, the town has more than 15 seafood restaurants. The **Essex Shipbuilding Museum** displays exhibits from the 19th century, when the town was an important shipbuilding center. *Rte. 133, Essex, tel. 508/768-7541. Admission: $2. Open mid-May–mid-Oct., Thurs.–Sat. 11–4, Sun. noon–5.*

Time Out **Woodman's of Essex** (Rte. 133, tel. 508/768-6451) claims to have fried the first clams in town back in 1916. Today, this large wood shack with unpretentious booths is *the* place for "seafood in the rough," and the menu includes lobster, a raw bar, clam chowder, and, of course, fried clams.

❼ Four miles north of Essex, the unimposing town of **Ipswich,** settled in 1633 and famous for its clams, is said to have more 17th-century houses standing and occupied than any other place in America. More than 40 homes in town were built before 1725. A *Walking Tour Guide of Historic Ipswich* is available at the Chamber of Commerce information kiosk. *Crane's Beach Rd. Open June–Labor Day, daily 10–4.*

Continuing north from Ipswich on Route 1A for 12 miles will take you past the salt marshes of Rowley and Newbury to **❽** **Newburyport.** Here Route 1A becomes High Street, which is lined with some of the finest examples of Federal-style (roughly, 1790–1810) mansions in New England. You'll notice "widow's walks," which afford a view of the port and the sea beyond, perched atop many of the houses. Like those in Salem, the homes were built for prosperous sea captains in this city that was once a leading port and shipbuilding center.

While Newburyport's maritime significance ended with the time of the clipper ships (some of the best of which were built here), an energetic downtown renewal program has brought new life to the town's brick-front center. Renovated buildings now house an assortment of restaurants, taverns, and shops that sell everything from nautical brasses to antique Oriental rugs. The civic improvements have been matched by private restorations of the town's housing stock, much of which dates from the 18th century, with a scattering of 16th-century homes in some neighborhoods.

Newburyport, Massachusetts's smallest city, is easy to walk around in, and there is all-day free parking down by the water. A stroll through the **Waterfront Park and Promenade** gives a super view of the harbor and the fishing and pleasure boats that moor there. Walking to the left as you leave the parking lot will take you to the **Custom House Maritime Museum.** Built in 1835 in Classic Revival style, it contains exhibits on maritime history, models, tools, and paintings. The audiovisual show is presented hourly. *25 Water St., tel. 508/462–8681. Admission: $3 adults, $1.50 children 5–15, $2 senior citizens. Open Apr.– Dec., Mon.–Sat. 10–4, Sun. 1–4. Closed Jan.–Mar.*

❾ A causeway leads from Newburyport to **Plum Island,** a narrow spit of land harboring a summer colony (rapidly becoming year-round) at one end and the **Parker River National Wildlife Refuge** at the other. The refuge has 4,662 acres of salt marsh, freshwater marsh, beaches, and dunes; it is one of the few natural barrier beach–dune–salt marsh complexes left on the Northeast coast. The bird-watching, surf fishing, plum and cranberry picking, and swimming are wonderful. The refuge is such a popular place in the summer, especially on weekends, that cars begin lining up at the gate here before 7 AM. Only a limited number of cars are let in, although there's no restriction on the number of people on the beach. *Tel. 508/465–5753. Admission: $5 per car (or $15 for a Duck Stamp, which permits free admission to all Federal Wildlife Refuges; or $25 for a Golden Eagle Pass, which permits free admission to all Federal sites). Open ½ hr before sunrise to ½ hr after sunset.*

What to See and Do with Children

The House of Seven Gables, Salem
Pioneer Village and Forest River Park, Salem
Plum Island, Newburyport
Salem Willows Park (at the eastern end of Derby St., Salem) has picnic grounds, beaches, food stands, amusements, games, boat rentals, and fishing bait.
Salem Witch Museum, Salem
Salisbury Beach, Salisbury, has a number of honky-tonk family amusement parks, water slides, food stalls, and various amusement arcades.
Tot Stop, at Museum Place in Salem, is a haven for toddlers, preschoolers, kindergarteners—and weary parents. The huge indoor playground has slides, climbing frames, tunnels, pedal cars, a sandbox, and child-size rooms furnished as kitchens, bedrooms, and more. There are playhouses, rocking horses, and toys *ad infinitum.* A quiet-room has board games, crayons, puzzles, and some electronic games. Any family vacationing with young kids will find this place a welcome break from conventional sightseeing. Parents can't leave children here, but there's a sitting area where grown-ups can work or read in relative peace. *Museum Place Mall, Church and Essex Sts., tel. 508/741–5704. Admission: $6 per child 8 mths–6 years (parents free); maximum $14 per family. Open daily 9:30–5:30 (Thurs. until 8.*

Off the Beaten Track

Although Salem is world-famous as the witch-hunt city, **Danvers** (Old Salem) is virtually unknown. Yet here are the real relics of the witchcraft episode. The house where the black slave Tituba told stories to two impressionable girls and began the whole business has been demolished, but the foundations were excavated in 1970, and can be viewed—they're located behind 67 Center Street.

The **Rebecca Nurse Homestead** was the home of aged, pious Rebecca, a regular churchgoer whose accusation caused shock waves, whose trial was a mockery (she was pronounced innocent, but the jury was urged to change its verdict), and who was hanged as a witch in 1692. Her family took her body afterward and buried her in secret on the grounds of this house. It has period furnishings and is gradually being developed as a model 18th-century farm. *149 Pine St., tel. 508/774–8799. Admission: $3.50 adults, $1.50 children under 16. Open June 15– Oct. 15, Tues.–Fri. and Sun. 1–4:30, Sat. 9–4, and by appointment.*

Shopping

Antiques The greatest concentration of antiques stores on the North Shore is around **Essex,** but there are plenty sprinkled throughout **Salem** and **Cape Ann** as well. Members of the North Shore Antique Dealers Association guarantee the authenticity of their merchandise, and a leaflet listing their shops can be obtained from participating stores. Try the **Pickering Wharf Antique Gallery** in Salem, where five shops house 50 dealers.

Art Galleries As an artist's colony, **Rockport** has a tremendous concentration of artists' studios and galleries selling work by local painters. Most are located on Main Street near the harbor, and on Bearskin Neck. The Rocky Neck Arts Colony east of **Gloucester** is another good place to browse and buy.

Specialty Stores Salem is the center for a number of offbeat shops that have a distinct relationship to the city's witchcraft history. The best known such store is **Crow Haven Corner** (125 Essex St., tel. 508/ 745–8763), where Laurie Cabot, Salem's "official" witch, presides over a fabulous selection of crystal balls, herbs, tarot decks, healing stones, and books about witchcraft. **Gornigo** on Pickering Wharf (tel. 508/745–0552), complete with a black shop cat, sells a marvelous array of scented herbs, herbal teas, potions, perfumes, runes, spirit lamps, and crystals. Crystals are a specialty at **The Crystal Chamber** (197 Derby St., tel. 508/ 745–9400).

Sports and Outdoor Activities

Boating Marblehead is the pleasure-sailing capital of the North Shore, but here and elsewhere it's not easy to find mooring space for your private yacht; many towns have waiting lists of several years. Town harbor masters will be able to inform you of nightly fees at public docks, when space is available.

Canoeing is less complicated; the best areas are on the Ipswich and Parker rivers. For saltwater canoeing and kayaking, the waters of the Essex River Estuary are generally calm and protected. The **Harold Parker State Forest** in North Andover and the **Willowdale State Forest** in Ipswich also permit canoeing.

Fishing Deep-sea fishing excursions are offered at various North Shore ports. In Gloucester try **Captain Bill's Deep Sea Fishing** (9 Traverse St., tel. 508/283–6995) for full- and half-day trips, and in Newburyport try **New England Whale Watch** (54 Merrimac St., tel. 508/465–9885).

Surf casting is even more popular—bluefish, pollock, and striped bass can be taken from the ocean shores of Plum Island; permits to remain on the beach after dark are obtainable free of charge by anyone entering the refuge with fishing equipment in the daylight. You don't need a permit to fish from the public beach at Plum Island, and the best spot to choose is around the mouth of the Merrimac River.

For freshwater fishing, the Parker and Ipswich rivers are both stocked with trout each spring, and many state parks permit fishing.

Hiking The best places to hike on the North Shore are in nature reserves with salt marshes. The Massachusetts Audubon Society's **Ipswich River Wildlife Sanctuary** (tel. 508/887–9264) offers a variety of trails through marshland hills, where there are remains of early Colonial settlements as well as abundant wildlife. Self-guiding trail maps can be picked up at the office (closed Monday). The Rockery Trail takes walkers to the perennial rock garden and Japanese garden; the Agawam Nature Trail focusses on local habitat. At the **Parker River National Wildlife Refuge** (Plum Island, tel. 508/465–5753), deer and rabbits share space with 25,000 ducks and more than 6,000 geese. The two-mile, Hellcat Swamp trail cuts through the marshes and sand dunes, taking in the best of the sanctuary. Trail maps are available at the office.

Spectator Sports

The one spectator sport of note on the North Shore is polo. The **Myopia Hunt Club** (Polo Promotions, Box 2103, South Hamilton 01928, tel. 508/468–4433) stages polo matches on Sundays at 3 PM between late May and October at its grounds along Route 1A in Hamilton.

Beaches

Here are some of the best beaches on the North Shore: **Crane's Beach** (Ipswich), **Parker River Refuge** (Newbury), **Plum Island** (Newburyport), **Salisbury State Reservation** (Salisbury), **Singing Beach** (Manchester), and **Wingarsheek Beach** and **Good Harbor Beach** (Gloucester).

National and State Parks

Of the numerous parks in the area, the following have particularly varied facilities: **Halibut Point State Park** (Rte. 127 to Gott Ave., Rockport, tel. 508/546–2997), the 3,000-acre **Harold Parker State Forest** (Rte. 114, North Andover, tel. 508/686–3391), **Parker River National Wildlife Refuge** (Plum Island, off Rte. 1A, Newburyport, tel. 508/465–5753), **Plum Island State Reservation** (off Rte 1A, Newburyport, tel. 508/462–4481), **Salisbury Beach State Reservation** (Rte. 1A, Salisbury, tel. 508/462–4481), and the **Willowdale State Forest** (Linebrook Rd., Ipswich, tel. 508/887–5931).

Dining and Lodging

The restaurant price categories are based on the average cost of a three-course dinner, per person, excluding drinks, service, and tax.

Highly recommended restaurants in each price category are indicated by a star ★.

Category	Cost*
Very Expensive	over $40
Expensive	$25–$40
Moderate	$15–$25
Inexpensive	under $15

*per person; add 5% tax

Highly recommended lodgings in each price category are indicated by a star ★.

Category	Cost*
Very Expensive	over $100
Expensive	$70–$100
Moderate	$40–$70
Inexpensive	under $40

*All prices are for a standard double room; add 9.7% tax

Danvers
Lodging
Quality Inn King's Grant. This modern building has tastefully appointed guest rooms with some reproduction antiques. Live entertainment is provided Friday and Saturday nights in the British Colony lounge, and the dining room re-creates 19th-century England. There's also an atrium with fish in the "brook," parrots in the air, and paths among the palms. *Box 274 (Rte. 128, Exit 21N), 01923, tel. 508/774–6800. 125 rooms, 2 suites. Facilities: restaurant, lounge, indoor pool, Jacuzzi. AE, D, DC, MC, V. Expensive.*

Essex
Dining
Jerry Pelonzi's Hearthside. This 250-year-old converted farmhouse is the epitome of coziness. Four small dining rooms have open fireplaces and exposed beams: The first is low-ceilinged with stencils on the walls; the others have cathedral ceilings with rough-panel walls and small windows. The newest eating area is in the loft. Entrées include baked stuffed haddock, seafood casserole, sirloin steak, lobster, and chicken. *Rte. 133, tel. 508/768–6003. Dress: casual. AE, MC, V. Moderate.*

Tom Shea's. Picture windows in this recently expanded, two-story, cedar-shingled restaurant overlook the salt marsh. Inside, walls are white, and the room has mismatched wooden furniture, with many hanging plants. Seafood is the main fare, including shrimp in coconut beer batter, scallop-stuffed sole, Boston scrod, lobster, and, of course, the fried clams for which Essex is famous. *122 Main St., Rte. 133, tel. 508/768–6931. Dress: casual. AE, D, MC, V. Moderate.*

Gloucester **White Rainbow.** The dining room in this excellent restaurant is
Dining in the basement of a west-end store downtown, and candlelight
★ gives a romantic atmosphere. Specialties include Maui onion
soup, grilled beef with a Zinfandel wine sauce, lobster *estancia*
(lobster sauteed with tomatoes, artichoke hearts, olives, scal-
lions, wine, and herb butter), and fresh fish of the day. *65 Main
St., tel. 508/281–0017. Dress: casual. AE, D, DC, MC, V.
Closed lunch; Mon. Expensive.*

★ **The Rhumb Line.** Despite its unimpressive location, this restaurant is worth the three-minute drive from the town center.
The decoration of the upstairs dining room gives customers the
impression of sitting on a ship's deck, with the wheel and com-
pass at one end, rigging overhead, captain's chairs at the tables, and seascapes on the walls. The selections include a
seafood casserole of shrimp, crab meat, and scallops in garlic-
lemon butter and white wine; roast duckling glazed with Grand
Marnier, honey, and marmalade sauce; and charbroiled steaks.
The bar food downstairs includes burgers, Mexican dishes, seafood, and steaks. *Railroad Ave., tel. 508/283–9732. Dress: casual. AE, MC, V. Upstairs dining room closed Oct.–Jan.
Moderate–Expensive.*

Captain Courageous. The most recent owner of this ideally situated restaurant has created a seafaring atmosphere with nets,
rigging, and paintings of old ships. In summer dining is on the
outside deck above the water. Seafood is the main fare, and daily specials include sautéed scallops, lobster, and scrod. *25 Rogers St., tel. 508/283–0007. Reservations advised. Dress: casual. AE, D, DC, MC, V. Moderate.*

Lodging **Best Western Twin Light Manor.** This is not your characteristic
chain hotel—it was a manor first, a Best Western second. The
English Tudor mansion was built in 1905 as a private home,
complete with elevator, children's playhouse, and seven-car
garage equipped with a turntable! Newer buildings nearby offer different styles of accommodations, and the complex is set
on 7 acres of ground, overlooking the ocean. The most interesting guest rooms are those in the manor itself; some are enormous and have nonworking fireplaces. Guests have golf
privileges on a local course, and the hotel is affiliated with a
Gloucester health club. *Atlantic Rd., 01930, tel. 508/283–7500
or 800/528–1234. 63 rooms. Facilities: dining room, golf, access to health club, 2 outdoor pools, games room, bicycles,
badminton, volleyball, croquet, shuffleboard, baby-sitters,
gardens. AE, D, DC, MC, V. Very Expensive.*

Vista Motel. The name describes it well, because every room in
this excellently situated motel overlooks the sea and Good Harbor Beach, just a few minutes' walk away. The rooms, perched
atop a small, steep hill, vary in quality depending on price, but
all are basically well furnished and spacious. Some have decks,
and some have refrigerators. *22 Thatcher Rd., 01930, tel. 508/
281–3410. 40 rooms. Facilities: outdoor pool. AE, MC, V. Expensive.*

Back Shore Motor Lodge. This lodge in East Gloucester overlooks the ocean from a rocky headland. All guest rooms have
sea views, and some have sliding doors onto decks at the front
of the building. Furnishings are good-quality motor-lodge
style, with some reproductions, and the color scheme is sea
green. *85 Atlantic Rd., 01930, tel. 508/283–1198. 23 rooms. Facilities: dining room, outdoor pool. Rates include Continental
breakfast. No credit cards. Moderate–Expensive.*

Marblehead **The Landing.** Right on the Marblehead harbor and still in the
  Dining historic district, this pleasant, small restaurant offers outdoor
dining on a balcony over the sea. Inside are wood chairs and tables, with lots of hanging plants. The chef prepares lobster,
scallops primavera, seafood scampi, Atlantic sole florentine,
Ipswich clams, and seafood kabob. A limited choice of steak and
chicken are also available. *Clark's Landing off Front St., tel.
617/631–6268. Dress: casual. AE, D, DC, MC, V. Expensive.*

  Lodging **Harbor Light Inn.** This is the best place to stay in Marblehead
  ★ and competes with the Clark Currier Inn in Newburyport as
one of the most comfortable and authentic inns on the North
Shore. Special features include some in-room Jacuzzis, skylights, rooftop decks, and spacious, modern bathrooms; traditional touches are found in the four-poster and canopy beds,
carved arched doorways, sliding (original) Indian shutters,
wide-board floors, and antique mahogany furnishings. In 1993,
the innkeepers bought the building next door, adding seven
big, beautiful bedrooms (with working fireplaces, four-poster
beds, and painted wood paneling) to the inn's roster. *58 Washington St., 01945, tel. 617/631–2186. 19 rooms, 1 suite. Facilities: pool, 2 parlors, dining room, conference room. No pets.
Rates include Continental breakfast. AE, MC, V. Expensive–
Very Expensive.*
Harborside House. Located in Marblehead's historic district,
Harborside House was built in 1850 by a ship's carpenter.
Susan Livingston has lived here for 28 years and has operated
the house as a successful bed and breakfast since 1985. The
downstairs living room has a working brick fireplace; bedrooms
have polished wide-board floors with Oriental rugs; and two
rooms overlook Marblehead harbor with its hundreds of sailboats. Susan, who works as a dressmaker, is a considerate and
interesting host, and her home is convenient to all of Marblehead's attractions. *23 Gregory St., 01945, tel. 617/631–1032. 3
rooms. Facilities: TV in rooms, shared phone, parlor, breakfast room, parking. No pets; no smoking. Rates include Continental breakfast. No credit cards. Moderate–Expensive.*
Pleasant Manor Inn. Off the main road between Salem and Marblehead, this rambling Victorian mansion has large guest
rooms (some with pineapple four-poster beds), and a carved
mahogany staircase. The wallpaper is on the shabby side, but
rooms are clean, the atmosphere relaxed and welcoming, and
the new manager, Lorraine French, prefers to keep prices at
their present reasonable rate, rather than to embark on a major
redecoration project. Amelia Earhart stayed in Room 32 in
1923, when the building first became an inn. *Rte. 114, 264
Pleasant St., 01945, tel. 617/631–5843. Facilities: TV and VCR
in rooms, parlor, breakfast room, tennis court, parking. No
pets. Rates include Continental breakfast. No credit cards.
Moderate.*

Newburyport **Scandia.** The restaurant is well known locally for its fine cui-
  Dining sine, and house specialties are veal and lobster sauté, and sea-
  ★ food linguine. The dining room is small and narrow, and dimly
lighted with candles on the tables and "candle" chandeliers. *25
State St., tel. 508/462–6271. Reservations advised. Dress: casual. AE, DC, MC, V. Expensive.*
  ★ **David's and Downstairs at David's.** These two restaurants at the
Garrison Inn are top of the line for both food and service. If you
dine upstairs in the formal room furnished with chandeliers
and white linen, damask chairs and drapes, such entrées as sau-

téed lobster with sea scallops, and mushrooms in anise cream; duck with ginger and scallion sauce; and chicken breast medallions with roasted garlic can be yours. Downstairs at David's is less formal, with exposed brick arches, a bar, and a lighter menu of steak, burgers, and fish dishes. An advantage of these restaurants is their child-care facility, where, for a nominal fee, kids can play and eat while parents enjoy their own meal in peace. Not surprisingly, David, the owner-chef, is a father of three. *11 Brown Sq., tel. 508/462–8077. Reservations advised. Dress: casual. AE, DC, MC, V. Moderate–Expensive.*

East End Seafood Restaurant. For a true dining "in the rough" experience, visit this restaurant just south of Newburyport in the village of Rowley. The exterior is somewhat shabby, but inside, the shedlike building is pleasantly airy, with wood paneling, cathedral ceilings, and rustic beams. Dining is at wooden picnic tables, and the fare is deep-fried seafood. Note that the place closes at about 8 PM. *Corner Rte. 1A and Railroad Ave., Rowley, tel. 508/948–7227. No reservations. Dress: casual. No credit cards. Closed Mon. Nov.–Apr. Inexpensive.*

Lodging **Garrison Inn.** This four-story Georgian red-brick building is set back from the main road on a small square. Inside, an elegant lounge and formal dining rooms are furnished with smart reproductions; the basement tavern is more casual, with exposed brick arches and wood-burning stoves in open fireplaces. Guest rooms vary in size; all have handsome antique replicas. The best rooms are the top-floor suites, set on two levels: Spiral or Colonial staircases lead up from the sitting room to the sleeping area above. *11 Brown Sq., 01950, tel. 508/465–0910. 18 rooms, 6 suites. Facilities: dining room , lounge, tavern, room service. No pets. AE, DC, MC, V. Expensive.*

★ **Clark Currier Inn.** This 1803 Federal mansion has been restored with care, taste, imagination, and enthusiasm, emerging as one of the best inns on the North Shore. Guest rooms are spacious and furnished with antiques: Some have pencil four-poster beds, one has a reproduction sea captain's bed complete with drawers below, and another contains a glorious sleigh bed dating from the late-19th century. There's a Federalist "good morning" staircase (so-called because two small staircases join at the head of a large one, permitting family members to greet each other on their way down to breakfast). *45 Green St., 01950, tel. 508/465–8363. 8 rooms. Facilities: TV lounge. AE, MC, V. Moderate–Expensive.*

Rockport **Brackett's Oceanview Restaurant.** A big bay window in this
Dining quiet, homey restaurant allows an excellent view across the
★ harbor. The menu includes scallop casserole, fish cakes, and other seafood dishes. *Main St., tel. 508/546–2797. Dress: casual. DC, MC, V. Closed Mon. and mid-Nov.–Mar. Moderate.*

My Place by the Sea. By the sea it is—this tiny restaurant is perched at the very end of Bearskin Neck. Inside, the small dining area has white wicker chairs and rustic beams; outside, the lower deck has tables overlooking the ocean. The restaurant serves mainly seafood, including baked scrod, swordfish steak, seafood fettuccine, and sandwiches. *Bearskin Neck, tel. 508/546–9667. Dress: casual.AE, DC, MC, V. BYOB. Closed mid-Dec.–May. Moderate.*

Portside Chowder House. This great little hole-in-the-wall restaurant is one of the few in Rockport that's open year-round. The tiny dining room with wooden beams and low ceilings has partial sea views. Chowder is the house specialty; also offered are lobster and crab plates, salads, burgers, and sandwiches. *Bearskin Neck, no phone. Dress: casual. No credit cards. Closed for dinner Oct.–Apr. Inexpensive.*

Lodging

★ **Yankee Clipper Inn.** The imposing Georgian mansion that forms the main part of this impressive, perfectly located inn sits surrounded by gardens on a rocky point jutting into the sea. It was built as a private home in the 1930s, but has been managed as an inn by one family for more than 40 years. Guest rooms vary in size, but most are spacious. Furnished with antiques, they contain four-poster or canopy beds, and all but one has an ocean view. In the Quarterdeck, a newer building across the lawn, all rooms have fabulous sea views; the decor here is more modern, and rooms are again spacious with big picture windows. The Bullfinch House across the street is an 1840 Greek Revival house, appointed with tasteful antique furnishings, but with less of a view. *96 Granite St., 01966, tel. 508/546-3407. 27 rooms, 6 suites. Facilities: restaurant, lounge, outdoor pool, gardens. Rates include full breakfast; MAP available. No pets. AE, D, MC, V. Very Expensive.*

★ **Addison Choate Inn.** This lovely, white clapboard inn sits inconspicuously among private homes, just a minute's walk from the center of Rockport. The spacious rooms, with large, tiled bathrooms, are beautifully decorated; the navy-and-white captain's room contains a dark-wood, four-poster bed with a net canopy, handmade quilts, and Oriental rugs. Other rooms—all with polished pine floors—have Hitchcock rockers and headboards, spool or filigree brass beds, local seascape paintings, and antiques. The two luxuriously appointed duplex carriage-house apartments have skylights, cathedral ceilings, and exposed wood beams. *49 Broadway, 01966, tel. 508/546-7543. 7 rooms, 2 apartments, all with bath. Facilities: breakfast room, parlor, outdoor pool. Rates include Continental breakfast. No smoking; no pets. MC, V. Expensive.*

Seacrest Manor. The distinctive inn, surrounded by large gardens, sits on top of a hill overlooking the sea. Two elegant sitting rooms are furnished with antiques and leather chairs; one has a huge wall mirror from the old Philadelphia Opera House. The hall and staircase are hung with paintings—some of which depict the inn—by local artists. Guest rooms vary in size and character: In the new wing they have more modern furnishings; upstairs, two have large private decks with sea views. Special touches are everywhere: complimentary morning newspapers, shoe shining, custom soap and shampoos, a nightly turndown service, and mints on the pillow, all accompanied by a Shakespearean motif. *131 Marmion Way, 01966, tel. 508/546-2211. 8 rooms, 2 with shared bath. Facilities: dining room, 2 lounges, gardens. No pets. Rates include full breakfast. 2-night minimum stay weekends. No credit cards. Closed Dec. 1–Apr. 1. Expensive.*

Bearskin Neck Motor Lodge. Set almost at the end of Bearskin Neck, the guest-room balconies here overhang the water. From the windows all you see is sea, and at night you can hear it lapping—or thundering—against the rocks below. Rooms are simply appointed with white and wood furniture and paneled walls. The exterior is gray cedar shingles, and a large deck over the sea at one end of the building can also be used by guests. *Bearskin Neck, 01966, tel. 508/546-6677. 8 rooms. No pets. No credit cards. Closed Dec. 1–Mar. 30. Moderate–Expensive.*

★ **Inn on Cove Hill.** This Federal building on a picturesque hillside dates back to 1792, when it was reportedly constructed with money from a cache of pirates' gold. Some guest rooms are small, but all are cheerful, pretty, and carefully appointed with bright, flowery print paper, patchwork quilts, and old-fashioned beds—some are brass, others are canopy four-posters. Rooms have polished wide-board floors, iron latches, wood bathroom fixtures, and pastel-tone Oriental rugs. *37 Mt. Pleasant St., 01966, tel. 508/546–2701. 11 rooms, 9 with bath. No smoking; no pets. Rates include Continental breakfast. No credit cards. Closed mid-Oct.–mid-Mar. Moderate.*

★ **Sally Webster Inn.** Sally Webster was a member of Hannah Jumper's so-called "hatchet gang," which smashed up the town's liquor stores in 1856 and turned Rockport into the dry town it remains today. Sally lived in this house for much of her life, and the guest rooms are named for members of her family. They contain rocking chairs; nonworking brick fireplaces; pineapple four-poster, brass, canopy, or spool beds; and pine wideboard floors with Oriental rugs. Bonnets and wickerwork hang on the walls; all rooms have candle-lanterns that can be lit in the evening. *34 Mt. Pleasant St., 01966, tel. 508/546–9251. 6 rooms. Facilities: dining room, lounge. No pets. Rates include Continental breakfast. MC, V. Closed Dec.–Jan.; weekends only, Feb.–Apr. Moderate.*

Salem Dining

Nathaniel's. This formal restaurant at the Hawthorne Hotel on Salem Common is hung with chandeliers. The menu includes lobster, swordfish in mustard cream, prime rib, and poached sole on spinach with champagne cream sauce. *On-the-Common, tel. 508/744–4080. Dress: casual. AE, D, DC, MC, V. Expensive.*

Chase House. This restaurant is extremely busy in summer, ideally located as it is on Pickering Wharf, overlooking the harbor. A giant swordfish hangs beside the chimney in the saloon, and the main dining room has low ceilings and walls of exposed brick. The menu offers steak, squid, flounder, and "old-fashioned seafood dinners" of clams, scallops, shrimp, fish, and lobster with onion rings. *Pickering Wharf, tel. 508/744–0000. Dress: casual. AE, D, DC, MC, V. Moderate.*

Lyceum. The Lyceum's great claim to fame is that Alexander Graham Bell made his first public phone call from this building in 1877. The decor connotes the '40s, with paneled ceilings, wood bar, fans, and old photographs. Entrées include chicken cutlets with lemon-cucumber sauce; swordfish steak; and black angus sirloin. *43 Church St., tel. 508/745–7665. Reservations advised. Dress: casual. AE, D, MC, V. Moderate.*

Ravi's Fine Indian Cuisine. The decor is, of course, Indian, and the spicy menu includes a large variety of lamb, chicken, beef, shrimp, and vegetarian dishes. *6 Hawthorne Blvd. (Rte. 1A), tel. 508/744–6570. Dress: casual. MC, V. Inexpensive.*

Lodging **Hawthorne Hotel.** The imposing red-brick structure is now the only full-service hotel in Salem—conveniently situated on the green just a short walk from the commercial center and most attractions. Guest rooms in brown and beige are appointed with reproduction antiques, armchairs, and desks (business clients are numerous). *On-the-Common, 01970, tel. 508/744–4080. 83 rooms, 6 suites. Facilities: restaurant, lounge, tavern, exercise room, meeting rooms, ballroom. AE, D, DC, MC, V. Expensive.*

The Inn at Seven Winter St. Built in 1870, this conveniently located inn has been accurately restored to re-create the Victorian era. Rooms, although a little dark, are spacious and well furnished, with heavy mahogany and walnut antiques, working marble fireplaces, and Oriental rugs on polished hardwood floors. Two large three-room suites are perfect for families, with fully equipped eat-in kitchens and a sitting room. *7 Winter St., 01970, tel. 508/745–9520. 7 rooms with bath, 2 suites, 1 studio. Facilities: breakfast room, parlor, deck, parking, in-room TV and phone. Rates include Continental breakfast. No pets; no smoking. MC, V. Expensive.*

Amelia Payson Guest House. This Greek Revival house built in 1845 has been tastefully converted into a bright, airy bed-and-breakfast inn near the common and all of Salem's historic attractions. Pretty rooms are decorated with floral-print wallpaper, brass and canopy beds, nonworking marble fireplaces, and white wicker furnishings. The downstairs parlor has a grand piano, while a reading room upstairs is filled with tourist information. *16 Winter St., 01970, tel. 508/744–8804. 3 rooms with bath, 1 studio. Facilities: breakfast room, 2 parlors, parking, in-room TV. Rates include Continental breakfast. No pets; no smoking. AE, MC, V. Moderate–Expensive.*

The Arts

Music   **Castle Hill** (Argilla Rd., Ipswich, tel. 508/356–7774) holds an annual festival, July 4 through mid-August, of pop, folk, and classical music, plus a jazz ball.

The magnificent organ at the **Hammond Castle Museum** (80 Hesperus Ave., Gloucester, tel. 508/283–2080) is used for organ concerts year-round, and in summer pops concerts are added to the schedule.

Theater   The **North Shore Music Theatre** (62 Dunham Rd., Beverly, tel. 508/922–8500) is a professional company that, from May through December, performs popular and modern musicals as well as children's theater. On Cape Ann the **Gloucester Stage Company** (267 E. Main St., Gloucester, tel. 508/281–4099) is a nonprofit professional group staging new plays and revivals May–September.

Nightlife

A selection of popular local spots includes: **The Grog** (13 Middle St., Newburyport, tel. 508/465–8008), which hosts live entertainment downstairs Thursday–Sunday nights and features a wide variety of blues and rock bands; downstairs at **Roosevelt's** restaurant (300 Derby St., Salem, tel. 508/745–9608), where local rock bands play Wednesday–Saturday nights; and **Blue Star Lounge** (Rte. 1/99, Saugus, tel. 617/233–8027), a rockabilly road house on a busy strip, playing country music Wednesday–Sunday evenings.

Index

Discover New England all over again this year

HALLIDAY'S NEW ENGLAND FOOD EXPLORER
Tours for Food Lovers

Now — a guidebook to New England for food lovers. In 12 tours through 6 states, discover the region's best markets, restaurants, farms, inns, even road-side stands in the literate, opinionated company of veteran food writer Fred Halliday. Packed full of culinary lore, food sources, and recipes, here's the best place to start the most delicious vacation of your life.

FODOR'S BED & BREAKFASTS AND COUNTRY INNS — NEW ENGLAND

This meticulously honest and thoroughly up-to-date guide includes critical reviews of more than 280 inns and B&Bs, plus everything you need to know about what to see and do and where to eat when you get there. The guide has 109 illustrations and its 36 pages of maps and charts instantly locate B&Bs with pools, golf, gourmet dining, and facilities for children, nonsmokers, and pets.

FODOR'S NEW ENGLAND '94
A Four Season Guide with the Best of the B&Bs and Ski Resorts

Nobody knows New England better than Fodor's, and in this discriminating, accurate, and up-to-the-minute guide you'll find all the best of New England — its top hotels, resorts, inns, and B&Bs in every category, great restaurants, cafes, and diners, wonderful shops for antiques and crafts, where to stay at 50 ski resorts, festivals and seasonal events, fishing, camping, and other outdoor sports, and 51 pages of maps.

WHEREVER YOU TRAVEL, HELP IS NEVER FAR AWAY.

From planning your trip to providing travel assistance along the way, American Express® Travel Service Offices* are always there to help.

BOSTON

One Court Street
Boston
617-723-8400

44 Brattle Street
Cambridge
617-661-0005

Collette Travel Service
10 Forbes West
Braintree
617-848-1810

Bloomingdale's
55 Boylston Street
Chestnut Hill
617-964-0622

Collette Travel Service
Augustine's Plaza
Saugus
617-233-9556

INTRODUCING

Fodor's
WORLDVIEW
TRAVEL UPDATE

AT LAST, YOUR OWN PERSONALIZED
LIST OF WHAT'S GOING ON IN THE
CITIES YOU'RE VISITING.

KEYED TO THE DAYS WHEN YOU'RE
THERE, CUSTOMIZED FOR YOUR
INTERESTS, AND SENT TO YOU
BEFORE YOU LEAVE HOME.

EXCLUSIVE FOR PURCHASERS OF
FODOR'S GUIDES...

Fodor's WORLDVIEW
TRAVEL UPDATE

Introducing a revolutionary way to get customized, time-sensitive travel information just before your trip.

Now you can obtain detailed information about what's going on in each city you'll be visiting <u>before</u> you leave home—up-to-the-minute, objective information about the events and activities that interest you most.

This is a special offer for purchasers of Fodor's guides – a customized Travel Update to fit your specific interests and your itinerary.

Travel Updates contain the kind of time-sensitive insider information you can get only from local contacts – or from city magazines and newspapers once you arrive. But now you can have the same information before you leave for your trip.

The choice is yours: current art exhibits, theater, music festivals and special concerts, sporting events, antiques and flower shows, shopping, fitness, and more.

The information comes from hundreds of correspondents and thousands of sources worldwide. Updated continuously, it's like having your own personal concierge or friend in the city.

You specify the cities and when you'll be there. We'll do the rest — personalizing the information for you the way no guidebook can.

It's the perfect extension to your Fodor's guide and the best way to make the most of your valuable travel time.

Your Itinerary:
Customized reports available for 160 destinations

ar
tou
9902
Regent's
The ann
in this an
domain of
tion as Joe
worthwhile. It
the performance
Tickets are usual
venue. Alternate
mances are cancelled
given. For more infor
Open-Air Theatre, Inner
NW1 4NP Open Air Th
Tel: 935-5756. Ends: 9-11-9
International Air Tattoo
Held biennially, the worl
military air display
demostra
tions, m
ban

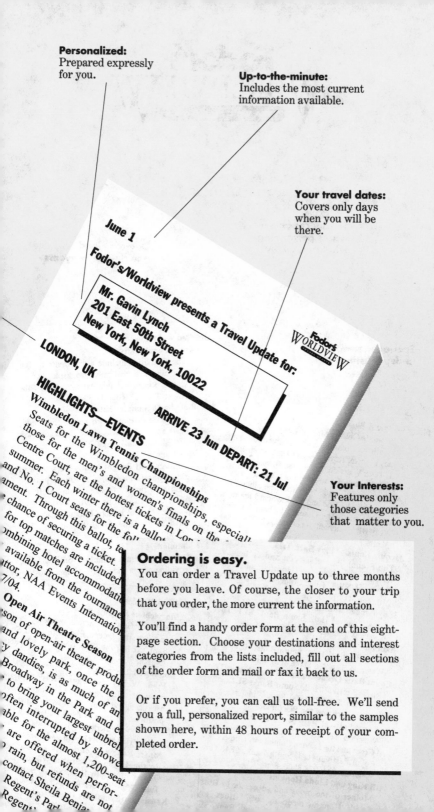

Personalized:
Prepared expressly
for you.

Up-to-the-minute:
Includes the most current
information available.

Your travel dates:
Covers only days
when you will be
there.

June 1

Fodor's/Worldview presents a Travel Update for:

Mr. Gavin Lynch
201 East 50th Street
New York, New York, 10022

Fodor's
WORLDVIEW

LONDON, UK

ARRIVE 23 Jun DEPART: 21 Jul

HIGHLIGHTS—EVENTS

Wimbledon Lawn Tennis Championships

Seats for the Wimbledon championships, especiall
those for the men's and women's finals on the
Centre Court, are the hottest tickets in Lon
summer. Each winter there is a ballot
and No. 1 Court seats for the fol
ament. Through this ballot, te
chance of securing a ticket
for top matches are included
ombining hotel accommodati
available from the tournam
ittor, NAA Events Internatio
7/04.

Open Air Theatre Season
son of open-air theater produ
and lovely park, once the
y dandies, is as much of an
Broadway in the Park and e
to bring your largest unbre
often interrupted by show
able for the almost 1,200-seat
are offered when perfor-
rain, but refunds are not
contact Sheila Benja
Regent's Par

Your Interests:
Features only
those categories
that matter to you.

Ordering is easy.

You can order a Travel Update up to three months
before you leave. Of course, the closer to your trip
that you order, the more current the information.

You'll find a handy order form at the end of this eight-
page section. Choose your destinations and interest
categories from the lists included, fill out all sections
of the order form and mail or fax it back to us.

Or if you prefer, you can call us toll-free. We'll send
you a full, personalized report, similar to the samples
shown here, within 48 hours of receipt of your completed order.

Fodor's WORLDVIEW
TRAVEL UPDATE

**Special concerts—
who's performing
what and where**

**One-of-a-kind,
one-time-only events**

**Special interest,
in-depth listings**

Children — Events
Angel Canal Festival
The festivities include a children's funfair, entertainers, a boat rally and displays on the water. Regent's Canal. Islington. N1. Tube: Angel. Tel: 267 9100. 11:30am-5:30pm. 7/04.

Blackheath Summer Kite Festival
Stunt kite displays with parachuting teddy bears and trade stands. Free admission. SE3. BR: Blackheath. 10am. 6/27.

Megabugs
Children will delight in this infestation of giant robotic insects, including a praying mantic 60 times life size. Mon-Sat 10am-6pm; Sun 11am-6pm. Admission 4.50 pounds. Natural History Museum, Cromwell Road. SW7. Tube: South Kensington. Tel: 938 9123. Ends 10/01.

Childminders
This establishment employs only women, providing nurses and qualified nannies to

Music — Jazz & Blues
Tito Puente's Golden Men of Latin Jazz
The father of mambo and Cuban rumba king comes to town. Royal Festival Hall. South Bank. SE1. Tube: Waterloo. Tel: 928 8800. 8pm. 7/15.

Georgie Fame and The New York Band
Riding a popular tide with his latest album, the smoky-voiced Fame and his keyboard are on a tour yet again. The Grand. Clapham Junction. SW11. BR: Clapham Junction. Tel: 738 9000. 7:30pm. 7/07.

Jacques Loussier Play Bach Trio
The French jazz classicist and colleagues. Kenwood Lakeside. Hampstead Lane. Kenwood. NW3. Tube: Golders Green, then bus 210. Tel: 413 1443. 7pm. 7/10.

Tony Bennett and Ronnie Scott
Royal Festival Hall. South Bank. SE1. Tube: Waterloo. Tel: 928 8800. 8pm. 7/11.

Santana
Royal Festival Hall. South Bank. SE1. Tube: Waterloo. Tel: 928 8800. 8pm. 7/12.

Count Basie Orchestra and Nancy Wilson Trio
Royal Festival Hall. South Bank. SE1. Tube: Waterloo. Tel: 928 8800. 8pm. 7/14.

King Pleasure and the Biscuit Boys
Royal Festival Hall. South Bank. SE1. Tube: Waterloo. Tel: 928 8800. 6:30 and 9pm. 7/16.

Al Green and the London Community Gospel Choir
Royal Festival Hall. South Bank. SE1. Tube: Waterloo. Tel: 928 8800. 8pm. 7/13.

BB King and Linda Hopkins
Mother of the blues and successor to Bessie Smith. Hopkins meets up with "Blues Boy" South Bank. SE

Music — Classical
Marylebone Sinfonia
Kenneth Gowen conducts music by Puccini and Rossini. Queen Elizabeth Hall. South Bank. SE1. Tube: Waterloo. Tel: 928 8800. 7:45pm. 7/16.

London Philharmonic
Franz Welser-Moest and George Benjamin conduct selections by Alexander Goehr, Messiaen, and some of Benjamin's own compositions. Queen Elizabeth Hall. South Bank. SE1. Tube: Waterloo. Tel: 928 8800. 8pm.

London Pro Arte Orchestra and Forest Choir
Murray Stewart conducts selections by Rossini, Haydn and Jonathan Willcocks. Queen Elizabeth Hall. South Bank. SE1. Tube: Waterloo. Tel: 928 8800. 7:45pm. 7/

Kensington Symphony Orchestra
Russell Keable conducts Dvorak's Dm

Here's what you get . . .

Detailed information about what's going on — precisely when you'll be there.

Show openings
during your visit

Reviews by
local critics

Exhibitions & Shows—Antique & Flower

Westminster Antiques Fair

Over 50 stands with pre-1830 furniture and other Victorian and earlier items. Thu-Fri 11am-8pm; Sat-Sun 11am-6pm. Admission 4 pounds, children free. Old Royal Horticultural Hall. Vincent Square. SW1. Tel: 0444/48 25 14. 6-24 thru 6/27.

Royal Horticultural Society Flower Show

The show includes displays of carnations, summer fruit and vegetables. Tue 11am-7pm; Wed 10am-5pm. Admission Tue 4 pounds, Wed 2 pounds. Royal Horticultural Halls. Greycoat Street and Vincent Square. SW1. Tube: Victoria. 7/20 thru 7/21.

Hampton Court Palace International Flower Show

Major international garden and flower show taking place in conjunction with the British ... floral exhibitions

Theater — Musical

Sunset Boulevard

In June, the four Andrew Lloyd Webber musicals which dominated London's stages in the 1980s (Cats, Starlight Express, Phantom of the Opera and Aspects of Love) are joined by the composer's latest work, a show rumored to have his best music to date. The 1950 Billy Wilder film about a helpless young writer who is drawn into the world of a possessive, aging silent screen star offers rich opportunities for Webber's evolving style. Soaring, aching melodies, lush technical effects and psychological thrills are all expected. Patti Lupone stars. Mon-Sat at 8pm; matinee Thu-Sat at 3pm. In-person sales only at the box office; credit card bookings, Tel: 344 0055. Admission 15-32.50 pounds. Adelphi Theatre. The Strand. WC2. Tube: Charing Cross. Tel: 836 7611. Starts: 6/21

Leonardo A Portrait of Love

A new musical about the great Renaissance arti... and inventor comes in for a London premier... tested by a brief run at Oxford's Old Fire Stati... ... autumn. The work explores the relations... ... Vinci and the woman '...

Spectator Sports — Other Sports

Greyhound Racing: Wembley Stadium

This dog track offers good views of greyhound racing held on Mon, Wed and Fri. No credit cards. Stadium Way. Wembley. HA9. Tube: Wembley Park. Tel: 902 8833.

Benson & Hedges Cricket Cup Final

Lord's Cricket Ground. St. John's Wood Road. NW8. Tube: St. John's Wood. Tel: 289 1611. 11am. 7/10.

Business-Fax & Overnight Mail

Post Office, Trafalgar Square Branch

Offers a network of fax services, the Intelpost system, throughout the country and abroad. Mon-Sat 8am-8pm, Sun 9am-5pm. William IV Street, WC2. Tube: C...

Albuquerque • Atlanta • Atlantic City • Ne
Baltimore • Boston • Chicago • Cincinnati
Cleveland • Dallas/Ft.Worth • Denver • De
Houston • Kansas City • Las Vegas • Los
Angeles • Memphis • Miami • Milwaukee
New Orleans • New York City • Orlando •
Springs • Philadelphia • Phoenix • Pittsburg
Portland • Salt Lake • San Antonio • San Di
San Franc... • Seattle • St. Louis • Tamp
Oslo • Was... • ...lu • Island •
Hawaii • Kauai • Maui • Abacos • Bimini
Ber... Countryside • Hamilton • Islar
Antigua & B... • ...vis • Tortc
Gorda • Barbados • Dominica • Grer
...cia • St. Vincent • Trinidad &Tobago
...ymans • Puerto Plata • Santo Doming
Aruba • Bonaire • Curacao • St. Ma
...ec City • Montreal • Ottawa • Toror
Vancouver • Guadeloupe • Martiniqu
...helemy • St. Martin • Kingston • Ixta
...o Bay • Negril • Ocho Rios • Ponce
...n • Grand Turk • Providenciales • S
St. John • St. Thomas • Acapulco •
& Isla Mujeres • Cozumel • Guadal
...a • Los Cabos • Manzanillo • Mazatl
City • Monterrey • Oaxaca • Puerto
...do • Puerto Vallarta • Veracruz •
...am • Athens •

Fodor's WORLDVIEW TRAVEL UPDATE

Interest Categories

For <u>your</u> personalized Travel Update, choose the categories you're most interested in from this list. Every Travel Update automatically provides you with *Event Highlights* – the best of what's happening during the dates of your trip.

1.	**Business Services**	Fax & Overnight Mail, Computer Rentals, Photocopying, Secretarial , Messenger, Translation Services

Dining

2.	**All Day Dining**	Breakfast & Brunch, Cafes & Tea Rooms, Late-Night Dining
3.	**Local Cuisine**	In Every Price Range—from Budget Restaurants to the Special Splurge
4.	**European Cuisine**	Continental, French, Italian
5.	**Asian Cuisine**	Chinese, Far Eastern, Japanese, Indian
6.	**Americas Cuisine**	American, Mexican & Latin
7.	**Nightlife**	Bars, Dance Clubs, Comedy Clubs, Pubs & Beer Halls
8.	**Entertainment**	Theater—Drama, Musicals, Dance, Ticket Agencies
9.	**Music**	Classical, Traditional & Ethnic, Jazz & Blues, Pop, Rock
10.	**Children's Activities**	Events, Attractions
11.	**Tours**	Local Tours, Day Trips, Overnight Excursions, Cruises
12.	**Exhibitions, Festivals & Shows**	Antiques & Flower, History & Cultural, Art Exhibitions, Fairs & Craft Shows, Music & Art Festivals
13.	**Shopping**	Districts & Malls, Markets, Regional Specialities
14.	**Fitness**	Bicycling, Health Clubs, Hiking, Jogging
15.	**Recreational Sports**	Boating/Sailing, Fishing, Ice Skating, Skiing, Snorkeling/Scuba, Swimming
16.	**Spectator Sports**	Auto Racing, Baseball, Basketball, Football, Horse Racing, Ice Hockey, Soccer

Please note that interest category content will vary by season, destination, and length of stay.

Destinations

The Fodor's/Worldview Travel Update covers more than 160 destinations worldwide. Choose the destinations that match your itinerary from this list. (Choose bulleted destinations only.)

United States (Mainland)
- Albuquerque
- Atlanta
- Atlantic City
- Baltimore
- Boston
- Chicago
- Cincinnati
- Cleveland
- Dallas/Ft. Worth
- Denver
- Detroit
- Houston
- Kansas City
- Las Vegas
- Los Angeles
- Memphis
- Miami
- Milwaukee
- Minneapolis/St. Paul
- New Orleans
- New York City
- Orlando
- Palm Springs
- Philadelphia
- Phoenix
- Pittsburgh
- Portland
- St. Louis
- Salt Lake City
- San Antonio
- San Diego
- San Francisco
- Seattle
- Tampa
- Washington, DC

Alaska
- Anchorage/Fairbanks/Juneau

Hawaii
- Honolulu
- Island of Hawaii
- Kauai
- Maui

Canada
- Quebec City
- Montreal
- Ottawa
- Toronto
- Vancouver

Bahamas
- Abacos
- Eleuthera/Harbour Island
- Exumas
- Freeport
- Nassau & Paradise Island

Bermuda
- Bermuda Countryside
- Hamilton

British Leeward Islands
- Anguilla
- Antigua & Barbuda
- Montserrat
- St. Kitts & Nevis

British Virgin Islands
- Tortola & Virgin Gorda

British Windward Islands
- Barbados
- Dominica
- Grenada
- St. Lucia
- St. Vincent
- Trinidad & Tobago

Cayman Islands
- The Caymans

Dominican Republic
- Puerto Plata
- Santo Domingo

Dutch Leeward Islands
- Aruba
- Bonaire
- Curacao

Dutch Windward Islands
- St. Maarten

French West Indies
- Guadeloupe
- Martinique
- St. Barthelemy
- St. Martin

Jamaica
- Kingston
- Montego Bay
- Negril
- Ocho Rios

Puerto Rico
- Ponce
- San Juan

Turks & Caicos
- Grand Turk
- Providenciales

U.S. Virgin Islands
- St. Croix
- St. John
- St. Thomas

Mexico
- Acapulco
- Cancun & Isla Mujeres
- Cozumel
- Guadalajara
- Ixtapa & Zihuatanejo
- Los Cabos
- Manzanillo
- Mazatlan
- Mexico City
- Monterrey
- Oaxaca
- Puerto Escondido
- Puerto Vallarta
- Veracruz

Europe
- Amsterdam
- Athens
- Barcelona
- Berlin
- Brussels
- Budapest
- Copenhagen
- Dublin
- Edinburgh
- Florence
- Frankfurt
- French Riviera
- Geneva
- Glasgow
- Interlaken
- Istanbul
- Lausanne
- Lisbon
- London
- Madrid
- Milan
- Moscow
- Munich
- Oslo
- Paris
- Prague
- Provence
- Rome
- Salzburg
- St. Petersburg
- Stockholm
- Venice
- Vienna
- Zurich

Pacific Rim Australia & New Zealand
- Auckland
- Melbourne
- Sydney

China
- Beijing
- Guangzhou
- Shanghai

Japan
- Kyoto
- Nagoya
- Osaka
- Tokyo
- Yokohama

Other
- Bangkok
- Hong Kong & Macau
- Manila
- Seoul
- Singapore
- Taipei

Fodor's WORLDVIEW **Order Form**

THIS TRAVEL UPDATE IS FOR (Please print):

Name

Address

City	**State**	**ZIP**

Country	**Tel #** ( ) -

Title of this Fodor's guide:

Store and location where guide was purchased:

INDICATE YOUR DESTINATIONS/DATES: Write in below the destinations you want to order. Then fill in your arrival and departure dates for each destination.

		Month	Day		Month	Day
(Sample) *LONDON*	From:	6 /	21	To:	6 /	30
1	From:	/		To:	/	
2	From:	/		To:	/	
3	From:	/		To:	/	

You can order up to three destinations per Travel Update. Only destinations listed on the previous page are applicable. Maximum amount of time covered by a Travel Update cannot exceed 30 days.

CHOOSE YOUR INTERESTS: Select up to eight categories from the list of interest categories shown on the previous page and circle the numbers below:

1   2   3   4   5   6   7   8   9   10   11   12   13   14   15   16

CHOOSE HOW YOU WANT YOUR TRAVEL UPDATE DELIVERED (Check one):

❏ Please mail my Travel Update to the address above **OR**

❏ Fax it to me at **Fax #** ( ) -

DELIVERY CHARGE (Check one)

	Within U.S. & Canada	Outside U.S. & Canada
First Class Mail	❏ $2.50	❏ $5.00
Fax	❏ $5.00	❏ $10.00
Priority Delivery	❏ $15.00	❏ $27.00

All orders will be sent within 48 hours of receipt of a completed order form.

ADD UP YOUR ORDER HERE. *SPECIAL OFFER FOR FODOR'S PURCHASERS ONLY!*

	Suggested Retail Price	Your Price	This Order
First destination ordered	$13.95	$ 7.95	$ 7.95
Second destination (if applicable)	$ 9.95	$ 4.95	+
Third destination (if applicable)	$ 9.95	$ 4.95	+
Plus delivery charge from above			+
		TOTAL:	$

METHOD OF PAYMENT (Check one):   ❏ AmEx   ❏ MC   ❏ Visa   ❏ Discover
                                      ❏ Personal Check   ❏ Money Order

Make check or money order payable to: Fodor's Worldview Travel Update

Credit Card #   **Expiration Date:**

Authorized Signature

SEND THIS COMPLETED FORM TO:
Fodor's Worldview Travel Update, 114 Sansome Street, Suite 700, San Francisco, CA 94104

OR CALL OR FAX US 24-HOURS A DAY
Telephone **1-800-799-9609** • Fax **1-800-799-9619** (From within the U.S. & Canada)
(Outside the U.S. & Canada: Telephone 415-616-9988 • Fax 415-616-9989)

(Please have this guide in front of you when you call so we can verify purchase.)

Offer valid until 12/31/94.